SAILING AROUND
THE WORLD

SAILING AROUND THE WORLD

◆

A Family Retraces
Joshua Slocum's Voyage

Guy Bernardin

Translated by Jeremy McGeary

SHERIDAN HOUSE

First published 2002 by
Sheridan House, Inc.
145 Palisade Street
Dobbs Ferry, NY 10522
www.sheridanhouse.com

First published in France under the title
Sur les traces de Joshua Slocum
by Editions Loisirs Nautiques

Library of Congress Cataloging-in-Publication Data

Bernardin, Guy
    Sailing around the world: a family retraces
Joshua Slocum's voyage/Guy Bernardin;
Translated by Jeremy McGeary.
    p. cm.
Translated from French.
Includes biographical references

        ISBN 1-57409-148-4 (Hardover: alk. Paper)
        1. Sailing. 2. Bernardin, Guy—Journeys.
        3. Voyages around the world. 4. Slocum, Joshua,
        b. 1844—Journeys. I. Title.
        GV811. B42 2002
        910.4'5—dc21   2002004517

Edited by Janine Simon
Designed by Keata Brewer

Printed in the United States of America

ISBN 1-57409-148-4

To all of you dreaming about following in Slocum's wake

Salut au Monde !

O take my hand Walt Whitman!
Such gliding wonders! such sights and sounds!
Such join'd unended links, each hook'd to the next,
Each answering all, each sharing the earth with all.

—Walt Whitman, *Leaves of Grass*

"To the one who loves the sea and boats
and understands them, at least in part,
the SPRAY will receive the full recognition
due to her."

—Cipriano Andrade, Rudder, 1909

Acknowledgments

◆

Special thanks to Jeremy Mc Geary, associate editor at *Cruising World* Magazine, who made the translation available to all of you and did such a wonderful job. Andrea and Carlos Badt allowed us to realize this wonderful project. All our deep love to Jinny and Bob Clarke aboard MAI-LING.

Along the way, there were so many talented and helpful people, ready to share a part of our trip. We apologize for the ones we might forget.

With us as part of our crew were: Veronica and Pedro Claverie, Catherine and Bertrand Dumont, Eric Vibart, Dominique and the Xingu's sailing team, the Guilbaud's family, Philippe Jeantot, solo sailor and organizer of the Vendée Globe, and his family, Bertie Reed's family, Eliane and Guy Viau, Tish Simpson, Steve Pettengill, José de Ugarte, Don Mason, Ned and Sue Reynolds, Marc Pardhaille, Mame Reynolds, Mrs Reiz, Robert Michaud, Commodore Ted Jones and Secretary June from the Slocum Society and their members, George Varga, Henry Hotchkiss and his Centennial Celebration Team, João Fraga, Nicolas Von Mally, the U.S. Embassy staff in Cape Town, Jacques Archambaut, Eben Human.

Thanks to the Cairns, Darwin, Grand Baie, Saldanha, Natal, Myrtle Beach and Royal Cape Town Yacht Clubs.

Also many thanks to the people at Fort Myers Boatyard, Wickford Cove Marina, Lagos Marina in Portugal and the incredible Port Olonna Marina at Sables d'Olonne in France.

Finally, a special thank you to Plastimo for their very helpful and useful equipment, to the photographers Barry Lamprecht, Onne Van der Wal, Frieda Squires from the *Providence Journal*, Daniel Allisy and to the many enjoyable people from the media and magazines publications around the world.

Contents

◆

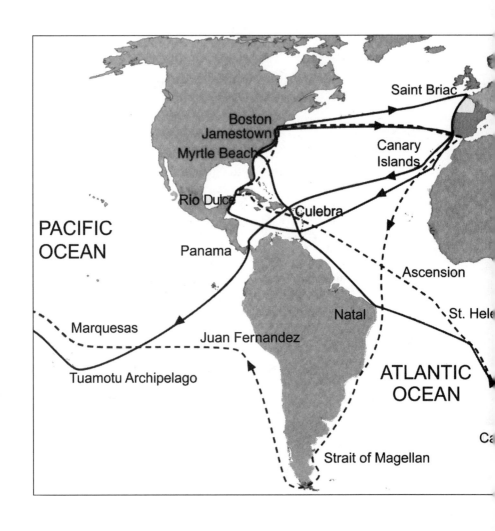

PACIFIC
OCEAN

ATLANTIC
OCEAN

Saint Briac

Boston
Jamestown
Myrtle Beach

Canary
Islands

Rio Dulce

Culebra

Panama

Ascension

St. Hele

Marquesas

Juan Fernandez

Natal

Tuamotu Archipelago

Ca

Strait of Magellan

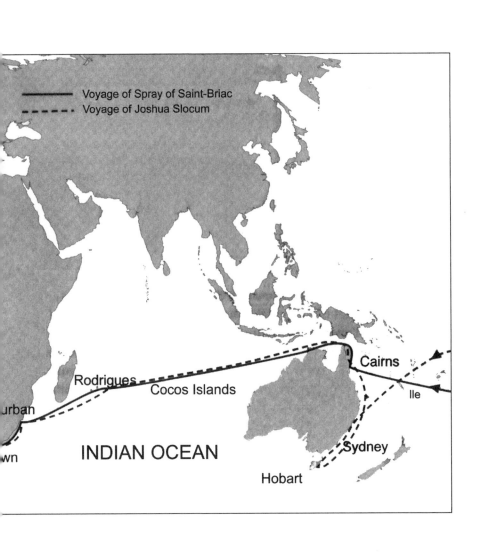

Introduction

◆

It was just after dawn off Rio de Janeiro's Copacabana Beach. The air was still and leaden, not unlike the dark water over which Guy Bernardin was almost willing his 38-foot RATSO to the finish line of Leg III of the inaugural 1982-83 BOC Challenge. Having left Sydney some 62 days before, one could hardly blame him for wanting to cross it.

I was on a photo boat just a few feet off RATSO's starboard quarter with a handful of journalists. Like RATSO, we were barely moving. There are images of that morning I'll never forget: the reflection of RATSO's sails in the shimmering water as the boat drifted up the coast past the famous beaches; the bold silhouette of dramatic Sugar Loaf mountain against a pale blue sky; the hot, heavy air, not a hint of breeze in it.

But what I'll remember most is the sight of Guy, hunched down to leeward, the genoa sheet in one hand, the steering wheel in the other. He was as much a part of RATSO—the backwards spelling of OSTAR, the solo transatlantic race which Guy had completed in 1980—as the spar from which the sails were set. We could've been on another ocean for all he cared. Singlehanded and singleminded, the essence of the solo sailor, he didn't know we were there. I was honored to be there, to witness the journey's end for a man who'd just rounded Cape Horn all alone, who'd just fulfilled a life-long quest.

I got to know Guy while covering the BOC for *Cruising World* magazine, and while reporting for a book on the race called *Out There*. Guy was always one of my favorite people to see and interview. He was sailing the smallest boat in the race and had absolutely no chance of winning. But it was clear from the outset that, though his effort was highly competitive, Guy wasn't in the event strictly for the competition. Like Bernard Moitessier and many of the French sailors he inspired, in the ocean Guy found not only a sporting arena, but in many ways a spiritual one.

After Leg II from Cape Town, South Africa, to Sydney, Guy described an incident that has to be one of the more amazing sea stories I've heard. He was seated in the cockpit in the aftermath of a gale that had packed 50-knot winds. Convinced that the storm was abating, he'd changed into dry clothes and was resting unharnessed when a huge, leftover sea broadsided RATSO and knocked her over.

Guy wrapped his arm around a winch but the force of the water pressure was too much. Instantly he was overboard, gone to the sea.

Later, he said, "I did not realize at the time that the boat was turning over. I felt well. It was like floating free in space. For a short time, I felt very nice."

Passive and even rejoiceful, for a brief instant Guy was ready to merge with the briny element that was already running through his veins.

Of course, then he came to his senses. He reached out and after a couple of grabs he snagged a line and held on for his life. Suddenly, RATSO sprung to and stood up, and when she did Guy found himself well aloft in the rigging of his still-floating boat. He slid down and landed back in the cockpit.

When he was finally ashore weeks later, he said, "That moment was the best souvenir of the voyage."

It was in that context, as the soulful offshore racer/philosopher, that I first got to know Guy. In the years that followed Guy's professional racing career took off, and the time for philosophical musing was increasingly taken up by the hours spent pursuing corporate sponsors.

When I heard Guy was buying a replica of Joshua Slocum's SPRAY, at first I was surprised. It seemed a strange turn of direction for a pro sailor competing at the highest ranks of the wild Grand Prix Open 60 scene. I'd thought of the Guy I saw that morning off Rio, intense and unrelenting.

But then I remembered the other Guy, the one who'd gone over the side in the Southern Ocean and emerged intact with, of all things, a cherished memory. Like Slocum himself, the case could be made that Guy was also a realist and a romantic, a doer and a dreamer. When I thought of Guy in that context and imagined him taking off aboard a sistership to SPRAY, it made all the sense in the world.

As is evident in the pages that follow, Guy turned out to be a pretty good writer, too, so he had another thing in common with Slocum.

A hundred years after Slocum, Guy followed the old navigator around the planet. There were similarities in the two voyages, the most obvious being the boats on which they were sailed. But there were differences, too, the largest being that Guy traveled with his wife and young son.

In the end, however, one of the coolest things about Guy's voyage aboard SPRAY OF SAINT-BRIAC is that he's captured the essence of his amazing trip in the book you now hold. On this adventure, unlike some of Guy's previous ones, we all get to share the souvenir.

Herb McCormick
May 2002

Preface

◆

When we decided to acquire a replica of SPRAY, we did so out of curiosity and in order to compare the boat with what Captain Slocum says about her in his book.

Subsequently, when we decided to sail around the world in SPRAY's wake, it wasn't to break records or out of a desire to achieve any kind of glory. We simply wanted to pay tribute to this great sailor and great man and to take advantage of such a wonderful opportunity to do something very special for our son, Briac, that will mark his future.

I believe that Captain Slocum represents a model of courage, enterprise, vigor, and hope. Right up to the end of his life, he was driven by that vitality that makes us dream. He never stopped struggling, whether it was against men, the elements or adversity, or even against progress that he perhaps could neither comprehend nor even see coming. In that respect, the *fins-de-siècle* of the nineteenth and the twentieth centuries have much in common.

Thousands of readers around the world have read his book and millions more will. The book is eternal, it's without a doubt the best gift he could have made us, as well as bequeathing to us the plans of his SPRAY.

We hope, through this book, to have rendered Joshua Slocum the tribute he deserves and given you the desire to follow him on the oceans.

PART 1

◆

Prelude to a Circumnavigation

1

"Looking for a Replica of SPRAY"

"Welcome aboard Northwest Airlines flight to Boston. We ask you to please secure your seatbelts in preparation for an immediate takeoff."

With a little jolt, the red and charcoal gray airplane started to roll on the tarmac and taxi toward the runway. The Charles de Gaulle terminal retreated, freeing our great metallic bird from its tentacles. The midday sun gently warmed the cabin and periodically shone on me through the porthole.

In my lap, waiting for me to open it, was the new French translation of the famous work of Captain Joshua Slocum, *Sailing Alone Around the World*. Patrick Leroux, a sportswriter, had given me the book when I visited him to chat about my future racing projects.

After lunch, my tray table at last stowed, I could relax, stretch my legs out, and recline my seatback. Extracting my glasses from their case, I stared for a long time at the photo on the cover before opening it.

I had read the original 20 years before, but the more pages I turned, the more I became engrossed and inspired by what I was learning. It was love at first sight, made all the more poignant because my recent experiences at sea, especially my adventures in spectacular Patagonia, brought me closer to this great sailor; I could better understand him intellectually as well as physically. I was awed by what he went through with SPRAY in the channels of the Strait of Magellan.

Comfortably ensconced in my seat, I let myself be carried away by his tale. From what I was reading, SPRAY seemed to be the ideal sailboat for cruising. It had shallow draft, lots of volume inside, and most important, it could sail itself with the helm lashed. It had everything to awake the curiosity of a budding circumnavigator and piqued me into searching for a replica.

All this was taking place at 30,000 feet above the Atlantic, which I could see clearly, its royal blue dotted with white flecks and, from time to time, the white thread of a wake trailing behind a ship.

It was a vague cloud of an idea. It needed time to float down to earth, to coalesce into a little seed, and to germinate and flourish into a palpable reality. Little by little, almost unconsciously, it began to take on substance and life as events unfolded in the course of the following months.

In the early 1990s, nothing was easy. The recent slump in the economy made it difficult to bring ideas to fruition, particularly in the world of sailing. Sponsors for an around-the-world race were difficult to find. Low prices combined with few and tough buyers made even real estate a tenuous proposition; our house had been on the market for two years. And then there was the boat in the yard.

In 1993, the manuscript I was working on was finished. The house was in the process of being sold and we had to vacate it before the end of May.

With more time on my hands, I concentrated on my search for a replica of SPRAY through advertisements and brokers. In the end, I placed a classified ad in *Soundings* magazine: "Looking for a replica of SPRAY." I knew that at least one exact replica existed. I had run across it, 20 years before, while passing through the Panama Canal with my first RATSO, a PIC 26 class which we were sailing from California to Brittany.

This boat was named SCUD. Her owner and skipper, George Maynard, had built her at Noank, Connecticut in the same way as Joshua Slocum did SPRAY. At the time, he and his family of five were sailing her around the world, without an engine. To transit the canal to the Pacific, he had fitted a mount to the large transom and rented a 25-horsepower outboard.

We were both sailing engineless, so we quickly struck up a friendship, and I agreed to help him make the passage through the canal. Those were days to remember.

The thing, now, was to find SCUD. It was a bit like looking for a needle in a haystack.

I saw several replicas but none that met with my expectations. And time was passing inexorably by!

A telephone call the evening of the day before I was to fly to Seattle and British Columbia to follow up another lead invigorated my search. An old skipper from Maine had seen my advertisement and gave me a contact who had found a SPRAY replica. "She's for sale, and actually under contract." But when it came down to it, he wasn't sure if the boat would really change hands.

I immediately dialed the number:

"Hi, could you give me the telephone number of the new owners of your old sailing boat?"

"It's still for sale. What do you want with it?"

"Oh, just to live aboard, may be go cruising!"

"That won't be very comfortable for you, because there's no interior. The boat has been doing day charters."

I thought to myself that that was just fine since it would render the survey easier and I could fit her out to my own taste without having to change too many things.

During the course of the conversation, which was held in the laconic style typical of Maine, I learned that the boat was none other than SCUD . . . the one I was looking for! I had to restrain myself so as not to let on how excited I was.

We arranged to meet so I could see her. For five months she had been out of the water, wintering in a shed.

The next day, I flew to Seattle to inspect another replica. It was an enchanting trip to a magnificent region studded with some 300 islands. The boat looked beautiful, sitting on the water in a little creek fringed with tall trees. I just had to find the owner, then a dinghy, and we came alongside her at her mooring. It was a quick inspection. Above the waterline, she was almost completely rotten. She was only 10 years old but the former owner had built her with untreated house construction lumber. Happily, a visit to Victoria and a delicious dinner helped me forget this frustrating incident.

Still tired from the long trip—Boston is as far from Seattle as it is from Paris—I rented a car and drove to the quaint little port of Camden, Maine.

There, in the dimness of the shed, I examined SCUD as best I could.

She looked good to me and I saw no obvious faults. Since she had to be put in a boatyard before being launched, we agreed to my having a second inspection before I made a final decision. On the way home, I was bursting with excitement. I felt I was on the brink of a new adventure.

Ten days later, the deed was done. We arranged for a truck to bring her to Wickford, near Newport, and SCUD arrived on the apron of the marina, although the driver had managed to forget the mast and rigging. We were in the midst of moving, as we had to vacate the house. In the way that things only happen all together, the sailboat in the yard found a buyer. That solved one of our problems and we couldn't have asked for better timing all round.

Annick and I, and our small son, Briac, now had a new home to move into—almost. We first had to fit out the boat. Apart from the settees in the main cabin, there was nothing below decks. Fortunately, Ned and Susan shared their comfortable house with us and let us store close to two tons of our belongings, largely books.

I set about building some lockers under the seats, a large and very rustic saloon table, and a mini library. Then I installed a Plastimo single-burner gas cooker, and finally some small storage hammocks. With the addition of a GPS and a VHF radio we were all set! Within two weeks she was in the water and, to our great relief, she floated.

Loaded with our belongings, the waterline submerged a good six inches. I found this somewhat unsettling. Having fought a constant battle against weight aboard all my previous sailboats, I was turning this one into a freighter. There was even stuff on the roof of the main cabin, to the dismay of others in the marina who were afraid these sea gypsies were going to lower the tone of their neighborhood.

All these preparations didn't proceed without a few small incidents: Briac, 11 months old, fell three times his height down the companionway ladder, landing, of course, on his head. The sight of his little cranium swollen and tender, as though there were water under the scalp, filled Annick with anguish and alarm. We rushed to the car and off to the doctor. He said that the wound wasn't serious and that the swelling would go down bit by bit, and it did. But it was a scare, and sobering.

The next day, I was alone on board, the rain pounding on the deck. When I tried to open the heavy wooden companionway hatch from the inside, it let go all at once, crushing my thumb against the stop. Ouch! It bled profusely around bits of exposed flesh. I wound a length of clean cloth around it and then drove to the hospital once more. I wasn't very proud of myself.

After an X-ray, a young intern gave me a few stitches. He was probably new to the trade; despite the local anaesthetic, his proddings with the needle made me jump out of the chair a few times.

With a bitter taste in my mouth, but embarrassed more than anything, I joined my family for a restorative lunch. The general consensus was that that was enough for the day, and we took the opportunity to go shopping.

I considered the boat was sufficiently ready to go sailing and, after a few trials in Narragansett Bay, we prepared to cross the Atlantic. We needed to take advantage of the early season before the hurricanes come up the East Coast of the United States. The boat was completely new to us in so many ways, and crossing the ocean would be the best way to find out what worked and what didn't.

It was the beginning of July. While around us tourist activity was building to its summer height, I spent my time checking off jobs we had already done and asking myself what was left to do. One particular task was to sell the car!

If we had been able to get ready to go in this short a time, it was thanks to the help of our friends. Ned lent me his truck to go and collect the mast from Maine, which took a full 36 hours on the busy highways. He let me into the secrets of caulking, though only a few spots needed it, and lent me several tools. Our friends Bob and Jinny were always on hand to help with small jobs or prepare a relaxing dinner. José Ugarte, who had just finished the singlehanded transatlantic race and was preparing for the Vendée Globe, gave us a Plastimo steering-wheel autopilot. I didn't yet know how the boat was going to steer once at sea and any assistance was welcome.

We still had to find a name for our new vessel. After a crew meeting, it quickly appeared that she could only have the one: SPRAY OF SAINT-BRIAC. SPRAY was Joshua Slocum's boat; it also described what part of her environment would be made of. And it was at Saint-Briac that I learned all about spray. Sitting on the water, tugging at her mooring, SPRAY OF SAINT-BRIAC had a proud and noble demeanor, and seemed impatient to head to sea.

Using Bob's car, we made the last provisioning run on the eve of our departure. To carry all the grocery bags onto the launch float, we used the marina's big-wheeled carts. With infinite care, I brought mine to the foot of the access ramp, then onto the floating dock. I left it for just long enough to help Annick bring down hers. The moment my back was turned, sensing liberty, my cart began to roll, faster and faster, before tripping over the dock edge and landing upside down in the water. Our first reaction was horror, and then everyone burst out laughing. We managed to round up all the packages and delicately picked them out. We had taken the precaution of wrapping everything in plastic garbage bags because it was raining, so nothing was lost or spoiled, and the air trapped in the bags made them float. Whew!

2

Getting to Know SPRAY in the Atlantic

The last weather bulletin we'd seen on television indicated nothing bad, and the barometer at 1020 Mb was relatively high. On board, there was that mixture of excitement and anxiety that comes with every major departure. I turned on the ignition key; after a few coughs, the engine started. Each time, it's a relief and a sort of miracle. I took a moment to check that the steering was working properly, and to sniff the wind: a light breeze from the southwest. "Ho! Cast off the mooring!" Judging by the gaiety with which the red buoy danced at the end of its tether, it was quite pleased to regain its freedom.

Briac was one year old. As though it were the most natural thing in the world, he had already acquired a good sense of balance and he instinctively applied the old salt's rule of "One hand for yourself and one hand for the ship." Smiling, curious, in T-shirt and shorts, he watched attentively everything that went on around him. He was particularly interested in the procedure for raising the mainsail, always a big performance. He was surprised, too, to see the boat, which had become his home, moving among the other moored boats. And then, the next thing we knew, Bob and Jinny were escorting us with their Morgan 42, MAI LING. Briac waved back when they said goodbye, happy to see us at last on our way across the Atlantic.

After the final emotional farewells, the sailing boats parted company and went their opposite ways. With a touch of sadness, we turned to watch furtively as MAI LING's silhouette disappeared and the low coastline of Rhode Island faded away on the horizon.

We were at last by ourselves aboard SPRAY OF SAINT-BRIAC, with a long crossing ahead of us that could prove full of surprises. The Atlantic by the northern route is very unpredictable. But as I watched Briac playing on the wide deck, I was sure that everything would go well. This little guy, without saying anything, got us to cross oceans, because he gave us confidence in the future.

The first thing to do now was get to know the boat. She was still a big mystery. We knew nothing about her; we had only sailed her for a few hours in the bay, and then not in very much wind. She was solidly built, and if worst came to worst, even without a rig, I was sure we would end up somewhere!

There was a small leak in one of the joints in the transom, a little above the waterline. As a precaution, in addition to the two pumps already on board, I had fitted a third, bigger one, with a discharge hose which could be passed out through a porthole, just in case . . .

SPRAY OF SAINT BRIAC
(Daniel Allisy)

On the first few days of sailing, the wind was light and SPRAY wouldn't steer well with the helm lashed. We therefore had to steer by hand and maintain a schedule of watches. When motoring, the AT 100 autopilot appeared to take it. I say "appeared" because with pilots I never know who is steering, but it seems to work psychologically, and that's the idea.

When the wind turned south-southwest and became stronger, the boat became harder and harder to steer. She had a tendency to luff, to climb up toward the wind. We had to fight to keep her on course, up to the point when the load on the helm was too much. We then had to take in a reef to reduce the amount of sail. In fact, the helm was always the first indicator of when we should put in one reef, then two, and eventually, furl the sail, which normally we would do when the wind reached about 35 knots. That was one of the first lessons SPRAY taught us.

Handling the mainsail when reefing required a lot of effort and strength, at least when we started. There was no winch, so everything had to be done by hand or with tackles. After a half hour of work, the average for taking in a reef, I was worn out. However, I modified the reef lines with a system of blocks, like I'd used on racing boats, and so I didn't have to furl away all of the cloth in the way it's normally done on this type of rig.

I never changed course to handle the sails except sometimes to drop the yankee or work on the bowsprit. That way the deck was more stable and I stayed dry. Because it was big and wide, the deck was a real pleasure to work on. SPRAY never heeled more than seven to eight degrees and she rolled little, which made life aboard very comfortable.

During this first gale, I stayed at the helm. In the end, I kept up only the big jib and the staysail we'd fitted before we left. This I kept quite flat, and sheeted to the centerline. Little by little, as the breeze strengthened, we trimmed the jib sheet. The boat held course with the helm lashed. For safety, I steered at night. My harness, with a shortened tether, kept me secure against the sudden movements and the increased heeling created by the breaking waves striking the hull. These could be dangerous and, from time to time, swept the deck from amidships to forward. I observed that the afterdeck by the helm stayed perfectly dry and protected. The poop lifted easily to the waves.

In the morning, I was tired and hungry, and Annick took over. It wasn't a simple matter because there was Briac. Left alone, he bawled, to put it mildly. We therefore had to dress him warmly and put him in his pack on his mother's back, at the same time as she was trying to steer and keep the boat under control. In the thick of the wind, with the rain driving in his face, he would beam from ear to ear. The same problem arose when we both had to work forward, as when sweating up the halyards. Taking him with us to the foot of the mast, all we had to do was hand him a rope end and ask him to help us by pulling hard on it. We could then complete the task at our leisure. Afterwards, the whole crew would go down into the cabin and, over a steaming cup, bask in the satisfaction of a job well done. Briac had to take part in everything. It kept him calm. The worse the weather, the more wind, the more Briac glowed with well-being. It seemed to energize him.

Little by little, the child settled into a routine on board. He would sleep for 10 hours straight and never needed an afternoon nap. He kept busy all day long and was never bored. In fact, at night, we were more relaxed. In spite of wind, thunder, lightning, and the boat being thrown in all directions, even beating to windward, Master Briac slept soundly.

Once we crossed the Gulf Stream, the air and water temperatures rose dramatically and we responded by shedding jackets and other cold-weather clothing. The downside was that the water temperature seemed to affect the caulked joints, because the water ingress became significant, especially around the sternpost. The pumps then began to earn their passage.

After several days of strong winds, during which two fronts passed through, I was extremely tired but I was reassured: SPRAY OF SAINT-BRIAC held her course and sailed by herself with the helm lashed. It was a tremendous relief as there was no more need to stand watches, tied to the wheel. A quick look around once in a while and I could pop back into the shelter of the cabin. During the last few days, we had lost the antennas of the Loran and the VHF from the top of the mast. They were fine up there for sailing in a sheltered bay, but on the ocean, SPRAY's old fashioned rig wasn't rigid enough and in a choppy sea the mast whipped around significantly. With this in mind, before leaving I had fitted two stainless-steel running back-stays, just in case.

The last front was the most violent, with quite a bit of water sweeping the decks which caused the loss of a few jerry jugs. Jibing under jib and staysail in the middle of the night was difficult. There was no problem with the staysail because it was already on centerline and had to stay there, but the jib was another matter. The blocks on the sheets had the knack of hanging up on the inner stay the moment the boat jibed. To top it all, the anchor point of the turning block suddenly let go. And there I was, screaming at the wind and rain to give me an extra hand, my own two not being enough to haul down this wretched rag. It was the kind of effort that brings you gasping to your knees with a sudden desire to gulp down half a gallon of water.

While SPRAY continued on her way on this new jibe, I had to re-adjust the position of the steering wheel. It varied from one tack to the other. Sailing boats act in mysterious ways, which often don't submit to rationalization or calculation.

The conclusion we drew after this first week of sailing was that SPRAY OF SAINT-BRIAC was a worthy successor to Joshua Slocum's own SPRAY. My problem was that I wanted more of what I'd had before. Going from an Open 60 to a boat of this kind, you sometimes want to pull your hair out. Patience, patience: that's the key word.

Just as the great sailor described it in his marvelous book, the boat sailed with the helm lashed. It was the most fantastic thing. I felt as if the hand of God was steering the boat. To roam the oceans was free-dom. The sailboat, all alone, with no outside mechanical assistance, steered herself. She became as one with the birds of the sea and I felt myself being carried on their wings across the vastness of the oceans. It filled me with a strength and a serenity which I had never known dur-ing all my previous voyages. I had nothing to do apart from adjusting the angle of the helm from time to time, and watching the sails and the course. Night and day, day after day, untiringly, SPRAY OF SAINT-BRIAC cut her wake across the face of the ocean.

I never ceased to be astonished by how she steered such a precise course. A windvane or an electric autopilot couldn't have done it bet-ter. All this without a sound and with no strain on the steering system. What other boat could do that?

I did, though, before the circumnavigation, have to modify the profile of the rudder to make it easier on the helm.

Because of the heavy weather conditions, we learned this magnificent boat's qualities and quirks. And so we gained confidence.

We continued to pump moderately, three or four times a day, about eight gallons at a time. It was nothing dramatic, just annoying. To raise everyone's spirits, I told about Joshua Slocum's first crossing as a cabin boy in a three-master from Nova Scotia to Dublin. The ship took on so much water that the waterline came up to deck level. It was only the cargo of lumber that kept her afloat long enough to finish her voyage without sinking. Our feet at least were still dry! We were also aware of the fact that our boat hadn't really sailed in the last 20 years, of which she'd spent 10 doing day charters in the bay. She seemed to have taken to sea again with considerable joy and revealed few problems.

But this first crossing turned out quite unpleasant, and it might just as well have been November. Day after day, the wind fluctuated across the westerly sector, from south to north, and we had to jibe frequently, a maneuver always tricky on this type of boat. A penetratingly damp mist enveloped us, often accompanied by drizzle, making navigation difficult and life aboard uncomfortable. After about ten days, the sun deigned to show itself, timidly at first, then gradually more boldly, which pleased us no end. As our surroundings brightened, so did our spirits.

We had brought on board dehydrated foods, in the form of complete meals. All we had to do was reconstitute them with hot water. The choice amounted to five or six different menus. We came to the conclusion that, unfortunately, their calorific value was somewhat reduced by the process. At the end of 30 days, we were not in the best of shape. Briac, however, with his special, rich diet, was in perfect health.

Despite trailing a fishing line, all we caught was one bonito. We scarfed it down! What a banquet! We felt reinvigorated, and dreamed about the next one.

Fine weather accompanied our arrival off the coast of Brittany. Off Ouessant, the French customs boarded and inspected us. Over a ridiculous matter of paperwork, having to do with SPRAY being registered, but not documented, they stayed with us for close to three hours. It was bad timing because it was dinner time. Briac hadn't yet eaten, his bedtime approached, and then passed. Throughout this time he stayed on his mother's back while she steered. Eventually, the customs officers departed into the night, leaving us utterly drained, hungry, and on edge. After 35 days at sea, this was exactly the kind of welcome we did not need. We had a hard time believing what they'd put us through. We had been so excited at the idea of at last reaching the Brittany coast, and this reception was a real wet blanket.

"Welcome to France," you can read in the logbook. Fortunately, the weather was good. As soon as Briac was in his bunk, Annick prepared a fine meal of spaghetti to fortify us and give us the strength we needed for the long night watches ahead. We settled down to relax, so we could devote all our attention to the navigation.

The next day we were sailing along the shoreline from Batz to La Horaine; we were excited to be introducing to Briac this region so dear to us. The following dawn, we reached the port of Saint-Quay. After many emotional reunions, we enjoyed a well earned meal, made with fresh food.

In the following months, which turned into a year, we worked on several projects as we moved from Saint-Quay to Saint-Malo, and eventually to Le Béchet, the little pleasure port of Saint-Briac. We had to change the standing rigging, as one of the shrouds had parted during the crossing—which isn't bad for 20-year-old galvanized steel cable. We also finished fitting out the interior with a wood and charcoal cooking stove that would complement our butane and propane burners. Forever after that we kept a supply of wood on board and, quite often, we indulged in making a fire, even in the tropics. It would fill the interior with the wonderful smell of woodsmoke while drying out the farthest corners of the cabin. What a luxury that was! In addition, the quality of the food cooked on it was much superior to anything cooked on gas. The fitting of the fuel and water tanks required a lot of effort and sweat.

There were still lockers to build, an SSB antenna to install, material to load aboard or to take off. Then, two dinghies came aboard in the shape of two wooden Optimists, and finally, we careened SPRAY on the beach at Le Béchet, under the benevolent watch of Mr. Lhotellier, the harbormaster.

After a last visit from the children of the Pleurtuit school, escorted by their teachers Mme Bodiguel and M. Ceron—who later sent Briac school assignments and followed up by mail and even by radio through our friend André—we were ready to set off on our great adventure.

3

Heading South

When setting out from Saint-Briac, we chose Sunday, July 10, the day of the Blessing of the Fleet, a Breton maritime tradition. At high tide, the harbor was bathed in the sunshine typical of high-pressure weather. A large crowd was there to witness the ceremony taking place on the waterfront. After the benediction, SPRAY set her bow toward the northwest, through the rocky channels, to begin her long adventure.

Our objective was to test both the boat and her crew in a circuit of the North Atlantic before eventually embarking on the circumnavigation.

Taking advantage of the benign weather and favorable tides, we worked our way around the coast of Brittany. We made a brief stop in Concarneau to spend a few precious moments with our friends, the Guinards, to see some old acquaintances, and to sign a number of books at the Maritime Book Show. We also took part in a regatta for traditional vessels held in the bay as a result of which a new barometer came to adorn the bulkhead in SPRAY OF SAINT-BRIAC's cabin.

After anchoring in the idyllic Glénan archipelago, we entered Port Olonna. Jacques Archambeau and his team proved once more how well they know the meaning of the words welcome and hospitality. To arrive in this Vendée harbor is to land among friends; months and years may go by, but the reception is always as warm. It's a wonderful feeling, and we are grateful to our friends for making it so.

Briac, now three, was assuming more and more the gait of a sailor. A true Breton, he took part enthusiastically in all of the boathandling activities.

A day spent at the home of Philippe Jeantot and his family allowed us to rehash old races and dream of future projects. Philippe had begun to cruise on one of his catamarans, with all the comforts of home, a washing machine, TV, video, computer . . . quite the opposite of SPRAY which is much more rustic and has no electronic gadgetry. Neither of us was racing now, but living out new and different adventures.

During our stay, we made the most of the fair weather to continue with our maintenance. We were never bored on SPRAY, as there was always something to do. For example, paying the deck seams is a thankless task, but there was no stopping Annick. She used her old coffee pot to melt the tar before pouring it, smoking, between the planks. I have to say that she did a fine job and she won the admiration of several local old salts.

The days went by, too quickly. We had to think about leaving, especially as the weather looked as though it was settling in favorably. There's nothing like a little nor'easter to help you to quickly cross the Bay of Biscay.

Thanks to the Brosset family, we were able to complete our provisioning easily. Among the stores we put aboard were several pounds of buckwheat flour for Sundays, when we looked forward to our Breton galettes. Protecting the flour from the humidity, though, would prove to be a problem.

After emotional farewells we cast off the lines. Escorted by Jacques Archambault and serenaded by crying gulls, we put to sea.

Sailing a replica of SPRAY isn't as simple as it might seem. I had to very quickly forget completely my years of racing, learn everything over again, and revert to my grandfather's philosophy, which was to respect the elements, the equipment, and the men.

Jean David, a longtime captain, was a wise and peaceful man, molded, like Slocum, by his many years at sea. He carried on the heritage of his father, Emile David, captain of square riggers and Cape Horner. Jean David had an ascetic appearance, chiseled, tanned features, the piercing gaze of an oceangoing bird from constantly scanning the surface of the ocean. His fine, pale blue eyes, were that clear color you find in the cold South Pacific, and in them always twinkled the little flame of youth, freedom, and desire.

I was very lucky to have known him and shared a little of his life during the school holidays I spent at his house. Le Béchet in those days was nothing more than a small fishing port. The tide set the rhythm of the movements of the boats and, at spring high tides, completely covered the pretty beach. The border of fir trees is no longer there, its place taken by concrete and a row of cabins. It's there that I served my first apprenticeship at sea, and also under it! I would have drowned had it not been for the rapid intervention of Mme. Berge and her friends. My grandfather, without getting angry, wasn't at all happy about the event and had me learn to swim before I could go on a boat again. That I did quickly.

He would have liked SPRAY. During our transatlantic crossing, I read one of the books that had belonged to him, *Around the World With KURUN* by Jacques-Yves Toumelin. The author had a poor opinion of Joshua Slocum's boat. But, marking a page in the book, I found a drawing of SPRAY my grandfather had made on tracing paper. From that, I took it that Jean David dreamed of sailing in this boat. In any case, he was with us aboard SPRAY OF SAINT-BRIAC, a little like the helmsman of the PINTA in Captain Slocum's account.

To sail SPRAY, above all you have to know her, to know how to listen and anticipate. To try to go against wind and tide was suicidal and could quickly have bad consequences. Her 30-horsepower engine wasn't powerful enough, so we soon learned to have an anchor ready to deploy and not to cut too close to the rocks.

One day, we were making slow progress in a very light breeze off Cap Fréhel. Despite repeated attempts, backing the jib and trying to push the boom across, we found it impossible to tack. We were heading inexorably toward the rocks at the foot of the cliff, just below Fort Lalatte. We couldn't use the engine because, as we left the lock at Saint-Malo, a piece of large-mesh netting had caught in the propeller. A fisherman was trolling in the area. I passed him a line. He succeeded in turning the bow around and we set off on the other tack, toward the open sea, to the lively satisfaction of the whole crew. As for our savior, he probably went off muttering to himself something like "If you don't know how to sail a boat, you should stay ashore." I understood then how big sailing ships came to be lost on that coast, with no wind, pushed irresistibly on by the swell and the currents.

"I learned more with SPRAY than on any boat I'd sailed on," Captain Slocum said on his return. Patience must have been one of his greatest virtues.

It was a new style of sailing, a different philosophy. I had to discover it little by little, learn it, and absorb it, not without some bouts of temper. Then, I began to appreciate the appeal and the sheer joy of this kind of cruising.

It was the end of August 1994, and, bathed in sunshine and pushed by a nice easterly breeze, we crossed the Bay of Biscay without incident to quickly skirt by Galicia.

"With this weather, do you think we might be able to anchor behind Cape Finisterre?"

As we passed the point, a sudden gust of wind caused SPRAY to round up suddenly. Luckily there was no one around and the rocks were a good distance away. Heaving on the wheel with both hands, I managed slowly to get the boat under control and bring her back on course, while at the same time the gust abated. I yelled once again, at the top of my lungs, that we really had to modify the rudder!

We found several sailboats in the pleasant and well protected anchorage at Puerto Finisterre and passed a quiet night there.

The next day, we set off for the Cies islands which we reached at the end of the afternoon. Rather than going there directly, we chose to go behind Point Subrido, where we spotted a beautiful large beach in the bay at Barra. The anchor went down a reasonable distance from the shore. A little out of breath, hands on hips, I took a look around. Surprise, surprise, it appeared to be a nudist beach! Apparently they were enjoying their privacy and freedom, because a large number were walking at a lively pace along the water's edge. Off we went anyway. At least we didn't have to deal with drying out the swimsuits afterwards.

The following morning we covered the few miles to Area das Rodas in Cies island, a spot that our friend Guy Viau had recommended warmly. Cruising with his family, he had spent several years exploring the Mediterranean and the Iberian peninsula. The scenic anchorage was all the more pleasant because we were almost alone. On shore, we were able to take long walks along well-maintained paths in the neighboring hills, and enjoy breathtaking vistas from their summits.

The ocean stretched as far as the eye could see to the west, and toward the land was a large bay with the port of Vigo. We relished our four unforgettable days there. At dawn, the mist would come in and envelop us, but by the end of the morning it would quickly give way to sunshine. We expected to see a lot of cruising boats, but in fact we encountered only a handful. Of course it was the end of the month, summer vacations were over, and the route for world cruisers was farther to seaward, leading to Madeira or the Canaries. The Portuguese coast in earlier times didn't have very much to induce you to stop, but now marinas can be found in Leixoes, Porto, Cascais, Lisbon, Lagos, Villamoura, and Portimão.

After a brief idyllic stay in Cies, which is in every way equal to any anchorage in the Caribbean, and with the weather forecast again favorable, we set off and proceeded to cruise along the Iberian peninsula. Each day was enchanting.

We were heading south. Just the sound of the word intoxicated us: south, *south*! The word suddenly became magic. Mile by mile, we left behind us the end of summer, the autumn, then the winter which would all too soon be taking over the high northern latitudes. The south meant warmth, fine weather, and the tradewinds with their flying fish and carefree sailing. It drew us in inexorably, helped by the Nortada, the Portuguese tradewind. This wasn't too strong and pushed us gently toward Cascais, where the anchorage is sheltered by the coast. Even so, toward late afternoon, strong gusts would blow down from the hills onto the fleet.

We received a very friendly reception at the yacht club, on the left of the bay, and the showers there were very hot. Cascais is a seaside resort and residential area an hour from Lisbon and is rich in architecture and fine villas. Its shaded streets are lined with outdoor cafes and restaurants where seafood is the staple on the menus. There's a nice little beach on which the fishermen pull up their boats whose yellow, green, red, blue, and orange offer an early suggestion of the Mediterranean.

We took the opportunity to go to Lisbon by the train, as it runs along the shore, a great way to take in the sights. It was Sunday, and everything in the city was closed, but strolling on and around the Praça do Comercio made us want to come back. We spent another day in Sintra, a town wedged in the hills amid luxurious vegetation which gave us a brief respite of coolness and shade. On rounding corners of its steep and winding lanes we would suddenly find small architectural treasures from centuries past, and impressive castles and monasteries, reminders of the age when Portugal was a kingdom.

The days passed quickly, under a sky that was a limpid, cloudless blue from morning to night. The dry air, combined with the wind, dried and cracked our skin.

Contemplating the beauty of the magnificent, perfectly clear starry nights made dreamers of us. For me, it brought to mind a scene from a movie about Admiral Nelson. He was on the balcony of his house in Lisbon, with Lady Hamilton, and they were both admiring the celestial view that they decided was "like no other place."

After we passed Cape St. Vincent, we decided to anchor in the bay of La Baleira, near a lovely beach. Apart from a few sailboarders making dramatic runs in the strong afternoon sea breeze, there was nobody there.

However, we began to discover one of the unpleasant aspects of cruising in this part of the world, which was to be under the continual scrutiny of the authorities. The moment we anchored, or set foot on shore, they were there, often in civilian dress. The repetition everywhere we went became at the very least annoying, and soured our exploration of this magnificent country. Happily, with the growing unity and conformity within Europe, things have become better in recent years.

Under the shelter of the high, ocher-colored cliffs, we sailed on toward the white city of Lagos, where the anchor settled on the sandy bottom off the beach, to the right of the starboard jetty of the harbor's entrance channel. This time, we were not alone, as there were about 10 cruising boats gathered there. Apart from the wind from the Nortada in the afternoon, the anchorage was pleasant and calm.

A new marina had just opened at the head of the channel and the staff came riding out in their Zodiac to invite us to stay there. But we were cruising, and preferred to anchor out and retain our freedom when it came to diving and swimming. In the past, the only marina had been in Villamoura, 30 miles to the east. This coast is quite inhospitable and a southeasterly swell often heralds bad weather. The only shelter to be found is up rivers, which entails crossing their bars and negotiating sandbanks, strong currents and channels that are badly buoyed, if at all. A large number of cruising boats had found them-

Briac under the coconut trees

———◆———

selves in dicey situations, but little by little, things are getting better and when assisted by a little prudence, the problems tend to be fewer.

We spent 10 idyllic days there during which time Briac got acquainted with the Optimist, and made rapid progress. During his swims at the edge of the beach he gradually regained his confidence in the water, every day putting his head a little deeper in the sea. He had to rid himself of a bad memory.

In 1993 he was two years old. We were tied up in the marina at Saint-Quay-Portrieux and a gull would visit him every day. The more they became friends, the closer they got to each other. What happened that sunny afternoon? We don't know. We suspect that the bird was on the floating dock, approaching the boat where Briac was standing on the deck, holding some scraps of bread in his hand. Annick and I were below with our cups of tea. Suddenly, there was a heavy thud, as though something had fallen on the deck. We looked at each other questioningly, listening for what might follow. But there was nothing, not a sound.

Immediately Annick went up the ladder to find that the deck was empty. She understood, leaned over the side, and saw the child under the water. His eyes wide with terror, he was desperately flailing with his hands for something to hold onto. Jumping on the pontoon, Annick thrust her arms in the water, grabbed her little one, and pulled him out of the water. She then brought him on deck and set about drying him off.

"It might be a good idea to take him for a hot shower."

What did I say! An indignant Briac shot me a look:

"No! I've had it with baths for today!"

For a long time he didn't talk about this traumatic event. It took close to two years, but little by little, a few words at a time and with long silences in between, he revealed what had happened. Since then he'd been afraid to put his head under water and swim. Each day in Lagos he became a little bolder and in the end, it was watching other children his age that gave him the most encouragement.

These 10 days were interrupted by a visit to Portimão. Dominique, a friend we'd known in Argentina, lived there, but we had no means of contacting him, neither an address nor telephone number. All we knew was that he raced in regattas, and very well at that. We thought we might find him if we hung around the waterfront or asked in the yacht club.

A small marina had been created at the top of the estuary, right in town, along the quays that were now almost deserted because of the decline of the fishing industry. Assisted by a strong current, we headed for it. As we approached the dock, a man walked up slowly, watching us carefully, before gesturing an invitation for us to tie up there. I replied as usual, no thanks, that doesn't interest us, we're just passing by. The guy, in denim shirt and jeans, wearing a baseball cap, stared at us for a moment while shading his face from the fierce sunlight with his hand, then shouted "Guy!"

"Dominique!"

Without expecting it and without arranging a meeting, we had found each other after many years!

Quickly, the fenders were in place, the mooring lines on the cleats, and SPRAY OF SAINT-BRIAC gently came to rest alongside the quay. We all shared a toast to friendship on board, followed by a lunch of grilled sardines and calamari on the terrace of a congenial cafe on the quay at Ferragudo, a village across the river.

Two days later we were back in our anchorage off the magnificent beach in Lagos, until a southeasterly swell prompted us to explore the river at Alvor, two miles away. There, we would be sheltered behind the two new breakwaters. We were delighted by the view that unfolded before us: a lagoon with perfectly calm water, out of the current that flows in the center of the channel, surrounded by hills and cliffs of dark ocher soil capped with shrubbery and sea pines. Above all, there was no one there, not one cruising boat!

A mile to our right, we could make out a white village, wedged in a fold in the cliff. It was low tide, and the river made a beautiful sight winding between sandbanks, some of them blindingly white. At high tide, terns, gulls, and cormorants would claim the remaining exposed areas as resting places.

Not knowing what I'd find higher up toward the village, I went in the dinghy at low tide the next day to familiarize myself with the course of the river and its channel. Checking the depth regularly, marveling at the light and the beauty, I kept on rowing forward. Soon, I made out the masts of a ketch, so there was enough water that far. I discovered that there was a sort of basin off the village where the fishing boats were moored. Delighted with this unexpected find, I quickly went back to SPRAY OF SAINT-BRIAC and her crew, who were trying to hide their impatience.

"So?"

"It's neat. Let's go. There's an anchorage and a village where we can do our shopping. Let's use the mid-tide so we can easily follow the channel."

No sooner said than the anchor was aboard, SPRAY's stem slowly followed the meandering bed of the river, and we were there, in one of our best anchorages ever, well protected and in unbelievable surroundings. Ever since, Alvor has for us remained one of the most pleasant places anywhere.

On all sides of the basin, which was roughly rectangular and no deeper than 10 feet, the scenery was lovely.

On one side, dominated by its church, the village of small white houses spread along the slopes of the valley with its brightly colored fishing boats huddled at the water's edge. There was the typical red and white lifeboat shed and inside it, we discovered a splendid wooden lifeboat trimmed with protective patches and strips of bronze and leather. It wasn't used any more, but once a year, in September, it would take part in the Blessing of the Fleet. You could still imagine the men, though, pulling vigorously on their oars, going down the river before confronting the bar and struggling against the dangerous rollers thrown up by the fierce gales. In some ways, those were the best times, when man pitted his own strength against that of the elements. From my seat in the cockpit, the village presented a lovely and restful sight glowing in the light of the setting sun.

On the south side, dunes separated the village from the long beach. On the west side, mud and sand banks dried out with the tide. North, dramatic vistas unfolded beyond vast, protected water meadows and old salt marshes surrounded by high dykes along which we would at times see cows plodding in single file.

The river wound like a long snake toward the northeast between cliffs in the valley it had created.

It wasn't long before we discovered lovely walks in the neighboring hills along paths which were most often deserted.

During the month that we stayed there, only three sailboats joined us for a few days. It was astonishing. It was hard to believe that we were still in Europe.

The village itself was invaded by tourists and foreigners who had invested in properties, among them many restaurant owners. On the sidewalks, vendors grilled sardines and all kinds of fish, as well as calamari and octopus, on great smoking barbecues. Fishermen caught the octopi in earthenware pots shaped like vases or small amphorae. They set the pots, tied together, on the flat, sandy seabed. The octopi took refuge in them and all the fishermen had to do was haul them up.

Once or twice a day, a flock of sheep, accompanied by an old shepherd and his lame dog, would pass along the water's edge across the foot of the village. The dog would take advantage of this spot to have a refreshing swim. After his master had thrown a few rocks and yelled at him, he would go back to work dragging his hind leg. Then, taking the initiative, he made the animals climb higher up the rocks and continue on their way to the nearby fold.

Briac was fascinated by the noisy three-wheeled delivery vehicles and the enclosed tricycle scooters that were the local vehicles of choice. Most picturesque, though, was the host of small motorcycles, some of which must have dated from the last war.

Making contact with the people was not easy. There was the language barrier, but it also seemed that the mentality in the Algarve was quite different from that in the rest of Portugal. The invasion of tourists didn't help. The inhabitants didn't seem quite at home, having been taken over by rather slovenly, beer-swilling hordes coming mainly from the north of England. Their houses were being torn down to make way for restaurants or boutiques and, one by one, they were being pushed out. The young were leaving the village to seek work in town, and the wooden fishing boats, each one painted in its own bright color scheme, were being replaced by plastic ones, boats in name only, not in character. Year by year, the graveyard of old hulls grew on the mud bank. The old fishermen were gone.

What impressed me most here was that the old had their place, which they accepted, and they were respected. They weren't shut away in retirement homes. As they say in Africa, "You shouldn't sell the old people, on the contrary, you should buy more of them." They have so much to teach us. Doesn't the knowledge and wisdom of the world reside in them? Every day, from sunup to sundown, they were there, helping to clean and repair the nets, baiting the long lines, and cleaning the fish. They watched, commenting, passing the time. At the end of the afternoon, they played cards or dominoes, only leaving their places to answer nature's call between the boats or in a crevice in the rocks. It was a simple life, with no frills, a step back into the past—but for how much longer?

Briac was visibly more content and more motivated in the presence of this continuous daily activity. Every morning, he went shopping with his mother in the new market building, where he would talk to people while Annick made her purchases.

We dedicated the afternoons to long walks, sometimes toward the hills, sometimes along the beach, and invariably ending with a swim in the ocean or the lagoon.

On other occasions, our path led us along the shore and we would return with a bucket of cockles; or, yet, with the Zodiac, we would go to the sandbanks which were still exposed at high tide to bathe, run among the gulls, or simply to relax in the hot sun. Quite often, we were alone on the little sandy islet which lacked nothing its Caribbean cousins had to offer. Eventually, Briac started to use the Optimist, sailing from one end of the lagoon to the other, under the proud, if not always confident, gaze of his parents who followed him at a distance in the inflatable dinghy.

It was almost paradise, what more could we have asked for? Why still go on farther? We found ourselves thinking that it would be difficult to find anything better . . . yet, we had to press on.

To begin with, we had to find a boatyard. A visit to Portimão, accompanied by Dominique, helped us to choose one: Portinave.

There, they had neither travelift nor slipway to haul the boat. Nothing of the sort. They did it the old way. At high tide, they set the keel of the boat on a kind of wooden sled, then put props around the hull. The whole rig was hauled by an ingenious system of cables and sheaves driven by an electric winch. The makeshift cradle slid on beams fastened to the ground, wood on wood. The whole apron of the yard being covered with these beams, they could steer the boat on its sled wherever they wanted to put it. When handling heavy vessels, of perhaps 250 tons, they would lubricate the beams with hot waste oil to make them more slippery. I was at first somewhat skeptical about it, but, after all, they had been doing it this way for a great many years.

And so SPRAY OF SAINT-BRIAC became reacquainted with traditional ways and found herself in the boatyard for an examination of her hull, several modifications to her deck and cabins, and an overall paint job. The rudder would come later. We also took the opportunity to replenish our stores. One particular task was to refill our butane gas cylinders and that brought us a surprise: Four pounds cost about three dollars and seven about four dollars—a bargain compared with French prices.

It was such a pleasure to be in a boatyard that worked in wood, where they received entire tree trunks and cut from them according to need. And what a privilege and an education it was to watch the carpenter at work and to follow the laying in of the planking.

To launch the boat, they lowered the whole assembly at low tide and waited for the rising tide to float the boat off. Nothing could be simpler, especially as time was never pressing there.

It was the end of October, and the weather began to deteriorate, marked by fronts of varying violence passing through. One night, the wind changed from southwest to northwest and gradually freshened. The sound of water splashing against the hull in an unusual way caught my attention. I pulled on my jacket and went up on deck to see what was going on. The boat was lying across the wind. My first thought was to look for the float that marked the anchor. We had buoyed it to make it easier to raise it because the impressive mechanical windlass, probably not much different from the one Captain Slocum used, wasn't neither very practical nor fast. It was as I thought. The buoy was caught in the dinghy painter, and that was now what was holding the boat to the anchor—a hefty quarter-inch line!

The problem was, the anchor was being pulled the wrong way and was dragging along the bottom, and our cozy little home was drifting slowly but ever so surely toward the sandbank behind us. Seizing the painter, and hauling on it like a madman seeing the end of the world approaching, I managed, with a little help from the boathook, to free the yellow float. Everything immediately resumed its rightful place and SPRAY was able to pull on her chain and anchor in the proper manner.

It's not difficult to find yourself aground or alongside your neighbor. Another incident confirmed how you have to always be prudent and alert. A few days earlier, when the Nortada was up early one afternoon, our American neighbor started to drag. Fortunately, the skipper was on board. When he raised his anchor, a fisherman, he noticed that the rope part of his rode had wrapped around its upper fluke and was pulling it in the wrong direction, upward. These little incidents of the cruising life show that you can never be completely sure that everything is going right. People have lost their boats to little details like that.

4

$\blacklozenge$

Briac's Second Transatlantic

Listening to RFI (Radio France International) at 11.40 a.m. GMT gave us no hint of anything special in the way of weather, and so it was with some sadness that we left this haven of peace and happiness, bound for Tenerife in the Canary Islands.

Within a few miles, we were once more in the great west-northwest Atlantic swell, which didn't help the sails set quietly. Without enough wind to keep them full it was truly awful. The mainsail with its spars, the boom and the gaff, described wild arabesques. Not only was that dangerous, it was also very testing for the rig and the gear. The best we could do was to try to lash everything down hard and wait for the wind to return.

After a few days of calms and variable winds, I reckoned we couldn't be far from the tradewinds. Then one morning, a few big clouds came toward us and . . . in an instant we were in a solid 30 knots under a squall, taken completely by surprise. Action stations on board! It was time to reduce sail because the boat was out of control. This operation quickly turned to pandemonium when the mainsail refused to come down. I ended up with sore fingers from trying to grip the fabric and sore arms from pulling it down. Relieved at last, the boat resumed her course, helped along by a fair northeast breeze of force 5 to 6.

The sun quickly came back and the white flecked sea took on a deep blue color. Several hours later, we saw the islands of Lanzarote and Graciosa to our south. With this fine wind, we would be in Tenerife the next day.

"Hey, the line's taut!" A quick glance toward the other end and "Fish!" the cry went up. The crew immediately took up their stations so as to try to bring the fish aboard. While I hauled in the line, Annick retrieved the sharp gaff from the passageway.

"Yeah! A dolphinfish, look at those amazing colors!"

Blue, green, yellow, silver—there is no fish more beautiful. The trickiest thing is to get it out of the water and over the lifelines . . . Bam! A well-timed swing of the arm and it landed on the deck, struggling briefly and changing color many times before giving up with a final shudder.

Fish are always welcome on board because they mean fresh food. We would take one, and then put the lines away until the next day. The lines were nylon cord about 200 feet long with a leader of stainless steel wire or heavy monofilament at the end. To this we attached a very simple lure, usually a multicolored plastic squid. Lacking one of those, which were the best, a piece of plastic supermarket shopping bag colored yellow, orange, or white, seized to the hook would do quite well. Later, I perfected my system using a shock cord hooked between a stanchion and the line. All I had to do was look at how stretched the elastic was to know if I had a catch. Quite often, a shark or a bigger fish would be faster than I was and leave us crying over an empty line.

I later fitted on the stern, between the davits, a round bar on which two black plastic cylinders, originally spools for small diameter line, could turn. They were ribbed on both faces. Using a piece of semi-rigid plastic tube, I could maintain enough pressure to prevent them from turning under the load of just the fishing line dragging through the water. Any greater load would make the assembly spin, setting off a tremendous rattling noise that sounded like a machine gun. On the cylinder, I only wound about 15 to 20 feet of quarter-inch line to which I would attach my trolling line. The first few times we almost jumped out of our skins at the noise, but it was very effective and we caught a lot more fish.

Meanwhile, we had the pleasure of eating the dorado, filetted and sauteed in the pan with garlic and shallots, together with pan-fried potatoes.

Pushed by the northeasterly wind we were approaching Tenerife and Point Anaga appeared soon, high, rocky, black, and menacing.

We would arrive in Santa Cruz at nightfall. That meant we'd have to eat later, after getting in, a plan that didn't sit too well with Briac.

The problem was, I wasn't too sure about where we would be mooring. Our friends Véronique and Pedro had described a place, but I had to admit, a bit late, that I hadn't understood them too well.

We began by taking a turn by the yacht club, while calling them on the radio, but nothing much seemed to be going on there. Eventually, someone indicated that we should go alongside at the marina three miles to the north. It was full and couldn't take us. We turned around, now in total darkness except for the bright lights on shore reflecting in the water. If worst came to worst, we could always anchor, but it was deep and there was a significant surge. No, we would try to find something better.

I managed to get in contact with our friend Carlos on the VHF. He said he would try to reach Pedro so that he, in turn, could get in touch with us, on channel 16. He told us, at the same time, that we should find a place in the commercial basin, just before the southern dock, behind a red boat. Great! With all these directions, we had better find something.

Once we were under way again, Briac didn't complain but seemed to want to chide me with a look—"I'm not sure about this"—obviously thinking about his dinner which had eluded him a little longer. We passed the club again and continued toward the head of the basin. In the powerful lights of the harbor, a red-orange mass loomed. It had the appearance of an ocean-going tug.

"Let's go and see!" It was indeed a tug. Pedro confirmed it, but suggested we should tie up astern of it. This wasn't going to be an easy maneuver, especially as a front had passed over us and a drenching rain rendered visibility poor and judging distances difficult. Véronique and Pedro, accompanied by a port watchman, were standing in the glow of the headlights of their car, like ghostly silhouettes or characters in a detective movie. They must have been perplexed by the slowness of our approach.

Eventually, after making a first pass to take a look, I chose a spot ahead of the tug. I wasn't too happy about the huge rubber sausages that served as fenders for cargo boats, but too bad, there was no swell and we could take another look in the morning. Briac, poor little chap, stood immobile in his waterproof jacket, stoically at attention on his bare legs, next to the closed companionway. In the howling wind and driving rain, he watched without a word. On top of everything, he was cold, hungry, and fighting off sleep. He won everyone's admiration.

"Come quickly, let's go eat at the house and get some rest there," shouted Véronique. We gratefully accepted her invitation and Briac miraculously came back to life. At that moment, a hot shower was our most fervent desire.

Thanks to our friends, this stay in Tenerife was pure enchantment for Briac. The next day, we went from the yacht club back to SPRAY OF SAINT-BRIAC aboard Pedro's fast motorboat. Briac didn't know which way to look: there was so much too see. Life in the port of Santa Cruz was very busy, what with the incessant movements of freighters, liners, ferries, hydrofoils, and the constant activity on the docks.

SPRAY OF SAINT-BRIAC found her spot behind the tug, right at the base of the first lighthouse of Santa Cruz.

Sailing along the coastline of Tenerife with Carlos and Véronique
(Pedro Doblado)

Imagine our surprise to see a blue Rolls Royce Corniche convertible draw up slowly and stop on the quay. It was Andrea and Carlos inviting us to join them for lunch in a country inn on this beautiful, sunny day.

Tenerife is one of the nicest islands we have visited. I'm not referring to the tourist areas, but to Santa Cruz, its market, the activity of the port, its commercial and residential streets, and above all the generosity of its inhabitants. There are wonderful walks toward Teide, an extinct volcano whose summit is often snowcapped in winter. On its slopes the climate, and with it the vegetation, varies as the altitude increases, and there are magnificent pine trees at the higher elevations. After we'd taken in scenery of vertiginous and breathtaking beauty, a visit to villages like Garachico or La Orotava let us explore the local culture and architecture.

It's an island with an eternal springtime climate where there's no other way to live than well!

"Come see, Briac."

Just in front of us, a superb three-master was maneuvering to come alongside the quay, with some of its crew standing at attention on the yards. It was the LIBERTAD, the Argentine sail-training ship. Briac, impressed, took in every detail of this magnificent vessel, which was a new experience for him.

"Do you think we can go and visit it?"

"I don't know. We'll see."

We were now really in good company and SPRAY OF SAINT-BRIAC, flying all her flags, looked more than a little proud.

Thanks to Carlos, who put a car at our disposal, we could do our provisioning with ease. The supermarkets were outside the town, as were the suppliers of fuel. The price of cooking gas proved to be much cheaper than at home.

The sea was calling us and we had to think about leaving. Christmas was coming, and presents arrived from Andreas, Véronique, and Bernadette. Imp brought one that touched me profoundly.

"Hey, come look, I've brought something for SPRAY."

Opening the trunk of his car, he showed me a superb 65-pound CQR anchor which could only mean he wished us one thing: Set sail, go explore the ocean, and seek good anchorages.

"If you want it, take it. It's my brother's. I phoned him in Australia and he said that I could give it to you."

It was hard to refuse, especially as all I had was a 45-pound Danforth that was marginal at best. In strong blows, the Danforth had a tendency to break out. Once we started using this new anchor, we had no more such problems. Perhaps it was because we had less wind. Who knows?

The day before leaving, we tried the SSB radio again. It worked, and André was listening, or more exactly I was listening because it was he who called. It continued to work throughout the crossing and the school at Pleurtuit received regular news of Briac and his adventure aboard his sailing ship.

For several days now, we had been waiting in rain and wind for the right break in the weather. Once it came, we immediately headed down to Galletas, a pleasant harbor south of the island, just beyond the airport, in the hopes of finding a place inside. It wasn't to be, and we had to anchor outside on a rocky bottom. Apart from some discomfort, though, the night passed without incident.

At dawn, we headed for the island of Hierro. We reached it at night and anchored at La Estaca. Here again there wasn't much room, there was a swell, and the holding was mediocre. Instead of visiting the island I stayed aboard to tinker and to keep an eye on another boat whose crew had deserted it for the day. It came close to us a few times as it swung around its anchor and dragged in the gusts of wind that hurtled off the cliffs. What fun! Happily, the chicken that Annick and Briac brought back was especially tasty when cooked over the wood fire.

The next day we raised the anchor in the hopes of keeping it for a while at the bottom of the bilge. The Atlantic stretched wide before us. The wind was light, which is normal that early in the morning. We were carrying 60 gallons of fuel and 75 of water, enough to reach Carriacou, our next stop, at least according to the plan. Carriacou is a small island north of Grenada, and has a reputation for still building wooden boats, which plainly interested me. We had chosen this island because we wanted to avoid those infested with tourists and charter boats, and we hoped we weren't making a mistake.

During this crossing, SPRAY was in her element, which is to say in a following wind with the helm lashed. We were therefore able to use our time for school, reading, maintenance, or simply leaning on the companionway coaming and dreaming. Fortunately, Dominique had raided his bookshelves to find us reading matter. Afterwards, we simply traded with other boats whenever we stopped. This way we always had something to read the whole time we were cruising.

This was the second time that Annick and I had taken the tradewind route. The previous time, 15 years before, hadn't left us with good memories. We had stayed a little too far north, on the English route as it's known, and encountered cold, a lot of rain, and contrary winds. This time we set a course of south-southwest before heading west.

From 25° North and 20° West and for eight days, we caught one dorado each day, sometimes two when we were slow to pull in the second line, and after that no more until arriving at Carriacou where we caught many barracuda. It would appear that fish have naturally defined territories.

We met quite a few sailboats, as many as four in one day. Some didn't run dead downwind, so they had to jibe regularly. They would therefore be crossing our path. It's possible they were part of a rally or a cruising race. Between events organized by the French and the British, there was a crowd on the ocean. This part of the Atlantic has become a busy highway!

We were content with averages of 125 to 140 miles every day. It was profoundly satisfying to watch SPRAY OF SAINT-BRIAC breast the sea with her full and powerful bow, leaving behind her a nearly perfect wake.

"Papa, papa, look, an island!"

All of a sudden, Briac became very alert and excited.

"Yes, it's Barbados, but we're not going there. Tomorrow, we should arrive in Carriacou and soon it will be Christmas!"

"Did I see it first?"

"Yes, you did."

Sure enough, Barbados, simply a bump on the horizon, was to our south. We had left Hierro 23 days before and had an uneventful crossing without any major problems.

In late morning, just before we arrived at the island, three lovely barracuda were laid out on the deck and we were watching the local sailing fishing boats, mainsheet eased out, drifting beam on to the wind in the channel that separates Carriacou from Union Island.

Once we'd passed Rapid Point and were under the lee of the shore, we dropped and furled the sails and prepared to anchor. We had difficulty containing our joy at reaching this next destination.

North of the jetty at Hillsborough, the anchor hit the bottom with incredible speed. For a few moments, we studied the shoreline looking for a place where we could land. I jumped into the dinghy with two barracuda, bound for the quay. We had too many fish, so I was going to give them away. A kid on the dock who had a fishing line wound around an old Coke can grabbed the first. He couldn't believe his eyes and made off excitedly, his arms wrapped around his prize. The second went to the port captain who promptly handed it to his wife who happened to be passing by. I learned that barracuda are especially good when made into a fish stew.

When clearing customs, I had to point out the Canary Islands on a world map hung on the wall. It was probably rare for sailboats coming from so far away to pick this place as their port of entry to the Caribbean.

I then went to immigration and also to the bank, because this first sortie on land wasn't free. It gave me the opportunity to see that this lovely village, with its pastel-colored wooden or cement block houses roofed with corrugated iron, had a post office, a bank, card-operated telephones and fax, and of course an open-air market. Everything was there to make a sailor happy. But that was more the concern of the rest of the crew, so I quickly went back aboard to give them time to make their purchases.

This was a most pleasant spot. Few cruising boats stay there, though several stop long enough to make their clearance before moving on. The activity in the harbor, though laid back and on a small scale, was constant and varied, the highlight being the typical Caribbean atmosphere that surrounded the arrival of the boat from St. Georges, Grenada's capital, with its cargo of passengers, animals, and merchandise of every description. In fact, the sole inconvenience was the anchor's annoying tendency to drag because the bottom, ten to twelve feet deep, was a layer of sand over rock or hardened lava. By diving, we found concrete blocks here and there to which we could tie a line or even shackle the chain.

The island's best anchorage was in Tyrrell Bay, a little farther south. It was crowded and to provision, you had to take the bus to the village. However, it was in this pretty bay that we saw the first builder of wooden boats, right under the coconut palms that lined the beach and the road. The place was quite primitive and interesting in many ways. We managed to collect several bags of wood chips, the best for starting the stove. There's nothing like it for drying out the boat, and on top of that, there's the smell and warmth of the burning wood. A fireplace on board . . . what luxury!

On the northeast corner of the island we found two more small boatyards, but there wasn't much activity.

After two days of rest, swimming, walks, and coming and going between the two anchorages, we left in rain and little wind for St. Georges, on the island of Grenada, to re-provision and find butane gas. Our objective after that was to get to the other side of the Caribbean, to the Bay Islands, off Honduras, a crossing which would amount to 10 days or so. We weren't much interested in staying on this side where it was now too crowded though, with a little exploration, you could still find some unspoiled corners.

In a violent squall, surrounded by a large number of sailboats and under the worried scrutiny of several skippers, we succeeded in setting our anchor in the middle of the lagoon.

St. Georges is a typical and lovely Caribbean port full of color and original colonial architecture. The walk from the lagoon to the center of the town is a sight not to be missed. It was such a pleasure to discover the fish market, and the fruit and vegetable market where the multicolored displays are permeated by the delicious aroma of spices.

After some hunting around, I found the place to get the four- and six-pound gas bottles recharged. It was a primitive procedure, but it worked: connect my small cylinder to a big one, then turn the big one upside down! If I remember correctly, it was near the Coke or Pepsi plant, which was also a depot for beer and soft drinks of all kinds, a sort of wholesale bar. I went there by taxi. To return, I took the bus from the stop right across the street.

In St. Georges, one of the main topics of conversation is security.

The day after we got there, a French sailboat had visitors in the middle of the night while the four people on board were sleeping. The intruders gave themselves away by brushing the arm of a sleeper. They just had time to flee, taking with them an electric flashlight, to light their way I suppose. The day before, I had seen a guy astride a sailboard hull, roaming between the boats. He looked to me as though he was studying ways of getting aboard, in particular the now fashionable sugar scoop sterns and bowsprits. Surprised to find me watching him, he immediately tried to explain his presence by offering me a few sad-looking fruits. He didn't impress me as being a salesman.

People padlocked their dinghies ashore and alongside their boats, and many were suspended from halyards at night. That didn't prevent theft from the more wily!

In the spirit of Joshua Slocum, who had used carpet tacks to deter the savages of Patagonia, I strung fine fishing line at calf height in various places around the deck and tied it to a one-gallon milk can that was barely balanced on the cabin top. I did the same for the dinghy, with an invisible line tied to a can set on the cockpit seat, in addition to its padlocked stainless-steel cable. When the can fell onto the deck, the noise would be enough to awaken a regiment, though not, perhaps, Briac. SPRAY is relatively low to the water, and the easiest way to get aboard, leaving aside the dinghy, is to use the chain bobstay that connects the bowsprit to the hull. I thought about wrapping it with barbed wire or something similar, but that wouldn't have done much aesthetically. The best solution, then, in the absence of an electric or electronic alarm, was a fishing line. It was a preventive and psychologically reassuring measure only, since in our entire voyage, we never had any regrettable incident. The danger is greater in certain tourist places, ports, or big towns, and doesn't always stem from the local inhabitants. In general, ashore as well as on board, one should be prudent and vigilant. Nevertheless, with cruising growing as it is, we can only expect theft from boats to increase.

We only stayed two days in that nervous and unpleasant atmosphere and quickly returned to the tranquility of Carriacou to prepare for going to sea once more.

5

From the Caribbean to Guatemala

We decided to leave on the morning of December 31. I have never enjoyed much New Year's Eve parties and the night would pass more quietly at sea. SPRAY concurred, she only wanted to be in the trades, and her wish was soon fulfilled.

There followed 12 days of peace and quiet in which we moved to the slower rhythm of the sea, so different from that in the anchorage. Briac got back to his routine of school and of games on the wide deck, which allowed him to run all round the boat while playing with his big trucks or his old wooden bus. Pushing on the bus with both hands, he would go round and around, stopping from time to time to regain his breath and reflect, or to watch a gull, a flight of flying fish, or a school of porpoises at the bow. And so life went on, simple and tranquil, to the rhythm of the elements and the cycle of the sun.

In the trades, there's nothing else to do, beside the occasional interruption by a squall, than to read and dream while contemplating the ocean's vastness. SPRAY OF SAINT-BRIAC continued calmly on her way. Other than the gurgling of the water along the hull, there was no sound. This magnificent wooden boat, her sails, the wind, and the sea, were all one in a way that was magical and unreal. We seemed to have entered another world and I never ceased to wonder at it.

She held her course without deviating more than 10 degrees either side of it, leaving behind her a perfect and almost undisturbed wake.

With SPRAY, I had discovered a form of perfection in sailing and I attained a level of serenity and a feeling of freedom that I hadn't dreamed of in a long time. This was the formidable legacy bequeathed by Captain Joshua Slocum.

During these 12 days, several freighters crossed our course. On the day after we left, we caught a dolphin, then three tuna the last two days at sea. They complemented our normal diet nicely.

Shortly before dawn we were within the range of the lighthouse of the northern point of Guanaja. Its beam swept the wave crests, highlighting their whiteness. Numerous threatening clouds, scudding rapidly toward the southeast, obscured the starry sky, a sign that a front was probably coming our way. We decided it was best to wait for daylight since the approach through the entrance channel was dotted with islets and a barrier reef surrounded the island. We hove to. Barely 10 minutes later, the sky started to unload tons of water, accompanied by tentative gusts of wind. I eased the mainsheet to keep the boat in control in the choppy and uncomfortable sea. While we waited for day-

Getting to know SPRAY
(Onne van der Wal)

break, the horizon began to clear in the east, and we ate a copious breakfast while thumbing through guidebooks to the region.

There are four islands: The farthest east, just ahead of us, was Guanaja; then came Roatán, Utila, and farther south, near the coast of Honduras, Cayos Cochinos. While the mainland coast was for the most part inhospitable, the islands offered good anchorages and plenty of them. For a long time, they had been the refuge of English pirates who preyed on Spanish galleons. The inhabitants, most of whom were black skinned, spoke an English patois as well as English and some Spanish. Spanish had become the official language but was mostly spoken by Honduran government officials. The rest of the population was white, many of them descendants of those old brigands. The Bay Islands are being more and more overrun by Americans who play a big part in the fishery, which concentrates on tuna and giant shrimp, and its dependent industries.

Most of the local black population lives in the small villages scattered along the coast; the high hills of the interior are covered with a luxurious vegetation which make them barely penetrable. Most of the dwellings are constructed on piles at the mouths of deep creeks. Communication and transportation are conducted by water through the bays or little channels that connect them, mostly by means of pirogues or cayucos dug out of treetrunks.

Attempts at tourist development have met with no great success but the construction of a new airstrip might have given it a boost. At the time, tourism was mostly centered around diving and several clubs had been developed for that purpose.

Guanaja is the highest island. It detached itself in front of us, a totally green mass set upon the blue of the sea. We quickly laid a course for the main harbor of Guanaja Settlement which had the standout feature of being on piles between two small islets. It reminded me of Venice. Narrow canals, wide enough for a cayuco to pass, wound between the jumble of wooden and cement block structures so close together that a fire in one of them would create a catastrophe. On the main island, at the head of the bay, several trawlers, bearing a strong resemblance to those on the American coast of the Gulf of Mexico, were unloading their catch at the processing and freezing plant.

"Yes, this is a good spot, let's anchor!"

The dinghy was next over the side but the trick was going to be finding a place to land in this confusion of pilings. I found one between two old hulks.

Now, we had to take care of the paperwork. A child wearing faded, dirty pirate's pants showed us where the office was. Though I tried to approach discreetly the wooden shack, I disturbed a chicken which, as it flapped its wings in retreat, screeched as though it would get hoarse, at least I would have if I'd tried to imitate it. The trusty port captain, seated near a broken fan, was wiping his brow and seemed quite happy to sign and stamp the various administrative implements. He wished us a pleasant stay in his beautiful country.

The place was truly unique and appealing. Cheerful children ran around our legs almost everywhere we went. We sensed here none of the surliness we'd encountered in some of the eastern Caribbean islands.

During our stay, we only saw a few cruising boats, most of them American, so there was always room in the numerous pleasant anchorages. The most popular place was undoubtedly French Harbour, on the island of Roatán, where there were about a dozen boats.

After a quick tour of the village I hurried back on board where Annick and Briac waited impatiently to hear my first impressions. Quickly, the whole crew returned to shore, to sniff out the local atmosphere and ferret around the little shops in search of a few vegetables, fruits, eggs, and perhaps, with luck, a piece of frozen meat. Because everything came from the mainland, there were often days when these were unavailable.

The anchorage near the village, while being both pleasant and a perfect vantage point, was in the path of the fishing boats so, the next morning, we moved to the well sheltered one at El Bight. Four cruising boats, five houses, and a tiki bar on a coral outcrop, which could be reached only by boat, were the only signs of civilization. Once the anchor dug in, our first look around revealed a magnificent pig in a pen that was half in the water and half on land. This enabled him to bathe and also to wallow in mud which, despite being somewhat thinned, was still smelly.

Just before leaving our previous anchorage in the village, we took the dinghy to explore El Soldado Canal which cuts across the island from south to north to the coast on the other side. SPRAY would have had enough water to make it through if it hadn't been for the floating dead vegetation. On the windward side of the island, the shoreline offered numerous small, pleasant and airy anchorages with beaches and remarkable diving spots in deep, clear water of surprising luminosity. The flora, fauna, and coral were every bit as plentiful and beautiful as in Belize or on the Great Barrier Reef of Australia.

A few days later, we went back as far as Savannah Bay. We anchored by ourselves off a picturesque village where we met an American retiree by the name of Bill who had settled there, far from everywhere.

For five miles along the coast, and parallel with it, stretches a chain of islets or keys, each with its white sand and coconut palms, protecting the shore and forming a vast sheltered sound. Most of these keys are owned by Americans.

One day, we witnessed the welcome visit of the banana boat. It came from the mainland, a good 20 miles away, a pirogue filled to the gunwales with barely enough space for two men to sit and paddle. We bought a stalk of bananas that would in time ripen on board. On another day, two fishermen came alongside us with fresh spiny lobster in the bottom of their cayuco.

A little sadly, we left again and headed west for Roatán where we expected mail to be awaiting us. Throughout our peregrinations, we had it sent to *poste restante* without much difficulty. The sole exception was South Africa where, depending on the place and the local official, they didn't hold it but sent it back or occasionally would forward it to a yacht club. Portugal surprised us by making us pay a small fee for our mail.

Going from anchorage to anchorage—that of Port Royal is magnificent, large and airy—we made our way toward French Harbour. Some bays penetrate far into the land and form veritable little fjords lined with dense tropical vegetation where howler monkeys and large numbers of parrots scream and squabble in the immense trees. At the head of Hog Pen Bight, Calabash Bight, and Oak Ridge, spiraling plumes of woodsmoke rose from cabins at the water's edge. We could envision the daily activities: the fishermen unloading their meager catch, the women doing the laundry or preparing meals, the children playing and swimming, the smell of the cooking. There was a light breeze and no mosquitoes. It was very pleasant and restful.

Just after leaving to starboard Little and Big French Cays, which mark the entrance of the channel to the French Harbour lagoon, there are two possibilities. At the red marker, or at least where it was, you can go to starboard and anchor among or in front of the boats there, in a vast area well aired out by the breeze. Alternatively, you can continue toward the very protected lagoon which shelters French Harbour Yacht Club. There you can either use one of the handful of docks at the yacht club or anchor off it in a tight space. We preferred by far the first option and anchored at the head of the fleet of about 10 boats. It was more to our liking because we could swim there or dive on the barrier reef in the shallow water behind which we found conch. We could also go to the Grand Hotel, which was completely engulfed in greenery, to buy stamps and post the mail or simply to stroll along the shaded walks.

Half a mile from there was the FHYC, set on a hill amidst trees, shrubs of all sorts, and flowers, and consisting of a restaurant, a bar, and a few rooms. It offered cruising sailors fax, mail, a book exchange, and various other services in a most pleasant atmosphere. For everything else, and to fill out the administrative paperwork at Coxen's Hole, the principal town, you had to cross the road to take the bus. You could go there by boat, if you wished.

We went several times by bus to the south of the island where there are lovely beaches. A few wooden structures set in the foliage, most of them in 1970s style, hint at tourism. We could have gone there by sea, along the coast, for there are some lovely spots to drop the hook, but it's less practical for the day-to-day activities because you have to take the bus to do any provisioning.

We didn't go to Utila, deciding instead to go directly to Cochinos. A lovely spot: two main islands are connected by a chain of keys such as you see only in dreams.

On Cochino Grande, there are but five or six houses, all of them lost in the vegetation, and one of which has rooms and a small bar and restaurant. To protect the coral seabed, it also offered several moorings at no charge.

Cochino Pequeño, less than a mile to the west, is protected by

UNESCO. In order to protect the bottom and not disturb the flora and fauna, anchoring or landing there is not permitted. Consequently, its beauty and serenity are guaranteed. We were there by ourselves to enjoy its marvelously clear and lovely water. These are certainly the most beautiful islands in all the Caribbean and we congratulated ourselves on coming so far to this little paradise. We were living in another world.

We had to force ourselves to resume our route westward, toward Guatemala and the Rio Dulce, about which we had heard so much.

6

♦

Journey to the Land of the Maya

At the end of the day the wind died until it was nothing more than warm, humid puffs. We elected, therefore, to go and anchor in the completely enclosed Bay of Puerto Escondido on the coast of Honduras. The only access is through a narrow pass between two rocks, on a course of 162 to be precise. It's absolutely incredible! Surrounding the lagoon is a beach bordered with coconut palms and behind that it's dense, tropical jungle. It's completely wild and untouched. There is not a single habitation, and the only sign of human life was a small sailboat tucked close to the cliff just inside the entrance. It left the next day anyway, without a word being exchanged.

Howler monkeys bickered in the big trees, their harsh and terrifying cries carrying over the water. There were also parrots, which sounded much merrier, and a multitude of birds maintained a constant cackling. The water was rather murky with sandy silt, probably due to the proximity of the Rio Tinto and because of the wind penetrating the entrance.

In the midst of all that jungle, the heat was heavy and humid. It was difficult not to heed the call of the beach, especially because it was dappled with dark, shady areas. It was over half a mile long and in places was covered with all kinds of flotsam, for the most part vegetation. We imagined ourselves like Adam and Eve, several years after having bitten the apple, in a paradise on Earth; everything seemed other-worldly. In the evening, as we were walking quietly along the water's edge, we were suddenly aware of a noise behind us. We turned around, and we couldn't believe our eyes. Silhouetted in the setting sun was a horseman wreathed in a halo of sparkling droplets kicked up by his cantering mount. It was a completely surrealistic apparition. Stunned, we thought we were witnessing the apocalypse.

It was unreal. We didn't know what to make of it and were a little on the defensive. He reined in his horse and approached us at a walk. We cautiously struck up a conversation, in Spanish. Polite words of greeting led to a few brief exchanges and ended with smiles. He had come from a fishing village on the other side of the lagoon, a few miles away, where he'd made some purchases, which lay across his horse in front of him. He was going back to his village a few hours away in the jungle, and this stretch of beach was the easiest part of his route. He assured us that there was nothing around there, only the dense and barely penetrable forest. With a big smile, he started his horse and soon disappeared into the vegetation.

When we set foot on the beach the following morning, we were assailed by swarms of no-see-ums, tiny, very aggressive flies which inflict painful bites. We had no choice but to stay submerged in the water and wait until they gave up and disappeared, at which point life once again became pleasant.

Around lunchtime, two fishermen came to rest in the shade of a coconut palm. They came from a harbor several miles to the west and had been working all night. A few fish were laid out among all kinds of stuff in the bottom of their plastic boat.

After three wonderful days, we had to put to sea again into the tradewind which, though feeble, at least allowed us to pass Cape Tres Puntas during the night. This is a long, low sand spit and approaching it required some vigilance especially as the currents are strong and unpredictable. After that, we patiently waited for daybreak before trying to enter the narrow channel that leads through the shallows to Livingston and the Rio Dulce.

At first light, we were most surprised to see a French naval vessel coming in from seaward. It passed quite close to us before disappearing behind the point into the naval base of Puerto Barios. It's crazy how the sight of a warship flying the French flag could lift our spirits and stir our hearts, especially this far from home.

Our problem was to find the entrance and the buoy. In the end, seeing nothing besides an almost submerged lobster pot float, I took some bearings from the land. Sure enough, there was the buoy dead ahead at 225°, just the way we like it, but in sandy and muddy water.

A good mile farther on, just after passing the range on Livingston, I turned to starboard to look for a spot in the anchorage, all the while trying to allow for the strong tidal current. After circling once, we decided on a place not far from the shore, to facilitate landing in the dinghy. The area seemed quite pretty and the village typical. Its distinguishing feature was the multitude of birds assembled there: cormorants, screaming and scavenging gulls, frigates, pelicans, white egrets. . . . At daybreak and day's end, in the trees and on the shore, it was an explosion of birdsong, a veritable symphony.

The anchorage was good. Nevertheless, it could be uncomfortable in the afternoon when the current was going the wrong way and the tradewind set the boat across it. As per routine, I went ashore to register our entry, but just before I reached the dock, a fellow on the shore indicated to me that I should return on board and wait there for the authorities. "They're on their way," he said, after glancing up the main street.

I just had to make a U-turn and wait, but not for long. In our entire voyage, this was the only time that we received a visit on board.

They came almost right behind me. They were courteous and friendly, but it wasn't just one but five officials who came aboard and immediately filled the main cabin. It was quite a crowd and I had difficulty finding a seat at the table. There were representatives from immigration, customs, health, police, and the port's naval commander. They conducted the whole business politely and in the best of humor.

"Everything is in good order. Come and fetch your papers in the afternoon."

It cost almost 100 dollars for all the permits. The departure, later, was a little less expensive. We received a sticker, which we were to place on a porthole, allowing free navigation for 90 days.

As soon as they had their backs turned, we abandoned ship, keen to explore the country and this village and to immerse ourselves in the enchanting Spanish-American ambience.

It's always exciting to come by sea to an unknown country. This village was particularly attractive and pretty, with several restaurants and craft and souvenir shops. There was also a nice hotel of about thirty rooms owned by a Swiss and whose architecture blended well with its surroundings.

We immersed ourselves little by little in an atmosphere that became more and more South American, as we were reminded by the presence of the military. The naval officer had pointed out to me that the war against the "revolutionaries" was still going on in the interior, to the north, when I told him of our intention to visit the Mayan regions.

After spending a marvelous week there, we set off on what would be one of the most beautiful experiences of our cruise as we ventured about 40 miles up the Rio Dulce.

The first stretch of the river ran between cliffs that formed a canyon about three hundred feet deep. They towered over us, their white masses covered with a luxuriant vegetation that provided a roost for a multitude of egrets whose white plumage dazzled in the sunlight.

As the gentle meanders of the Rio Dulce unwound, waterfalls appeared, tumbling down the rock faces. Gradually, the sea water gave way to fresh water which was good both for us and for the boat, and we used it lavishly.

The sound of a powerful motor interrupted the serenity and set the birds to flight in a majestic clatter of wings. Round a bend, belching black smoke, came a launch of the Guatemalan Navy filled with young men in T-shirts and jeans. We figured out that they were French sailors on a guided tour, and we saluted them as they passed us a few yards off. They looked at us in surprise, and when we pointed out the Breton flag fluttering in the shrouds, they let out cries of joy and waved madly to the bewilderment of the Guatemalan sailors who regarded us with incomprehension. We were far from Brittany, but we returned there for a few moments on that Sunday afternoon.

Just before reaching Lake Golfete, to starboard are hot-water springs which form natural bathtubs between the rocks. All we had to do was to anchor nearby, push aside the branches a little, and, surrounded by glorious vegetation, take a nice hot and invigorating bath to the accompaniment of birdsongs of all kinds.

As evening was approaching, we anchored at the entrance to El Golfete, behind the small island of Cayo Grande. There are plenty of good anchorages in the lagoons adjacent to the lake and in the water courses that run into it. It was great fun exploring them in the dinghy, ducking under the overhanging branches and weaving between the waterlilies in bloom.

All together, there are few hazards if you pay attention. There are a few species of land and water snakes, carnivorous water turtles, a few crocodiles, spiders, parrots and manatees, but few mosquitoes, at least at that time of year.

We went up one of these tributaries. Once past the vegetation, we ended up between pastures where long-horned cattle were grazing. Gaunt-featured horsemen were trying to herd them, assisted by their scrawny dogs.

Two Indian children approached us timidly in their little pirogue. We chatted. A column of smoke rose from the hut where they lived, which was hidden from sight behind some large trees. Their father made model cayucos and would have liked us to buy one. We would have preferred a full-sized one, as big as theirs. Before they went back home, Briac gave them some sketchbooks, pencils, and some clothes. A little later, the parents came to give us the price of a new cayuco, which we found a bit expensive. They thanked us on behalf of the children and left, smiling broadly.

Shortly before anchoring, we had met an American cruising boat. Its crew warned us not to leave the boat unattended if we wanted to visit the nature reserve, a few cable lengths from our current anchorage. That made us nervous, but the night was calm and peaceful and passed without any problem.

While we were weighing anchor, a manatee with big, bulbous eyes swam by us nonchalantly and without apparent fear before disappearing in the dark green water.

It took us several hours of motoring and sailing to cross El Golfete and find the course of the Dulce with its low banks lined with old, bare trees, their roots in the water. Behind them was dense vegetation and beyond that, pastures of tall grass stretched out across the hills. As we approached Fronteras and Relleno, the two villages on either side of the bridge that spans the river, we saw magnificent mansions of an architecture that blended admirably with their surroundings. In our wildest dreams, we would never have imagined coming across such luxury along this river.

Soon, Mario's Marina appeared on the right. It could hold a good 30 boats side by side, separated only by their fenders, and several boats were anchored just off it with plenty of swinging room. There was more air on the river and we could use the various services offered by the marinas just as easily. The place was isolated anyway, and all communications were made by water.

A little farther on, on a small peninsula, was the Catamaran Hotel, made up of very nice bungalows and with its own small marina. It was a charming spot, breezy and pleasant and we could anchor off it, as we could anywhere in the river.

When we arrived, we anchored off Fronteras, a typical Central American village, captivating with its vivid and varied colors. We enjoyed ambling between the market displays, often right on the dusty ground, discussing prices and watching the women's faces light up with joy when we purchased a few fruits or vegetables. There was a market every day and many vendors came from far away, arriving very early in the morning to reserve a space to display their meager wares, even if it was on the ground. The atmosphere was unique and unforgettable.

By searching for it, we could find anything we needed and at a good price, even though the quality left something to be desired. In fact, and this was a surprise, the high-quality fresh products were all exported. In Guatemala, the land of coffee, all we could find was instant!

If in Livingston the population was mixed and mainly black, here it was Indian or half-caste, with a few whites of Spanish descent.

We took this opportunity to have a local carpenter make a table to go on the deck. As on Joshua Slocum's SPRAY, a seat runs across the aft side of the aft cabin trunk. When sitting there on the water, we felt like old geezers in a public garden. A table was definitely in order.

It's probably one of the best things we've done to the boat. Made of tropical hardwood, it's six feet long by 18 inches wide, with a flap to make it 14 inches wider. We fitted it across the deck and bolted it down, and it immediately added a new dimension to life aboard, particularly at sea. From that time on, we lived entirely outdoors. At sea, with few rare exceptions, we took every meal outside. I could use the table for cleaning and cutting fish and even as a workbench. Annick also prized it for various sewing jobs, including sail repairs, and Briac could do his schoolwork there and play for hours.

All of a sudden, we started having problems with the outboard motor's fuel system. Twice, I took it to a mechanic, a nice young man. In the end, he fitted a filter in the fuel line and that solved the problem.

From Fronteras, buses leave for the capital, Guatemala City, and other areas of the country. We decided we would take one, but first we set off to discover all the Rio Dulce's charms and sail its navigable length up to its source at Lake Izabal.

The latter is 25 miles long by 10 wide at its widest point. It is relatively deep, from 30 to 50 feet in the middle, but the muddy bottom near the shore offers unreliable holding. It stretches lazily between two chains of mountains, the Sierra de Santa Cruz, at about 4,000 feet, to the north, and in the southwest, the Sierra de Las Minas which is much higher, reaching 7,500 feet.

In the afternoons the wind, coming from the Atlantic and blowing up the river, could quite often reach 25 knots, making the surface of the water rough and unpleasant for sailing, except when going downwind of course. This wind died immediately at sunset, leaving the nights calm and pleasant.

From time to time, we came across large rafts of floating plants. We would think we were entering shallow water, but that wasn't the case. They came down from the many tributaries and were drifting around the lake until eventually coming to rest against the shore.

Fishermen set baited lines at night and when they pulled them up at dawn, before the mist had completely risen, the scene was quite magnificent and unreal.

Before setting off to explore the lake, we visited Fort San Felipe, which guards the entrance. Spanish galleons came up into the lake to fill their hulls with treasure and were very attractive to English and Dutch pirates. The fort was built to control access and protect the ships, at least, that was the idea. Its first stones were laid in 1595 and it was taken and retaken, demolished and rebuilt several times. It was finally and splendidly restored in 1955. You can anchor right next to it. It is a magnificent spot, especially as the rebuilt old stone quay gives access to a nature park through which you can follow lovely shaded footpaths into the fort itself.

As the sun rose over the sierra, we raised the anchor and moved on to moor at the other end of the lake, in the Bay of Puerto Refugio. Despite the name, there is no port, just a few fields surrounding a *finca* and several outbuildings. We were alone and we spent a pleasant and very tranquil evening watching the action, which amounted to birds and a few domestic animals.

The next day, we changed anchorages to a little bay near the mouth of the Rio Palachic, so we could go up it in the dinghy, to the crew's great delight. They're always keen for new adventures like this, especially Briac. At age 4, he handled the inflatable and its 9-horsepower motor very well. He steered us between banks edged with shrubs, tall grasses and reeds, and our passage put lots of birds to flight, among them magnificent egrets.

Briac was very alert to the least suspicious movement, both on the muddy banks and in the water. He knew that he could very likely see a crocodile—there were theoretically large numbers in these parts—as well as turtles.

"There, there, I saw one!"

"No, it's a submerged tree trunk."

After going up a couple of miles, a little disappointed and at the same time relieved, we had to head back. The vegetation had become denser and denser, often growing across the stream so that we had to cut a path.

But Briac was happy in the end because, in the village of El Estor where we anchored for the night, in the square opposite the church, there was a pool in which two alligators lay, looking studiously bored.

The locals swam and bathed right in the lake or the river. The women, bare to the waist, chattering and laughing, did the laundry while the kids ran, dove and bickered among themselves. Everything here was so natural and easy going that it seemed time hadn't affected the way of life at all. It was the same as two hundred years ago. SPRAY's silhouette blended perfectly into this scene.

I was becoming preoccupied. I felt that the boat was no longer reaching her normal cruising speed, and the problem seemed to be getting worse. I thought it might be best to go back down the river to a place where we could eventually check it out and correct it.

Nevertheless, we wouldn't give up the idea of spending 10 days in the interior of the country. We went back to the Rio Dulce, sailing by Fort San Felipe while it was bathed in the light of a magnificent sunset. We decided to go to the marina at Susanna's. It's inside a small lagoon completely enclosed by vegetation but great trees fortunately brought a little breeze and coolness. Here, we could safely leave the boat. The following morning, we took the ferry to the village and jumped on a bus going to Guatemala City. We didn't go all the way to the city but changed buses to go to Cobán. What a dumb idea that was! The next bus, which picked us up at the side of the road, was packed. Eventually, after three hours of standing in the central aisle, fighting to keep my balance on the numerous bends in the steep road, and suffering from the heat and the humidity, we got off in order to take another bus. Ten minutes later, while we were walking in single file on the main street of the town, another vehicle stopped. To our great surprise it bore the sign "Expreso." It was going to Cobán, it was three quarters empty, and, best of all, it was like a Pullman, and very comfortable. What a relief for my back!

Cobán was a beautiful, colonial-style town, high up, with dense vegetation and shaded, flower-lined streets. We quickly found an inn, a former convent of magnificent Spanish-style architecture with delightful patios. The bedroom, formerly a nun's cell, was cool, simple, and comfortable, and invited rest.

Before stretching out, though, we went first to the restaurant where we tasted local specialties, served by a young, dark-haired woman wearing a traditional Maya costume colorfully embroidered. We were right in the town center, and a tour through the neighboring streets allowed us to visit some shops, admire several buildings, and note the location of the market which seemed to be very large. Cobán is a big town and its market is impressive as much for its large number of stalls as for the crowds it attracts.

After Cobán, we had no other choice for making our *grand tour* but to take the buses that serve the small villages lost in the wilderness of the plains and mountains, on roads that quickly became dirt tracks winding over hill and through dale, wide enough only for one vehicle. This calls for a stout heart. A meeting with a truck coming in the opposite direction required the two drivers to use much ingenuity, and much backing and filling on the edge of the precipice, to pass each other. The dust came in through the open windows which at least let out some of the obnoxiously loud music. After the mountain roads, the bus crossed the rivers by fords, in water up to the axles. The gearbox ground. The engine of this old American school bus glowed red under the impatient foot of the driver, tired and frazzled by the long hours at the wheel. Behind him, the passengers each tried to find and hold onto their space, even if only to park one cheek on the end of a rickety bench to which three people had already attached themselves. A fatalistic and resigned atmosphere prevailed even while everyone was impatient to reach the end of the journey. It was only a short while ago that buses in this region were attacked and robbed by guerrillas. We didn't dare raise the subject . . .

At the bus stops in the small villages, children would come up, offering for sale fruits, small sandwiches, pastries, or drinks, but not with any great success.

When they came to Briac, they would stop, stupefied and baffled. They stood looking at him in rapture, without saying a word, and seemed to completely forget their business. It was only when the bus began to move off that they came back to life and rushed for the exit and, once outside, gazed back at him with their black eyes. Often in the street, and especially in the markets, the same phenomenon would be repeated, both among the children and also with the old women. They would stop in wonder and, smiling radiantly, place their wrinkled hands, religiously, on his head.

Briac appeared to them like a being from another world, a blond angel. Faced with this attitude, we worried and increased our vigilance but, as it turned out, all was well, and Briac made many friends around the market stalls.

What surprised us when we reached the higher elevations was the vast patchwork of cultivated fields, separated by piles of rocks. At over 6,500 feet of altitude, where the sun's rays barely penetrated the white blanket of mist, women toiled, bent double under their big black hats, creating a scene of unforgettable beauty.

At that evening's stop, Ustapan, we had first to find lodgings, then something to eat in one of the tiny dives to be found in the dark and narrow lanes. After a long day on the bus with only a couple of sandwiches for lunch, we badly needed sustenance, and we didn't try too hard to determine exactly what was on our plates.

We had to get up at three in the morning to catch the only bus of the day going to our next destination. And so we began to learn the way hotels operate in this part of the world. They had cut off the water and it was impossible to find anyone. They were probably hiding in the depths of the kitchen or cowering beneath the rudimentary reception desk!

After this early-morning departure, which allowed us to watch the new dawn followed by a magnificent sunrise on the passes of the surrounding mountains, we arrived mid-morning at the bus terminal in one of the most beautiful small towns in existence: Chichicastenango.

The bus stop was in a field dusty to perfection and bursting with activity. Smothered in the sooty fumes of badly maintained diesel engines, dozens of spluttering buses came and went in a concerto of aggressive horns and a riot of gaudy color.

Our first concern was to find something to eat, which we did in a small restaurant, near the terminal and not too far from the market. A crowd had gathered outside. A guy was stretched out on the ground . . . dead. Nobody seemed unduly troubled: They covered his head with his jacket and went on with their lives. *Está muerto*!

Chichicastenango's various and colorful markets draw large numbers of foreigners and tourists who come to look at and purchase Mayan crafts. All the inhabitants of this region dress in traditional costumes. Their beautiful features match the luxuriance of their clothing and when a smile breaks out across their round and tanned faces, it's like the sun coming out—dazzling!

The Indians walk many miles to bring the products of their labor to market in the hopes of getting a good price for them.

Without a doubt, one of the most beautiful sights is the flower market; it's a unique and ravishing scene. The steps of the church, itself a building of a great architectural purity, are crowded with women surrounded by multicolored blooms, with incense sticks burning in front of them. This fabulous sight, rich in color and humanity, takes place twice a week, on Thursdays and Sundays. When planning our trip, we had taken into account the market days, so we found frenetic activity in these normally much sleepier towns.

In the market, there were also places to eat. On the ground were small braziers, on which vegetables and pieces of meat simmered in pots. Women squatted next to them, watching the cooking and stoking the fires with sticks. Most of them were plump, and they were dressed in long skirts of multicolored stripes, an ample shirt, blouse or bodice of vibrant color, and with headscarves often covered by a black felt hat. Enveloped in the scents of fresh vegetables and spices, they offered a variety of soups and stews and pieces of grilled, peppered chicken, to prospective clients, addressing the men with a flirtatious, singsong "caballero."

Young girls, always chattering, smiling, or laughing merrily and carrying on their heads large pitchers striped in two colors, fetched water from the fountain. They wore colorful blouses and sandals and aprons to protect the fronts of their long skirts, the colors of which varied according to their home towns and regions and also identified tribes and ancestors.

It was delightful, strolling along the alleys among the stalls in this multicolored crowd, even though there were, to our taste, a few too many tourists. In the afternoon, we were once again on the road, which had become more comfortable and partly tarred. We were bound for Quezaltenango.

This is a much bigger town, and the administrative center for the region. Old buildings and an imposing cathedral dating from colonial times surround the magnificent central square which consists mainly of a shady park where you can sit, relax, and watch the daily life unfolding all around. At the tourist bureau, we were told that we could find lodgings in a small mountain village, so we got on another bus going to San Francisco El Alto, high in the sierra.

Each bend in the winding road revealed a magnificent view. It wasn't market day—a little calm wasn't a bad thing—and the town was deserted apart from a few mangy stray dogs. In the middle of the afternoon, the best thing to do is find some shade and take a siesta. Only tourists, therefore, walk about in the steep lanes under the full sun. We were alone as we strolled around looking for a hotel and a place to eat.

There was a small hotel on a corner, but it appeared closed. A neighbor snoozing nearby opened one eye and uttered a very deep "Pablo." Pablo appeared, buttoning up his shirt; "*Si, si, está abierto*, but on days when there's no market it's usually quiet!" Since market days were on Fridays only, he had lots of time to rest!

The rooms were large and had big bay windows and we had the choice of them since we were certainly the only clients in the establishment.

After we ate in a snack bar behind the church and poked around in the streets and, sitting on the steps in the square, admired the imposing panorama of the surrounding valleys, we went to bed. The next day, we had to rise at five to catch the bus to take us down to the main road, where we would board the express to Solala and Panachel.

We had paid the night before, which seemed to be the only formula in these parts, except that here, they cut off the water in the morning, even for the toilet. The luxury was that we had one in the bathroom. Things were made worse because Briac, who had been sick through part of the night, had thrown up in the washbasin and in the toilet. When we woke up, Annick went to the reception and succeeded, through persistence, in getting someone out: "*Si, si, no problema*"—but still no water.

When we went out through the front door, which happened to be wide open, we didn't meet a living soul!

A little while later, we were on the express bus for Panachel, which is a tourist resort and spa on Lake Atitlan.

This town presented quite a different prospect, with large and beautiful villas around part of the lake, across which ferries and motorboats cut their wakes. There are hotels of all classes, restaurants, shops where they exploit the Mayan theme to the maximum, and street vendors. In short, a brief return to civilization. Well, actually, to our civilization, because in the region we'd just come through, they have never ceased to maintain as far as possible their traditions, their culture, and the way of life of several centuries of ancestors.

It wasn't hard to find a comfortable hotel room. As we were about to take up our paltry baggage, and above all head for a nice shower, the receptionist had the quaint notion to ask me to settle in advance. This one undid himself in his zeal. I responded that I would only pay on leaving in the morning.

"But sir, it's a rule of the hotel."

"Then I'm leaving now. I'm getting fed up with the water being cut off in the morning. I'll pay you tomorrow, on leaving, and if we have water." Faced with such determination, the employee acquiesced and even became quite friendly.

As for dinner, while the restaurant was attractive, the meal was a dismal failure. The menu announced roast chicken and we ended up with pieces fried à la Colonel Sanders. From our short experience, I think that hotels and restaurants can be a problem in this country, or maybe we needed more time to get used to them.

The next day, we were once more on the road, headed this time for Antigua. This city, the former capital of Guatemala, is rich in architecture, with a number of churches, palaces, monasteries, and convents, as well as the university. Antigua was an enchantment to explore. Some of its fine stone structures had survived the terrible 1773 earthquake. Today, it feels good to stroll and loiter in these paved streets, to visit the cathedral, and to breathe the air filled with the perfumes of flowers and plants. Surrounded by so much culture and the rich Hispanic past, you thrill at each house with its interior courtyard, at each street corner, and at each face. Here is a place—one more for the list—where I could live well. All is peaceful and tranquil and everyone attends to their own business. The cafe terraces induce relaxation, contemplation, and meditation. That evening, happy and at ease, we went to our room and fell asleep very quickly.

The atmosphere in the dusty square reserved for the buses was, as always, charged. The competing bus crews vie vociferously for business: "Guate, Guate!" the drivers or their helpers cry to attract customers and lure their unwitting clients to the adventure that awaits them. We just had time to understand what was being said, find the right bus, hustle aboard it, and cram ourselves onto a bench, which was loose because it was missing two mounting screws, before it took off at speed. I began to understand the sayings "*Dios te guarda*," or "*Dios es con ellos*" written above the driver, usually accompanied by a photo or a religious icon. The drivers, anyway, seemed to have such a faith in God that they thought themselves immunized against death. So, they overtook on blind bends and careened pedal to the floor down serpentine mountain roads. Everyone aboard seemed resigned and fatalistic, as though sharing this faith. The problem was, the same belief was shared by the driver of every bus, truck, and car going in the opposite direction.

I didn't feel the same enthusiasm in the least and I began to consider these journeys by road particularly dangerous. Also, our metabolisms were beginning to rebel against the inadequate food and the rhythm the bus timetables imposed on our movements. So we decided to head back toward the boat.

After Guatemala City, a new express bus, certainly more comfortable and perhaps a little safer, brought us back to Fronteras. We couldn't help but notice that the big highways were littered with plastic jugs, paper, and trash of all kinds.

Greatly relieved, we arrived at our point of departure. After buying a few groceries and calling the marina, we were aboard the pirogue being ferried toward our boat.

On the menu that evening, to restore us, was frozen chicken, though that was an optimistic description as the appliances only run between the numerous power cuts. Not long afterwards, I became quite ill with a high fever that lasted several days despite the care patiently lavished on me by Annick and her assistant, Briac. Fortunately, we had left the marina and gone back to the anchorage, near Mario's marina, where we had the good fortune to get to know a French couple. The wife was a nurse and had on board stuff to get me back on my feet.

We were enchanted by our journey into this country, but a little disappointed with its people who, while friendly and charming, seemed always to be under the spell of the repression that has for so long been their lot in South America.

After several days of rest, putting SPRAY OF SAINT-BRIAC back in order, and a last visit to Castillo San Felipe, we went quietly down the river toward its mouth. Of the large number of boats there that year, the majority of them American, some had come to take refuge during the hurricane season. Within the fleet, the cruisers had formed a small society, and organized events for mutual assistance and to alleviate the day-to-day ennui of the place. For example, anyone flying to the United States would take everybody's mail so as to mail it directly on getting there.

Our propulsion problem seemed to be getting worse and worse and we were barely able to get to Livingston where we anchored for a few days to deal with the exit paperwork. We decided then that instead of going straight to Florida, we would return to French Harbour because there was a fellow living aboard a sort of tug, who called himself a mechanic. I was hoping that he could tell me what the problem was. It wouldn't be a bad detour, anyway, because it would allow for a better course toward the Yucatán Channel, between Mexico and Cuba, and we might avoid tacking too much.

Our decision was confirmed when a front arrived, bringing with it winds in the west to northwest sector: following winds. Perfect!

Two days later, we saw the island of Roatán. There was very little wind on the back of the front and we had to wait for the trades to return. Our propulsion was zero by then. I wondered if the problem was with the propeller, which had adjustable blades and could have gone out of adjustment. Good thinking, I was close, but not quite!

Thanks to the VHF, we were able to talk with the guy in question. He waited for us and, with his dinghy, helped us get through the pass and up to the anchorage. It's narrow and right in the axis of the tradewind. It had taken us 36 hours to cover the last 20 miles of which we made two in 20 hours of tacking. When we thought we were on the final tack, the wind veered more and more as evening approached, and we had to start over. The cross current didn't help. With this succession of tacks, I felt we were in full training for the next America's Cup.

Eventually, at daybreak, we were off the pass. Mike nudged his dinghy up to our transom and pushed. Slowly, he drove us toward our former anchorage.

After discussing the symptoms with him, exploring the possibility of careening, and figuring the delays in getting spare parts, it seemed more sensible, safer, and quicker to put back to sea, head toward Florida, and do the work there, especially as we needed a haulout anyway.

7

Return to the United States— the Intracoastal Waterway

Once the tradewind returned we wasted no time in taking to the pass again but this time under sail, so ending the humiliation. We sailed along the south of the island, past magnificent beaches and, at the end of the afternoon, we left its protection to find a steady northeasterly wind. Once more, the tranquility of sailing on the open sea with the helm lashed settled on us. It was, however, momentarily interrupted the following morning by the discovery of a nice little hole high up in the mainsail. That wouldn't do, so we dropped it. Annick got out the sewing kit and very soon the sail was set and drawing again. No, you can't let these little problems get you down!

At the end of the afternoon, a beautiful dorado came aboard to the cheers of the crew. Nine days later, at night, and after a period of light and variable winds, we entered the bay at Fort Myers and dropped our anchor close to Sanibel Island, not far from the road bridge that connects it to the mainland.

We were back in the United States, with its avenues, cars, trucks, the superb Florida mansions, and the characteristic noise of traffic.

We needed to find a boatyard. Bob had recommended Fort Myers Boat Yard, but it was a long way up the river, there were bridges to negotiate, and we had to do it all under sail.

We visited two yards in the bay, at Fort Myers Beach, but they didn't inspire me. After breakfast, to the amazement of the crew, the skipper announced that we were going up the river.

The anchor once more came on deck, but not without some reservations on the part of the hands. After making radio contact, we presented ourselves on schedule at the first bridge, so that it would open.

"Okay, here we go!"

The channel was narrow and the current was running quite fast, but the wind wasn't strong enough for me.

The bridge pilings approached quickly, tension mounted on board. Would we make it through or not?

A hundred and fifty yards away, SPRAY OF SAINT-BRIAC wouldn't have it and she jibed in a wind change. All she did was luff up, come head to wind, and ask politely if we would like to anchor her. And so, as far as the plan to go up the river was concerned, SPRAY had decided against it.

The bridge operator, who hadn't understood this sensible maneuver, could only close the bridge. Thinking that we were waiting, she reopened it 15 minutes later. On the radio, I explained to her that we had a little problem and that we were awaiting the towing service. The yellow and black Sea Tow boat, looking very spiffy, arrived quickly and soon had us in tow. It left us two hours later half way to the boatyard in a place in the river where we could anchor. Outlay for the operation: 250 dollars. A good start!

I believe in retrospect that the boat, by refusing, like the horse before the jump, had perhaps helped us avoid greater difficulties, because when it came down to it, making the trip under sail wasn't going to be straightforward.

"So, we'll see how things turn out tomorrow."

The anchorage, outside of the buoyed channel, was very pleasant and we spent a quiet and pleasant night there. At nine in the morning, in a nice little crosswind, we set sail. After about two hours, when we came to two bridges, one close to the other, and some 500 yards from the boatyard, we anchored and dropped the sails. We readied the dinghy with its 9.5 horsepower motor, and tied it alongside at the stern. It was worth a try . . . and it worked! We raised the anchor and got under way. I stayed in the dinghy while Annick took the helm and Briac, promoted to tactician, showered us with directions.

It was good that we did this because the swirling currents of air, accentuated by the presence of buildings on the bank close by, would have given us lots of trouble in the narrow passage under the bridges. Haltingly, the motor straining, we arrived at the boatyard. Tony, the manager, was there to take our lines in anticipation of our haulout the next morning. Boy, did it feel good to be on a dock!

Fifteen days later, we were back afloat. We tried the engine with the same result: no propulsion! I had taken off the propeller, changed the nylon bearings, and greased it. On land, it seemed to be working and activating all the blades. But now, nothing. Tony came to take a look and found the problem. The propeller shaft had come loose and had a little play fore and aft, not much, but it was enough.

We weren't idle during this stay on land. We painted outside and in, examined the whole deck and rig, as well as the dinghies, the engine. SPRAY OF SAINT-BRIAC was like new!

We were ready to set off again and cross Florida by the ingenious Intracoastal Waterway. By using this system of natural bodies of water and linking canals, you can go from the south of Florida as far as Canada without having to face the ocean. We were about to learn another type of navigation, in the well-buoyed and maintained channels used by the majority of Americans who cruise from north to south and vice versa according to the season. The entire length of the route, there is little problem anchoring or finding comfortable marinas. The height of our mast being less than 65 feet meant we didn't have to lay it on the deck, so there was no significant obstacle in the way of this new adventure. Nevertheless, there was a little stress, because you had to be vigilant at the helm and there were many lifting and swing bridges on the way. The speed with which these responded, and therefore how quickly we progressed, depended on the goodwill and zeal of the various operators.

The month of April was coming to an end, the days were getting longer, and it was already pleasantly warm. The scenery along the canal was changing. The suburbs of Fort Myers gave way to open fields where cows watched us pass by and birds squabbled on the banks. Now and then, one or more turtles, startled by our approach, scuttled to hide in the depths. The trim village of La Belle had even put a guest pontoon at the disposal of transient boats, but we needed to make several circles in the water before the bridge opened to let us through. At day's end, we anchored in a bend surrounded by low green hills where cattle came and went at their leisurely pace, and settled down for the night.

The next day, we crossed Lake Okeechobee after having followed its bank for a while among bare trees. We also saw alligators drying off in the midday sun or taking siestas, to the great delight of the crew who were always on the lookout for that kind of show.

In the lake, it's best to follow the buoys. Though there's water, you're not immune from hitting some kind of obstruction. Throughout the day, boats of all kinds passed us or overtook us; the most troublesome obviously were the powerboats because of their large and devastating wakes. Happily, some of them were polite enough to slow down sufficiently early that we could avoid being tossed in all directions. In the evening, we anchored at the exit from the lake so as to be ready to continue on our way through this pastoral scenery at the first opening of the lock. And so we crossed Florida and, after going through the last locks, we were back at sea level and heading for Stuart. Large, beautiful, and sumptuous villas now bordered the canal: Florida in all her splendor is an impressive sight.

At the two bridges in Stuart, one a highway, the other a railroad, a dozen boats were waiting patiently to get through, most of them that is. Suddenly, the strident siren sounded to announce that the traffic was stopping and that the bridges would open. Everyone got ready, in line astern. We were last in line.

Before the bridge was completely open and the light turned green, everyone moved forward. What was going on? Before the three or four last in our line reached the bridges, the boats coming the other way burst through! A big powerboat just missed our port side while a large ketch maneuvered to starboard and barely managed to clear the bridge before we brought our 18 tons at full power between its pilings. The light on the railroad bridge was red, and turned green just as we entered it. I had no idea what was happening.

"In 13 years on the job, I've never seen anything like it!" complained the bridge tender over the VHF, which he'd left on. In this America that's so well organized, it was a surprising state of affairs.

In any event, I had no choice but to continue, especially as the other boats coming toward us were now waiting their turn, grumbling. On reflection, once the pressure was off, I had time to reflect on it and I figured out that the boats coming the other way had the right of way because the current was carrying them. Our group shouldn't have gone through.

The first in line was a little private tugboat. He had gone through the lock with us earlier and seemed to be in a hurry. Was he afraid he'd miss the opening of the next bridge? Anyway, when the first one opened, he forged on through before the draw was barely wide enough for him to get under. Without thinking, everyone followed him, provoking a flood of adrenaline and some frayed nerves. A few planks lost some paint!

Eventually, after passing through many bridges and crossing quite strong currents near the inlets that give out to the ocean, we ended up anchoring at Fort Pierce, to port, just off the road, at 27° 14'N, 80° 13'W.

We were held up there for several days by fronts coming down from the north.

The next day was a happy one for Briac: we asked a uniformed officer where the post office was. He turned out to be none other than the sheriff, and he drove us there in his car. He didn't turn on his siren, but for Briac it was a dream come true.

We'd had enough of bad tempers at the bridges, so we went by sea as far as Charleston, where the Around Alone was finishing. This is the solo round-the-world race in which I twice took part, in 1982 and in 1986.

We made the most of a three-day calm by getting out to sea by the next inlet. Getting in or out in bad weather is pretty difficult, especially with this low coastline and shallow waters. I understand why folks stay inside the Waterway.

Thanks to the Gulf Stream, we made rapid progress and arrived in the middle of the third night. The least that I can say is that this landfall wasn't too easy the first time, especially without a detailed chart and with a front approaching.

In the maze of channels we were fooled by a green light which in fact we should have used in alignment with a slightly higher green light—very clever American know-how—and we ran aground on a sandbar on a falling tide. All we could do was set an anchor to hold us, because the 25-knot wind and the waves were tending to push us farther onto the bar. Once we were sure SPRAY OF SAINT-BRIAC was safe, we went to bed to wait for daylight and the next tide. In the channel we saw Jean-Jacques Provoyeur's boat being towed to the marina, having just finished the race. A few hours later, in brilliant sunshine, we got ourselves off without difficulty and headed toward the anchorage, just off the same marina.

We were overjoyed to meet friends from way back. Herb McCormick was running the press office with panache, Billy Black was taking photos, Peter Dunning was, as ever, at his post at the race communications center and, of course, there were the racers.

Christophe Auguin had won for the second time. His boat, immaculate even after sailing round the world, was waiting for the start of the next race.

The great bearded and beaming visage of Jean-Luc Van den Heede greeted us and he did the honors with his boat for Briac, who was in seventh heaven. He would have liked to have visited them all, or very nearly. Steve Pettengill demonstrated his onboard computer and Briac didn't miss the least detail. He thought these sailing boats were magnificent. He never stopped asking questions and, once back aboard SPRAY OF SAINT-BRIAC, began making drawings of the boats.

For my part, I went back aboard feeling a little nostalgic. That's a race I would like to do again, it's the best of all of them. What a rapid evolution these boats had come through since the first around the world race!

Charleston is a pleasant town, with ornate colonial houses of wood or brick, typical of the southern United States. All along the waterfront, superb promenades have been created and we took advantage of them whenever we could.

We couldn't stay long and attended neither the dinner for the veterans nor the prize-giving ceremony. From Charleston to Beaufort would take two days by sea. After that, we would take the Intracoastal Waterway as far as Norfolk.

It was the end of a lovely day. I sat close to the helm, the beauty of the sunset washing over me. Annick was making dinner and Briac was drawing. Everything was marvelously tranquil. Suddenly, from each side of SPRAY, at sea level, two jet fighters roared by, so low I couldn't see them behind the sails. More than the sight of them, it was the terrifying noise that made us jump. Better not be susceptible to a heart attack! Why were they there, just to seaward of Carolina Beach? Were we in a military zone? For a long time we couldn't settle down to our normal routine, the fright was so great.

After a stormy night passage and in very bad visibility in rain, we entered the channel in the Beaufort inlet. We decided to anchor in the first propitious spot and wait for the sun to return. It rained without stopping all day long; a nice wood fire was in order. It warmed us to the core, and, since we had the time, we prepared a meal of galettes!

The passage to Norfolk was magnificent: sandy banks with great pine trees, isolated wooden houses, stags and does running free, a host of singing birds, egrets and herons foraging in the tall grasses on the water's edge, squirrels running and leaping. It was a peaceful and reassuring journey.

We took advantage of a stop in Bellhaven, in the heart of North Carolina, to restock with food and fuel. It was really a leap deep into a strange and alluring America. In order to go through the Great Dismal Swamp Canal, we took the fork toward Elizabeth City. It's an ornate town, lively, and most hospitable in that it provides a guest dock where you can stay and take the time to visit. The old canal, which you get into through a very well kept lock with well-maintained green lawns and flower beds, leads through luxuriant greenery, with just enough room for two boats to pass if they hug the banks. We sailed deep into the countryside that, in that springtime of 1995, was green and beautiful.

Since it was late, we set two anchors in the middle of the canal. There wouldn't be any traffic anyway because the locks were closed until the morning. SPRAY OF SAINT-BRIAC was therefore able to take her ease in peace and safety in perfectly still water.

There was a change of scenery when we passed through Norfolk, the principal naval harbor on the East Coast. The sheer number of ships of all types and sizes is really impressive. Passing the port's miles of docks left us feeling small, so we chose to go and anchor far from it all, in a creek at the mouth of the Lafayette River near the entrance to the harbor. This was well protected and not very deep. The problem was to find a place to land, as is often the case in this country where so much is privately owned. In the end, Annick and Briac jumped from the dinghy onto the rocks near a bridge and were able to get on the road to the supermarket, two miles away. I picked them up in the same place on their return.

On Sunday, May 20, we took advantage of a high-pressure weather system to set off again, bound this time for New York and ultimately Newport, the end of this first voyage. If the weather pattern remained normal, there would be time before the next front.

We had lunch, which consisted of taboule and mackerel in white wine, near the immense tunnel/bridge that connects Norfolk to Cape Charles. The Intracoastal Waterway continues through Chesapeake Bay and then reaches New Jersey down the Delaware Bay. It's longer, and anyway we preferred the sea route. Its navigation is easier and its slower rhythm would allow Briac to get back to his reading, his exercise books, and the story time that he liked more than anything. Annick was then reading and explaining for him *The Life of the Whalers* and *The Sea Wolf* by Jack London. For my part, I could slack off, keeping one eye on the course because of the presence of shallow water along the coast, and the other on the page of my book.

The next day there was a significant change; the water temperature became very cold and we immediately noticed it when we showered. It was no doubt the reason that two fine sea bass accepted an invitation aboard.

Perhaps due to the cold Labrador current and the clear atmosphere, the sunset was absolutely magnificent, like those we would see every evening in Newport. It reflected off the glass of the buildings in Atlantic City which we could see on the horizon. That night, though, despite the warm clothes we hurriedly dug out, we felt the cold. The temperature dropped close to freezing. During the day, in the sunshine, the temperature rose again to 80°.

At dawn, we saw Sandy Hook and, way in the distance, the skyscrapers of Manhattan began to appear. All our eyes were on this fabulous and legendary bay, which had figured in the hopes and dreams of so many immigrants.

The sun was behind us and reflected with a hard and dazzling glare off the buildings. The light, southwest wind made the sailing easy.

Soon, we entered the approach channel, under the noisy and majestic Verrazano Bridge. After that, the bay widened with, to starboard, downtown Manhattan, the World Trade Center, and Governors Island where the Coast Guard is headquartered. To port were Ellis Island and New Jersey, and a little farther up stood the Statue of Liberty.

We didn't want to miss anything of what was going on before our eyes and, the closer we approached, the greater our excitement and eagerness. It was an overwhelming and emotional experience.

The scenes unfolded before us as if in a movie. This arrival in New York is probably one of our best memories. It reached its climax when we entered the East River and its current swept us into the city to be surrounded by its increasingly deafening noise, which was quite terrifying when we passed under bridges, especially the Manhattan Bridge, with its subway trains and traffic. It was really impressive. And then there were the helicopters wheeling overhead, landing and taking off in clouds of dust and litter, the continual strident din of ambulances and police cars, and the constant lines of vehicles along FDR Drive among which we could easily pick out the familiar yellow taxicabs. In the

Sailing up the East River in New York

midst of all this din, there were people taking their ease, sitting on benches calmly eating their sandwiches or doing a little midday courting. And throughout was the characteristic architecture, where ancient and modern coexist. It's beautiful, very beautiful. Our breath taken away, we passed by this prodigious spectacle as if on a moving sidewalk.

Navigation didn't pose much difficulty, but we had to keep an eye out for debris and floating logs. After Queensboro Bridge came the Upper East Side, a residential area. We tried to spot the street where we had lived twenty years before. Manhattan is marvelous and unique. It certainly touches me more than any other city, and I love it with a passion.

Little by little, the sounds of the city faded behind us where the river narrowed as it passed between Queens to the right and the Bronx to the left. The current here was much stronger and it was difficult to steer the boat in a straight line. Struggling to avoid a head-on encounter with one of the numerous barges being pushed or towed by small tugs, we had the unpleasant sensation of trying to paddle in rice pudding.

After we left the East River, the command came from the bridge, "Raise the sails!" and the crew set to work. We felt as though we were nearing the end of our voyage.

We enjoyed a fine southwesterly breeze, the advance sign of an approaching front. Among a host of boats sailing on the sound, SPRAY OF SAINT-BRIAC, inspired once more, helm lashed, ate up the miles. Off New Rochelle, a large tug crossed us and its crew, recognizing SPRAY's lines, saluted us with blasts of the siren and waved in greeting. During the course of her voyages, SPRAY OF SAINT-BRIAC often received recognition from vessels of all descriptions.

Everybody was happy; we were about to end our first sail around the Atlantic. Then, after a spell in the shipyard, we had to prepare for the long voyage, the circumnavigation. Wasn't that the best thing we could give Briac? Share with him the experience of spending three years at sea. Maybe he would never go back to sea after that, but that's not important. The lessons learned in this school of discovery would be with him for life.

Meanwhile, this last night was going to be trying, because we had to maintain a constant watch. The wind began to seriously build once we were out of Long Island Sound, and we had to take a reef when we set our course toward Newport. Wind abeam, a bone in her teeth, SPRAY, at full power, pushed aside the sea, anxious to get to the finish so she could enjoy a well-earned rest. We were tired and numb with cold, and it was a great relief when we lowered the sails. Under power, we entered the anchorage in Jamestown. We called the harbormaster on channel 71 and he directed us to a mooring. It was over, for the time being anyway. The first stage was completed and it had provided a wealth of experience and discoveries, leaving us feeling better than when we left. Above all, I knew what modifications I would have to make to the boat to make her more efficient and better suited to facing the ocean.

"Conanicut Marina, could we have the launch, please? And what day is it?"

"It's Wednesday, May 23, and the launch is on its way."

To be in Jamestown again was a little like returning home, because we have so many friends there: Mame Reynolds, Jinny and Bob, Susan and Ned. It's the same in Newport, with Mamita, the Dumonts, and many others. The reunions were joyful occasions.

We were awed by the big, beautiful trees and the splendid, freshly mown lawns that surrounded the lovely wooden houses so typical of New England.

Three days later, we were back in the shipyard in Wickford Cove Marina and in the hands of George, without a doubt the most energetic and most professional boatyard owner I've ever met. He is simply unbelievable, and it was a great pleasure to see him again.

To help me with my work, Ned recommended I contact Don Mason. Don is a character, a law unto himself. He works when he wants to and for whom he wants to. To my good fortune, we got on well and his help was invaluable. The first thing we had to do was to drop the rudder, to ensure it was in good condition, but above all, to modify it. It was too long, fore and aft, for its height, and developed so much pressure on its surface that it was counterproductive. Our new boatyard buddies, Helga and Jochen, who had just come from a cruise around South America and Patagonia, agreed with me. Jochen, an engineer, had built their handsome aluminum sailboat, ANDROM-EDA. We also had to replace a hardwood slab on deck which served as the collar and bearing for the rudderstock, not to mention a host of smaller jobs. At each stopover there was always a long list of things to do and redo.

The biggest task was that of the rudder, which we had to remove from its stock so we could work on it more easily.

"We have to saw off the stainless steel straps!"

After looking at it, Don, unperturbed as ever, stepped in:

"Yeah! No problem, saw away, we'll find a welder afterwards!"

This simple little job on the rudder took several days, what with Don's comings and goings, looking for this part or that tool; but it progressed.

He made a very fine bronze heel fitting, on which the stock could rest, and then, as soon as the welder had come to do his job, the rudder went back into its place. It looked much better, at least, and I was sure that in the water it would be more efficient. To think that the previous owners had sailed her with a rudder like that for all those years! There had been other little things which had surprised me somewhat and which needed to be fixed. The boat was now in better condition to face the open sea, the North Atlantic in particular. We expected to make other improvements when we could find a builder of wooden boats, probably in Portugal.

At the same time, we brought aboard a yankee and an asymmetrical spinnaker, as well as an 18-horsepower outboard motor, just in case, far from everything, we had to tow or push SPRAY OF SAINT-BRIAC. We would now have a more powerful and reliable motor than our 30-year-old 9.5-horsepower Yamaha which, though it started on the first pull, had a small problem from time to time with the spark in the lower cylinder. Apart from that it was perfect and gave me high regard for Japanese technology.

Every evening, after dinner, we would walk in Wickford's streets. It's surely the prettiest village in this area, and has changed little since it was founded. Its wooden, seventeenth-century clapboard houses are classified as historical monuments. Painted pastel blue, white, pale yellow, or brick red, surrounded by their lawns and shrubs, enclosed by little wooden fences, many of them are shaded by splendid trees, among them fine oaks and chestnuts. There is no restaurant open after 8.00 p.m. and no bar. It's utterly tranquil. We like Wickford very much, its calm, gentle New England atmosphere, and its quality shops, like the Gourmet Store and Ryans Supermarket, so prized by their customers that they think nothing of driving many miles to go there to shop. The Gourmet carries a line of high-quality and sought-after French specialties.

We took a break of a few days and went to Montreal, where I had been invited by CONAM, an association of amateur builders and sailors, to give a conference with a film and sign my book *Potpourri au Cap Horn*. This foray into Canada also gave us the opportunity to see our friend Hervé Guilbaud and his family who live in Montreal.

With Béatrice as our guide, we explored this friendly and very pleasant city and the evening was spent in the company of 250 people speaking with a Quebecois accent.

On the way back, we stopped in a Canadian village where we found very high quality firewood and kindling. On top of that, to our great surprise, we found the buckwheat flour for making galettes that turned out to be some of the best we ever had.

To make it easy for us to run our last errands, George had lent us his Mercedes.

Eventually, after 10- and 12-hour working days, we were ready to leave the boatyard. Framed in the lens of the very professional Frieda Squires, SPRAY OF SAINT-BRIAC went back into her element. Just before we left, *The Providence Journal*, the region's largest newspaper, gave us part of its front page and all of the third. The television channels 6, 10, and 12 soon followed.

While waiting to leave, we went back to Jamestown where, thanks to Bob's intervention, we were able to use Graham's mooring.

We only stayed two weeks, long enough to fine tune our preparations and to buy stores, fuel, water, and the spare parts we would need for the rest of the voyage. We had by then decided that we really would to try to reenact Captain Slocum's voyage of which it was now the centenary (1895-1898).

At least we knew one thing: the date of our return to Newport, which would be June 27, 1998. All the rest was up to chance!

After a pleasant meal with Jinny and Bob, we spent a wonderful afternoon at the Dumonts, feasting on the local lobsters, talking about the past, the present, and the friends who'd gone away in whatever direction their travels had taken them. Then, just a few hours from our departure, Catherine showered us with useful gifts.

Henry Hotchkiss, president of the association organizing the Slocum centennial in Fairhaven, paid us a quick visit. To our great surprise, he spoke marvelous French and used it to wish us bon voyage.

With the cooperation of the weather, we decided to leave on the next day, July 13, celebrating, in a way, our national holiday . . .

PART 2

◆

Following Joshua Slocum's Trail

8

Hurricane Chantal in the Atlantic

Accompanied by our friends Bob and Jinny Clarke aboard MAI-LING, we left the moorings in Jamestown and headed toward the open sea. From the moment we were abeam of Castle Hill, a fair southwesterly breeze filled our sails. Jinny passed across a harness that she had spent the night before making for Briac, and then they left us. It was an emotional parting for all of us.

The breeze strengthened and for the first three days it held, allowing us to cover 420 miles, according to that amazing instrument, the GPS.

On the morning of the fourth day, which was grey and misty, a strange noise caught my attention. It sounded like an engine but even though I wasn't yet fully awake I knew that it couldn't be the freighter we had passed a little while before. Then I saw it, a speck in the sky approaching rapidly at low altitude. A large United States Coast Guard aircraft roared overhead. I was a little surprised to see this apparition so far from land—we were about 350 miles north of Bermuda—and I wondered what was coming next. The plane made a wide arc, then came back toward us and turned on its lights. Apparently, it wanted to communicate with us. Without taking my eyes off the plane, I felt for and pressed the switch of the VHF radio. As the aircraft passed overhead in a din of engines, a voice came over loud and clear.

As soon as it was finished, I picked up the mike and pressed the transmit button.

"Coast Guard, this is SPRAY OF SAINT-BRIAC, over."

Several years earlier, not far from the same area, and in bad weather, I had been contacted in the same way. Radio reception, and more so transmission, only worked when the plane was directly overhead. This time I was surprised because, although I could no longer see the aircraft, a perfectly audible voice was still coming from the radio.

After I had identified us and stated our course, the voice asked me a question which took me aback:

"Can you render assistance?"

"Of course, depending on its nature and whether I am able."

"About 30 miles to your southeast is another sailboat which is also headed to the Azores. It has engine problems. Would you have a spare diesel filter?"

Somewhat baffled by this new development and the question I replied, "I'm sorry, but I don't have anything like that on board."

Which in fact was true. For one thing, I didn't yet know that a Racor filter had an internal element that needed changing. I wouldn't know until very much later—after I'd owned the boat for five years. As for the filter on the engine, I had changed it once in Brittany, in 1994, but since then I hadn't found a similar cartridge and it wasn't until we reached Australia that I found one and was able to change it. Apart from my supply of oil filters, I had nothing else.

The plane left. Two hours later, by which time we were moving under power, but slowly because the wind was beginning to fill in from the east and therefore on our nose, it reappeared and went through the regulation ritual once more. I switched on the radio.

"SPRAY OF SAINT-BRIAC, can you render assistance?" It was almost getting comical.

"What can I do for you, sir?"

"Since you are going the same way, to the Azores, could you catch up with the other sailboat and take it in tow?"

"Have you seen my boat? It has an old-fashioned rig, weighs 18 tons and its engine has barely 30 horsepower and gives us four or five knots in a flat sea. How do you think I could take another boat in tow in this wind and sea? What sort of boat is it?"

"A 38-foot sailboat. But don't bother, we understand. For your information, there's a hurricane watch for this area within 48 hours."

This was the coup de grace!

"OK, thanks for the warning."

Heck, that was something else. We would have to keep tabs on the situation on the SSB radio on 8765.4 KHz at 10:00, 16:00, and 22:00 GMT.

This gave us something to worry about. Possibly, the plane was patrolling so as to locate ships at sea and advise them. The weather was still overcast and, to cap it all, the wind settled in the east.

In view of the way these things usually develop, and since we had to choose a tack to be on anyway, I felt that our best route for avoiding the storm was to head southeast. The other approach was to head back toward the American coast and hope to get into the safer semicircle of the storm. But how could we know what track it would follow?

The radio confirmed it. Hurricane Chantal was heading toward us on a north-northeast track. Chantal's position on this Monday was 17° 35'N and 67°W; we were at 38°N and 62°W. We were in for it!

The next day, the wind continued to veer south-southeast, but it wasn't too strong, so we were able to head more or less east-northeast, which was not exactly where we wanted to go. Chantal was approaching as though to go around us and pounce on us from the north.

Position: 37°N and 65°W, and we were at 37°30'N and 61°W. The pressure on our nerves began to rise, the opposite to the barometric pressure. We were facing a very real danger; nevertheless, the crew remained calm and confident.

On the Wednesday, there was a mixture of clouds, rain, and sunshine and the wind was generally from the south and building. We could feel it coming.

Chantal: 37°N and 68°W. It seemed to have turned a little back toward the west. We were at 37° 20'N and 60°W.

The barometer continued to fall and we reduced sail as the wind rose. Then the barometer dropped rapidly: 6 millibars in four hours. The storm was approaching in earnest now and the wind took on a high-pitched and keening note.

What would Slocum and my grandfather have done in a situation like this and in this type of vessel? The decision was made: we dropped the mainsail, furling it tightly on the boom and lashing it down securely. We did the same with the yankee. We replaced the staysail with a smaller and stronger one and double-sheeted it each side to hold it on centerline. We worked feverishly in mounting gusts of wind that began to whiten the sea, streaking it with spray torn from the ever higher wave tops.

I steered SPRAY OF SAINT-BRIAC dead downwind and asked Annick to get out our four big mooring lines which were about 120 feet long and nearly an inch in diameter. I tied them end to end and after taking care to tie one end to the starboard cleat and the other to the port one, streamed them behind the boat. The loop formed by the warp was long enough that its center lay about three waves astern. We could have added a tire, but I thought that we would get by with what we had.

In all my voyages—close to 300,000 miles, most of them single-handed—this was a first. This boat, too, was a first. Normally, I keep some sail up and don't slow the boat down more than is necessary. SPRAY was different. She was an old lady, and if we wanted her to take care of us, we had to take care of her. In any case, I wasn't racing. I didn't want to end up exhausted, famished, and wet through from having to constantly steer. Also, I didn't want to take risks. I followed my grandfather's teaching: Act with prudence and respect both the boat and the elements.

I stayed in the aft cabin, on my bunk, ready to jump up to deal with any emergency, while Annick and Briac stayed in the main cabin.

The wind now howled with abandon, tearing off the wavecrests and hurling the spray in horizontal sheets. The huge seas were breaking and roaring all around us. With the wheel lashed, SPRAY moved slowly forward with an easy motion like a gull sitting on the sea, making between three and five knots by herself. Taking advantage of a lull between waves, I leapt on deck, ran to the main cabin, and dove down below to check in on my crew. I also wanted to eat, because that's important at times like this. All was well below. Annick was already cooking without much difficulty and Briac was sitting quietly at the table drawing and coloring in books. In fact, it didn't seem much more uncomfortable than when we were on the mooring in Narragansett Bay.

But, the moment we opened the companionway hatch to let in some air and took a look outside, what we saw was a Dantesque spectacle of wild wind and riotous sea. Monstrous waves, breaking suddenly with a deep, muffled roar would hurl themselves toward SPRAY as though to engulf her and then, at the last minute, they lifted her transom and disappeared beneath it. The aft deck remained dry, and only amidships did any water come aboard, and this quickly drained away through the scuppers on either side.

There was nothing we could do, or needed to do, but contemplate this remarkable and disorderly seascape. I went back into the aft cabin to read or sleep while waiting either for something to happen or for the weather to improve. From time to time a wave would slam us hard, making the boat lurch and me hold on and worry for a moment, but nothing untoward followed. I glanced at the barometer and saw the needle was on 1001 millibars . . .

During the night, the wind shifted to the northwest. SPRAY took her cue from it and carried on toward the east-southeast without my having to intervene.

By the following morning, everything was much quieter. The barometer had surged upward to 1017 millibars and it was still rising slowly.

With all sail set, SPRAY felt as though she'd regained her youth and was in a hurry to forget the previous day. The sea was still rough and uncomfortable, and the going was hard on the rigging. The mainsheet fitting on the boom broke and the spar thrashed about dangerously. We quickly grabbed a specially made strap which let us reattach the sheet so SPRAY could resume her course. Just before we left Jamestown, Steve Pettengill had taken me to his garage, a veritable nautical treasure trove, and told me to take anything I thought might be useful on my voyage. That's how I came by that strap, for which I thank him!

The weather improved and over the following days became quite pleasant. After the terrible weather we'd been through it was like getting a new life. Under a light southwesterly breeze, the asymmetrical spinnaker drew us along gently and surely, much to the delight of Briac who loved this lovely, colorful sail.

He was four years old and growing into a fine little boy. This was his second west to east Atlantic crossing. Since the first day at sea when he was a little off color, he had been in great shape and didn't stop from seven in the morning to nine at night.

Annick had at last found a remedy for seasickness. The day before we left, she put a Scopolamine patch behind her ear. After two or three days, she felt no more ill effects at all. She spent more time with us and the atmosphere aboard improved, especially for the captain. There's nothing worse than to be in charge of a boat and have really seasick crew on board.

Later, the Atlantic became unstable when a series of fronts passed. It wasn't too rough, but it was unpleasant, with rain and variable winds so that someone had to be at the helm and we had to work with the sails a lot if we were to make headway in the right direction. We also had to watch out for the boom, which, when there wasn't enough wind, would swing across the deck as the boat rolled in the swell. Eventually, working in the dark one moonless night, I rigged a preventer to hold it steady.

We became more and more fatigued from the strain of watching the unlit compass mounted on the cabin top while lightning flickered on the horizon. By flicking on the flashlight for a quick look at the compass, glancing at a star, and feeling for the wind on my neck, I could get my bearings in the dark night, but only for so long.

Under these conditions, the nights spent steering were long. I welcomed the arrival of the next watch so that, before I had to come on deck again, I could stretch my legs, rest my eyes, and perhaps gulp down something warm like Chinese soup which on occasion might have a treat like an egg in it.

At last, I would watch with relief as the sky lightened in the east, little by little, like a theater curtain rising. The darkness would give way to day at a growing pace until suddenly, as if part of a well produced show, the sun would come up. Its glare, magnified by reflection off the water, was dazzling and forced a retreat behind sunglasses together with a hat or visor. Then daytime sailing took over, and all was once more tranquil and serene.

In humid and overcast weather, not at all what we expect in early August, we spotted the island of Faial emerging from the clouds to our south. It had taken us 22 days from Newport.

Not being familiar with the harbor, we took a few turns around it to get our bearings. Then someone told us we could tie up alongside another boat at the customs dock while we completed the entry formalities.

I didn't care to venture into the crowded marina where it would be difficult maneuvering SPRAY, so we stayed alongside the lifeboat at the end of the quay, hoping that it wouldn't be called out in the small hours.

We loved Horta from the minute we arrived, not least because of the contrast between this little corner of Europe and the places we had just come from. We especially liked the market with its displays of vegetables and the fresh fruits that came from the neighboring island of Pico, whose summit we could occasionally see when the weather was clear. The meat was delicious. I still remember the succulent little sausages and the juiciness and flavor of the pork chops. After our sea rations, all this wonderful, fresh food was a treat.

The weather remained unsettled and would be gray, rainy, and sunny all in the same day, so we made the most of it by going to see an exhibit on the centennial of Joshua Slocum's voyage. It was a fine show, with prints and photographs from the era, an excerpt about Pico from Slocum's book printed on a poster, and an interview from the newspaper of the day, *O Telegrafo*. There had been a regatta the week before we arrived, the "Joshua Slocum Regatta," singlehanded of course. The idea was to hold it every year from then onward. João Fraga had organized these events and we had a pleasant and memorable evening dining with him at the Castle restaurant.

Five days are not enough, and it was with some sadness that we left Horta and its hydrangeas, and we promised to return for a longer visit.

We were bound for Cape St. Vincent, the southern point of Portugal. The Sailing Directions advise setting a course north of the direct route so that you won't have to sail close hauled when you meet the northeasterly winds as you approach Portugal. The Nortada (the Portuguese tradewinds) shift to the north closer to the coast and can be strong at times. Sailing a little north from Horta gives you a better angle and a more comfortable ride.

From the second day at sea, I began to suffer from a severe headache and it became quite worrying. It could have been due to the strong sunlight, magnified by the reflection off the sea, because there had been little wind and a flat sea and I had spent the entire day at the helm. I have never experienced such pain, and I was convinced my head was about to burst. Pills did nothing and cold compresses brought only momentary relief. I tried to rest as much as I could, stretched out in the shade, but I felt worse lying down. I did only the most important jobs and for the rest let SPRAY take care of herself. In the middle of the ocean, there was little else I could do.

The sailing was beautiful in this light, northeast wind, though I would probably have preferred some overcast and a little less heat. Briac played on the deck in a rubber dinghy which we'd turned into a bathtub, splashing around for hours. One day he watched fascinated as four beautiful, black sperm whales cruised lazily by a short way off. After spouting a few times, they disappeared.

Because I was worried about my health, we decided to stop in Lagos instead of pressing on to Gibraltar. At dawn, the anchor settled on the sandy bottom off the beach, to the left of the jetty. Once the tender was in the water, we went to the beach next to the fort. While Annick and Briac visited the ancient covered market, I paid a courtesy call on the authorities who were now located in the grand new marina building. After a quick, refreshing swim we rowed back to SPRAY to lunch on grated carrots and hard-boiled eggs. The fresh food seemed to relieve the pain.

After that, I felt that a nap would do me good, because between crossing the shipping lanes and nearing the coast, I'd had little sleep. It didn't last long. The Nortada came up quickly, streaking the sea with whitecaps. Taken by surprise, SPRAY began to tug at her chain, to fetch up, and to sheer. The Danforth lost its grip and she began to drag, beam on to the wind, toward the open sea and Africa. There was no immediate danger, but . . .

"Raise the anchor!"

With two of us hauling on the chain, the anchor soon appeared, shiny from being dragged through the sand—it had never been so clean. After we'd got back our breath, started the engine, and chosen another place to moor, the anchor once more went to the bottom, this time under the brown cliffs, near a little creek.

The next day, we decided to go to Alvor. It was exciting to pass between the jetties once again and into the lovely anchorage in front of the village. There were many more sailboats than the last time we'd been here, thanks to the new Lagos marina. We found our favorite spot in the river, at the edge of the current. We planned to stay only long enough to rest before continuing on to Gibraltar.

On Thursday, August 24, we put to sea again. The wind, already light, soon died completely so that at the end of the afternoon we were becalmed in fog. We were just off Faro and we decided to put in there. We entered the channel against a strong current, and were afraid for a time we wouldn't make it in. But, turn by turn of her propeller, SPRAY screwed her way in until, once free of the current, we could steer for the island of Culetra where Guy Viau had told us there was a good anchorage. He was right. We spent the night there with about twenty boats.

Early the next day, this time with a fair tide, we put to sea again. Once more there was little wind so we headed for Tavira. The small mooring area was at the junction of two rivers and fully in the current, which is tidal and strong at times. We managed to anchor at the head of the fleet, where it would be calmer, in water just deep enough for SPRAY. The town was a good mile away, and to get there we had to use the dinghy. We enjoyed visiting the fishing port and the old town and loitering in the streets lined with old buildings. The people were friendly; the fishermen were quick to smile and offer a few words which, though we tried, we didn't understand.

Four very pleasant days later, we set off again for the Rock.

During the night, off Cape Trafalgar, the wind shifted to the east and began to build rapidly. The sea began to make up, too, and the short waves made progress difficult and uncomfortable. After reducing sail and tacking a few times in an attempt to find an acceptable course, I decided to give up and look for shelter along the coast of Andalusia. We were west of Barbate, quite far offshore, so we turned to go north.

The large, rocky bay of Cádiz was soon to starboard. At daybreak, we thought about entering it, but since we didn't have a detailed chart of this region, we headed for the mouth of the Guadalquivir River and another of the anchorages described by Guy. We finished up opposite Sanlucar, near the nature reserve. It wasn't perfect, but we made do for the night while deciding where to go next.

Just before sunset that evening, wild boar and deer came to the beach looking for food left behind by the day trippers, who can only get there by boat and are not permitted to spend the night. It was a rare and fascinating sight, a little like a Nature Channel documentary playing before our eyes, with its soundtrack the cacophony of hundreds of birds gathered near the fish-filled waters. A large number of fishing boats, which were much larger than those we had seen in Portuguese waters, passed by, making the water quite choppy. From here, it's possible to go up the river as far as Seville, and some people do that and winter at the Club Nautico or the Gelves Marina.

In the end, the weather showed no sign of changing to bring any improvement in the Strait of Gibraltar, so we gave up and turned back toward Tavira.

There are miles and miles of beaches along this coast where there are neither people nor any sign of habitation. Apart from a few places that day trippers can reach, it's deserted. A dune runs along behind the beach and behind it a body of water that separates it from the mainland and civilization. The only way to get to the beach is either by private boat, or by one of the ferries. Where ferries operate, there are restaurants and bars for the holidaymakers, who usually stay close by. Families would be nearest, then, farther away, the naturists, at first in groups or pairs, then singly. These last often appeared like sentries; as we passed by, they would stand up, one at a time, behind the top of the dune! After that would be more miles of sand and dune until the next populated area. It was like that all the way from Faro to the mouth of the Guadalquivir.

I expect that Joshua Slocum would have forgiven us. If he had been confronted by headwinds in the Strait of Gibraltar, and they're not uncommon there, perhaps he, too, would have put in to Cádiz.

From anchorage to anchorage, we made our way back to Alvor and then quickly on to Portimão. Here we went to a boatyard to prepare the boat for the next crossing, which would be to the Canary Islands.

For a month, SPRAY OF SAINT-BRIAC was the object of our tender ministrations and also came under the expert hands and eyes of José and his yard workers.

We scraped the hull bare, something which apparently hadn't been done in a long time, and after checking the caulking, we repainted it completely. Among other things, we fitted two new Plastimo compasses, with built-in lighting.

When the work was done, we left SPRAY in the yard, rented a car and drove to France to see our families. This gave us an opportunity to travel through the interior of Portugal and Spain, something that's easy to miss when you sail around the coasts!

We were enchanted by Evora, Evora Monte, and Estremoz, beautiful towns and castles steeped in history. Evora dates from the Middle Ages and captivated us with its lanes, its ancient houses, and its parks and churches. In one of these was a crypt that contained thousands of human skulls, a truly impressive sight, but it gave us goosebumps.

Evora Monte is a castle whose turrets dominate the surrounding hills and valleys and it offers a spectacular panoramic view. The village inside its walls, with its sun-faded houses, has hardly changed in centuries. We saw no sign of tourists, not even a postcard vendor. The place was stuck in another era.

The medieval town of Estremoz is enclosed by ramparts. Lovely buildings surround its central plaza where we had a wonderful time walking around in the market, especially the bric-a-brac stalls. Once again, we were transported into the past.

Careening SPRAY in Spain.

We were surprised by the great open spaces we found in Spain, which are not unlike those in New Mexico, Texas, or Nevada, but on a smaller scale. Here and there were tiny villages with imposing churches. Some of the larger towns were unattractive except that they usually had well preserved old sections in their centers.

9

Objective Tenerife

Once we got back to Alvor, we stayed there to wait for a window in the weather that would allow us to set off for Tenerife. The weather here normally deteriorates at the beginning of November, but this year it began to do so early, and rapidly. Everything on board was ready, down to the water, the fuel, and the fresh food, which we topped up daily. Listening to the radio and reading the local paper did little to raise our hopes. The Azores high pressure was too far north and the lows had no choice but to pass to its south, through the region where we were.

We killed time with long walks in the beautiful countryside among the gently sloping hills that surround Alvor. We observed with interest the great variety of birds, storks, herons, and egrets which probed with their long beaks for their daily sustenance in the teeming life of the salt marshes. Without trying to imitate them, at low tide we would hunt for cockles which we would eat on a bread spread with salted butter, or with spaghetti in garlic butter.

At other times, we would walk along the beach, watching the powerful rollers break and surge foaming, up the gently sloping sand, or inspecting whatever flotsam may have been washed up the night before. We recovered several containers, buckets, and buoys which we found quite useful.

We continued to swim almost every day even though the water was getting cool. We couldn't complain as the temperature was still the same as in summer in Rhode Island!

The depressions marched by in steady succession, bringing strong winds and rain. We were still there at the end of November.

One night, a sudden and violent gust of wind lashed SPRAY. In the squall, amid sheeting rain and lightning, the boat dragged wildly and fetched up on a sandbar before the second anchor could be put out. I had left for France the day before and Annick and Briac were alone on board.

The boat didn't seem to be damaged and, little by little, as the tide went out, she settled with a six-degree list and stayed put. There was nothing to do but go back to bed, which Briac had already done, and wait for daylight, but what excitement!

Happily, our friend Dominique was there, Three days later, after digging a channel for the keel, and with the help of his crew, he freed her on an extra high tide. SPRAY regained her freedom and, after that, hung on two anchors.

Christmas came by and while we were still waiting, we celebrated with Dominique and Michele.

Still the heavy rain came down, causing floods in Portugal and Spain, and great numbers of oranges appeared along the beaches, washed down by the swollen rivers. This hadn't happened in more than a hundred years. Carlos, waiting for us to arrive in Tenerife, couldn't understand it; we were supposed to have been there the first week of November.

Discouraged, and needing a change of venue, we decided to go to El Rompido on the Spanish coast where Wolfgang, who owned a small boatyard, would put us on a secure mooring in the river. We took advantage of a lull between two depressions and arrived there without any problems despite the difficulty of passing over the shallow and poorly buoyed bar. The next day, 50-knot winds battered the mooring area. The already strong current was boosted by the torrential rains, and between the two, SPRAY felt as though she was in a washing machine. We were tossed about like never before. The dinghy, at the stern, was damaged and nearly sank. What a night it was! We tried hard to play scrabble, but we couldn't concentrate, so we went to our respective bunks, hoping it would soon be over.

The region suffered considerable damage. Part of the marina at the yacht club, a few miles away, had been destroyed, there was much flooding and several roads had been cut. The boatbuilder had never seen anything like it and feared for his large glass windows.

Other boats, anxious to make the crossing, remained harbor bound like we were. Some of them tried anyway but turned back to take shelter. Others made it to the Canaries but only after long and difficult passages. It was no kind of weather to put a SPRAY outdoors!

As long as the weather remained the same, the long walks went on, this time on the beach which ran along the far side of the dunes. It was 15 miles long, and apart from a few fishermen riding mopeds, there was not a soul on it. We imagined ourselves like castaways on a deserted planet, standing before this boundless ocean where, occasionally, we would see a trawler towing its net not far from shore, or a sailboat moving slowly along the horizon. It was exhilarating, walking along this long ribbon of sand. Beautiful shells lay everywhere, and all sorts of mysterious flotsam and jetsam aroused our curiosity.

We used the time to tour Andalusia and visit the magnificent city of Seville, Cádiz whose fortifications along the sea reminded us of St. Malo, Granada with its many architectural treasures, the snows of the Sierra Nevada, and finally Gibraltar, where we spent most of our time waiting at the Spanish customs on our way out. This beautiful and interesting region will forever be engraved in our memories. In springtime, the Route of White Villages, as we called it, where all the houses are painted white and surrounded with flowers along the roads and in the meadows, was unforgettable.

We had the privilege, and it's one not to be missed, of watching a display put on by the Andalusian equestrian academy. The dedication to perfection in education and training, the sublime elegance of the gestures, the pure beauty of the animals, and the richness of the costumes and the teams transported and enchanted us.

On returning to El Rompido, we careened SPRAY on the slope of the dune, on the river side. We were surprised to see that in so short a time, a veritable carpet of grass had grown on the hull. It was probably a phenomenon peculiar to that body of water. We decided to go back to Alvor, our favorite place on this coast.

If entering El Rompido wasn't easy, getting out was even less so. This time the ranges were behind us and thus more difficult to follow,

Siesta time in Sanlucar, on the
Guadiana River, Spain

———◆———

especially as the tide was setting us across the channel. After touching
bottom several times, we at last reached deep water, to our great relief.
Our first objective on the way was to go back up the Rio Guadiana, to
the border between Spain and Portugal.

The entrance, between two long breakwaters that stretched out
into the sea, was well buoyed. After checking in with the Portuguese
authorities, we went to moor just north of Ayamonte on the Spanish
bank, opposite a boatyard a little beyond the fishing dock. It's a pleasant village, bright with flowers, where the bars invite you to relax and
snack on their succulent tapas.

Every day on the Guadiana was enchanting; it was like passing
through paradise. The nearby arid hills were starkly beautiful, there
were so many colors and scents, and the tranquility was so pervasive
that even the slow chugging of our motor couldn't disturb it. Once the
anchor was down, the simple act of silencing the engine put us in perfect harmony with our surroundings and at peace on the clean, sweet
water that flowed slowly at the whim of the tides.

The gorgeous sunsets lit the entire landscape in delicate colors, to
the accompaniment of a chorus of birdsong. Nearby, in a big nest made

of branches, was a pair of storks and we could see through binoculars two small beaks aggressively demanding their food.

At dawn, we went a little farther up, and moored not far from where a tributary joined the Guadiana. When we set out to explore it, we came across a ruined mill. All that remained were the foundations and the millpond, which still held water and was ringed by a bank of highly polished pebbles. Natural shallow swimming pools had formed in several places where the cool water flowed gently between boulders and banks of the wonderful pebbles. We did our laundry here, just as Portuguese laundresses had in times gone by. In beautiful sunshine, we also brought out our cushion covers, sheets, towels, and all the soft furnishings to give SPRAY a big spring cleaning in this dreamlike river overhung with leafy branches. We were alone. There was nobody around on land or on the water. It was a true spring of life and happiness. Briac made the most of it, running into the clear, calm water, diving, and trying to catch in his hands small fishes that swam between piles of the smooth, white stones. We spent the whole day in this idyllic spot.

About halfway up the navigable length of the river two towns face each other: Alcoutim on the Portuguese side and Sanlucar on the Spanish. The first was very busy with several businesses around the square, the other seemed to be asleep and we had to search for the grocery store.

It was fascinating to compare the different architectures and cultures, not to mention the characters, of these two pleasant spots. We leaned toward the Spanish town which was more tranquil and perhaps more sociable, and we could at least converse with the people. Each had its castle, a reminder of the period, not so long ago, when they viewed each other across the point of a sword. The one in Sanlucar, perched high on its hill overlooking the river, offered a panoramic view of the region.

Both municipalities—I don't know which one was first—had installed guest docks and these were occupied by several sailboats. We could also anchor on one side or the other, or even in the middle if we were undecided, the question then only being which courtesy flag to fly. Now that both countries were in the European Union, we could, with no problem at all, take an aperitif in one town and have coffee in the other while in between stopping back on board for dinner. The terraces of the bars in Alcoutim were always busy and we found the people from the boats there in a friendly, relaxed, and very British, atmosphere.

As all good things come to an end, the time came to return downstream and get back to our voyage. Sailing along the coast we were happy to get back once more to Alvor, its river, its sands, its lovely hills, its village and its fishermen. Now, it had been invaded by tourists on land and sailboats on the water. It hadn't taken long for those in Lagos to hear about Alvor and come here to anchor. There were British, Dutch, Germans and a few French. It was beginning to get crowded and we could remember when, two years before, there was scarcely anyone there.

We were pleased to meet up once more with an older English couple, Diana and Mike, their dog, Peanut, and their two cats, Baggywrinkle and Gingernut, animals they'd rescued during their cruise around the Mediterranean. They'd left home 16 years previously and didn't seem to be in any great hurry to get back. We also met up with Dominique again, still winning regattas and with his head still full of ideas.

After a few days of good times in Alvor and its surroundings, we had to think about SPRAY and we returned to the Portinave boatyard in Portimão.

José, the eternal cigarette butt in the corner of his mouth, checked over the caulking to make sure everything was in good shape. The paint was wearing quickly and, since the primer was orange, we decided to make a change and paint the hull in this bright color, which would also make us very visible at sea. The bulwarks would remain white. We removed the chainplates to get them galvanized and paint them with epoxy, and checked every inch of the rigging and every shackle and block.

Returning to Alvor, we topped off the various stores so as to be ready to leave earlier than we had the year before.

On October 10, 1996, we raised the anchor, which was covered in a sticky and stinky mud. We had the technique down by now and only used the manual windlass to help in extreme conditions. With patience, it came up by hand without difficulty, but it did take two people.

Our friend, Fidel, was fishing in the channel, between the two breakwaters, in his green, yellow, and red-painted wooden rowboat. We hailed him one last time and I'm sure he shouted something like "Bon voyage."

Soon, inspired by having the wide open ocean before them, the whole crew worked together to hoist the sails, despite a lack of wind.

"Let's try to set the old light genoa."

Briac, now five years old, took part in all deck activities, knew how to tie knots, and sailed and rowed his Optimist like an old salt. On top of that, he had a keen eye and he was often the first to notice a loose reef tie or anything else that wasn't right, or even a supermarket on the shore. From the age of two he had been in charge of stopping the engine.

The breeze filled in from the north-northwest and slowly built, to the point that the "jumbo" shredded. We recovered the remains, set the yankee and staysail, and resumed our course to the south.

Toward two in the afternoon, we crossed paths with a few freighters and were somewhat surprised, and a little unhappy, to see five 55-gallon drums floating by.

After the fine weather of the first few days, a southwesterly front, bringing a solid 35 knots of wind, obliged us to drop the sails and apply our new technique of running off under sheeted-in staysail and trailing warps. Unlike Captain Slocum, I prefer doing this to using a sea anchor. We would lose a little more ground but the boat was less exposed and, most important, the rudder was less vulnerable. The seas quickly became steep and short in violent gusts of wind. I took the helm for a while, until I was confident everything was under control, then lashed it and went below into the warmth of the cabin.

The next day, the wind died down quickly but a sea confused by crossing swells made it difficult to lay a course toward the southwest. We soon found it necessary to use the engine as a way to make life aboard more bearable.

We were still a good distance from the Moroccan coast and we passed many freighters and fishing boats while crossing a region that was particularly agitated presumably by currents because there was virtually no wind. It was quite something, and I certainly wouldn't want to be there in bad weather! The chart didn't note anything out of the ordinary, but for anyone who might find it of interest, it's located at 31°17'N and 10°43'W. Even when the fair weather returned on this leg of the voyage, the heavy swell remained and the pitching and rolling put a strain on the rig.

This time around, we were ahead of schedule and decided to put in at Lanzarote, which we didn't know, at least by boat. Just as we did in the same area on our previous passage, we caught a fine dorado the evening before arriving at Arrecife.

While we waited for daybreak, we hove to a short distance from the harbor entrance, entering at about 8 a.m. after a good breakfast. At first sight, the anchorage appeared full of sailboats of all nationalities. We found a spot between a British boat and a Canadian one to set our anchor. We were very careful about it as we didn't want to make them nervous.

The port was well protected and the town attractive and engaging, with a lovely beach. Briac and the rest of the gang went there almost every afternoon to swim, to play, and to use the very clean showers.

On the opposite site of the harbor and fort, in front of the town, a new and interestingly designed marina was under construction.

We took a bus to explore this special island with its lunar landscapes of solidified lava and were impressed with its barren beauty.

After paying a visit to the yard where they build wooden boats, which is always of special interest to me, we moved to the southern end of the island, first to the anchorage at Papagayo and then to Playa Blanca. The latter is a small tourist town of pleasant proportions and its narrow harbor is busy with ferries to Las Palmas and Fuerteventura. We anchored, therefore, near the buoyed cables that mark off the swimming area at the beach. The water here was so clear we could easily watch a small crab as it scuttled along the bottom. During the three wonderful days we spent there, we swam around the boat because the surf on the beach was often too powerful to enjoy it.

In excellent weather and with a fair east-northeasterly wind, we left this enchanting spot with its green-shuttered, white-painted houses to head for Tenerife where Pedro and Carlos were waiting for us to arrive, only late by a year.

Just before sunset we were quite surprised to see, poking up from the horizon, the tip of Teide volcano. I went below to calculate the distance, because I didn't expect to get there until late next day. Eighty miles! It was amazing. That was the first time I had ever seen anything at such a great distance. If it was a mirage, then everyone saw it, and quite clearly, too! To end the day on an especially high note, we landed a tuna big enough for the three of us.

After a delightful night's sailing, under a magnificent full moon, we entered the south basin of Santa Cruz harbor. At the far end, to the left, a new marina was still under construction, but we preferred to moor alongside the concrete quay.

We soon found our friends, Veronique and Pedro, then after work, Carlos came to join us, and offered us the use of an apartment, as a change from the boat. That was a touching gesture and we much appreciated it. Accustomed as we were to SPRAY, and though we were sad to abandon her, we accepted the invitation. I felt sure our beloved boat would understand and not begrudge us the few nights ashore when we slept in a beautiful, big bed. Briac was quite excited about seeing his friends again and with the prospect of a change in surroundings.

Along the quay it looked like a gathering of traditionally rigged vessels. The biggest among them, EYE OF THE WIND, was taking passengers to the Caribbean on her way to Australia. Briac received an invitation aboard to play with the captain's young daughter. How thrilled he was to be on the deck of such a magnificent sailing ship that seemed to have come right out of his story books. Tenerife was an unending succession of discoveries for him, with so many landscapes, boats, cars, and friendships all in an atmosphere of profound happiness. For us, Tenerife was one of the most beautiful islands, and sojourns, of the voyage.

We made sure to go on an expedition to Tiede and its snow-capped peak. We accompanied Doris and Klaus, a friendly German couple sailing on a 27-foot, superbly-built boat that's fitted out without bulkheads. Klaus, an ingenious builder, comes from East Germany and was very happy about his new freedom. He was building a fiberglass dinghy on the quay, using an English cruiser's boat as a mold. We picnicked between two banks of cold and penetrating fog and then drove to Orotava and back.

After a visit to Bernadette in Puerto de la Cruz and a last meal with our friends who had treated us to such a memorable stay—during which I ate my favorite dish, boiled octopus—we left this much-loved place. We were bound for another island on the other side of the Atlantic: Culebra, which lies between Puerto Rico and St. Thomas.

10

◆

The Tradewind Route
to Culebra

On Sunday, November 24, in beautiful weather and a northeast wind, we left the port of Santa Cruz. As it often does between the mountainous islands of the Canaries, the breeze built quite rapidly so that we had to put in a reef. But more important, it let us log 140 miles in the first 24 hours.

That first night of sailing was like a fairly tale, illuminated by the moon and with the sound of the waves for a lullaby. It also brought us to the Tradewind Expressway. On the following day we saw seven sailboats and on the next day, seven more. And they weren't the same ones! They were with the Atlantic Rally Cruise, bound for St. Lucia, in the Windward Islands. More than 200 boats left Las Palmas, Gran Canaria at the same time.

Our radio schedule with André went well. It was quite a thrill to hear his voice from so far away as he passed along news of Brittany. We were able to keep him informed of our progress. Unfortunately, these transmissions wouldn't always be so reliable all around the world because of the capricious way that radio waves function.

My fishing line system on its storage reel, which I had recently installed under Klaus's interested eye, began to prove its effectiveness. We literally jumped when it went off like a machine gun. We immediately looked astern to see a beautiful dolphin trying to free itself by jumping violently out of the water.

"Fiiiiish!" the cry went up.

The crew all sprang to their stations in readiness. I hauled in the line quickly to maintain tension and at the same time asphyxiate the fish by dragging it along the surface. Annick grabbed the gaff and Briac commented excitedly.

"It's a big one!"

With this very simple system, we caught more fish than usual during the crossing and lost fewer lures. We limited ourselves to one per day, which was enough to provide two meals as well as appetizers of raw fish marinated in lemon juice.

We caught 13 fish in the first part of the passage and after 46°West we didn't get a single bite. This was the same geographical boundary as on our previous crossing.

Our daily lot alternated between fair weather and overcast punctuated with squalls and a more or less big swell, making life aboard quite uncomfortable. The tradewind routine of the lashed helm established itself from the outset. Life aboard returned to normal and Briac once more settled into his schoolbooks.

Time for school

Every day the timetable was much the same. Annick, the schoolmistress, sat at the table in the open air to wait for her student; Briac came up the companionway ladder with his backpack full of books, took a deep breath and surveyed the weather. He then sat on one of the small benches José made for us in Portimão, pretending he was on the school bus. He often chatted with an imaginary pal about how dreary it was having to go to school every day. Finally he came to sit down close to the teacher who would reproach him gently.

"Well, Briac, you took your time today."

"It was snowing and the bus was late!" the pupil would reply. Or, "The bus was on strike." (That's the kind of thing he'd pick up from Radio France International news). Every day, it was a different excuse.

After class, Annick would go down to the galley to prepare a little snack for the crew, and became Briac's mother once more. He would climb down the ladder to put away his books as if coming home from school.

"So, how was your morning, Briac? Did you study well?"

"Oh, man! Teacher was really hard on me today, not really nice. But, I learned a lot anyway."

Briac's timetable was simple. School in the morning. After lunch, his mother read and explained stories by authors like Jack London, Robert Louis Stevenson, and Henry de Monfreid, as well as books on the lives of whalers or pirates, in English and in French, and occasionally in Spanish. After tea at four p.m., Briac would come to see me in the aft cabin where I would read from one of his favorite books. In the evening, after dinner, he had one last story with his mother. She would start telling it but he would soon integrate himself into it and become the main character in the role of Superman or Zorro.

He had no computer, television, or video player, only a radio that his great grandmother had given him on which, nine times out of ten, he listened to classical music. He learned to appreciate it at a very early age because Annick made him listen to it a lot of the time when she was expecting him.

The rest of the time, the boy played with his cars, animals, and wooden blocks. He had a tool set which he'd been given on his fourth birthday: screwdriver, hammer, pliers, saw nails, and screws held no secrets for him. The miracle is that he never hurt himself.

From the moment he set foot aboard, Briac acquired a natural sense of balance, which let him coordinate his movements perfectly with those of the boat. He had a fine sense of observation and learned very easily and by himself, just by watching. He tied knots, and without much teaching from me, learned how to drive the outboard, and to row, scull, and sail his Optimist.

A quick study, he was always asking questions. Life for the three of us, 24 hours a day, created an atmosphere in which month after month his growth and his self confidence were encouraged.

During the long days at sea, Briac would be discussing with us everything that went on around him, what he heard on the radio, and the stories he listened to every day.

One of the first stories I told him, obviously, was that of Captain Joshua Slocum.

Once upon a time, and this is a true story, there was a little boy named Joshua. He had several brothers and sisters and his mom and dad had a farm in Nova Scotia, in Canada. They worked hard to feed their family. One day, they decided to go to where the mommy had been born, in the village of Westport on the island of Brier in the Bay of Fundy. There, you know, the tides are as big as they are in Brittany. You remember, at Saint-Briac, the water comes up very high, right up to the cabins on the Salinette and afterwards, it goes down a long way, uncovering sandbars where you can dig for clams. You remember those thin, shiny little fishes which jumped under the shovel and you had to catch them quickly before they slipped away and disappeared into the wet sand? What fun that was! Well, in the bay in Westport it's the same, and there are lots of currents.

His father made boots for the sailors and fishermen and Joshua often had to help him. He hardly knew what school was.

One day, in the cellar, he built a lovely schooner out of scraps of wood. His father was furious when he saw it. He snatched it up and threw it on the ground, where it smashed, bringing the tears streaming down Joshua's face. He was mad at his father and was unhappy for a long time.

Joshua loved his mother very much and spent a lot of time helping her. Sadly, worn out from her hard life, she died and went up into the sky, you know, like your great grandmother, Didine.

On her death, Joshua left home, found work on the fishing boats, first as a galley boy, then made a transatlantic voyage on a three-masted sailing ship that only stayed afloat because of its cargo of lumber.

He changed ships, made a voyage around Cape Horn, and learned navigation. At the age of 21 he became an American citizen, and that allowed him to command a coaster on the west coast of the United States. That's a sailing vessel that trades along the coasts. After a season of fishing in Alaska, he lost his boat but managed to save his cargo and bring it to San Francisco. On his return, he obtained a new ship which he took to Sydney, in Australia.

There, he met Virginia, a beautiful, young American woman. Three weeks later, they were married and they spent their whole lives sailing together, on many ships. They had many children, some of whom didn't survive and they went, too, into the sky.

They kept up this way of life for twenty years, sharing the hard ways of the sea. Virginia rode horseback and knew about firearms. On board, to amuse herself, she would often use a pistol to shoot sharks which one of the children would attract by towing a piece of meat on a line behind the boat. One of their sons was named Garfield, you know, like the cat!

At one point, Joshua built a boat, deep in the jungle where he was surrounded by snakes and other dangerous animals. In exchange for this work, he was given a sailing vessel, the PATO. He left with that boat for a season of fishing off Alaska, caught lots of fish, and made a lot of money.

Once in Honolulu, a fast three-master which carried the mail to Australia left one bag on the dock! Slocum intervened: "Throw me the bag, I'll take it to them!"

Everyone on the dock was skeptical, because PATO wasn't what you'd call a fast boat. But he left them to argue the toss and eventually caught up with the ship as it was leaving the pass. After this exploit, he sold his boat for a good price and bought another, the AMETHYST, on which Garfield was born.

After several long voyages, he sold it again and bought, with two partners, his best ship, NORTHERN LIGHT.

You know, Briac, life aboard ship wasn't easy, and sometimes they had mutinies: the men didn't want to work or obey orders, and wanted to take over from the captain. Joshua Slocum would then take his guns, often supported by Virginia, also armed, and arrest the leaders and clap them in irons in the bottom of the hold, like in prison.

Portrait of Joshua Slocum
(E.P. McLaughlin,
Sheridan House Archives)

———◆———

Trade was difficult and they had to sell the beautiful three-master,
NORTHERN LIGHT, *in New York. But he soon bought the* AQUIDNECK *and
left to trade in South America. It was in Buenos Aires that Virginia, ill and
exhausted, died.*

*The ship was moored in the Rio de la Plata. They had agreed that if
something bad happened when Joshua was ashore, his son would hoist the
flag that represented the letter J. As it happened, when he saw the flag, he
was able to get back on board just in time. Virginia gave her last breath,
surrounded by her husband and her children.*

*You know, Briac, Joshua was very upset by this loss. Later, his son
Garfield said that his father was "like a ship without a rudder!"*

*They returned to the United States. Some time later, Captain Slocum
married one of his cousins and they sailed for Argentina aboard the* AQUID-
NECK. *Business was harder than ever, with more crew problems, sickness,
and troubles with port authorities. He was even attacked aboard his own
ship. He had to shoot at his assailants, killing one of them, for which he
was acquitted by a Brazilian court. Finally, the ship foundered on a sandbar and the waves destroyed it.*

He wasn't going to be defeated by this latest blow and, with pieces of the planking and lumber from local trees, he built a small sailboat. He rigged it like a Chinese junk, with slatted sails, and christened it LIBER-DADE. *In this craft, probably one of the first cruising sailboats, they returned to the United States.*

Once there, he wrote the story of his voyage and looked for work which, at the end of the nineteenth century, was hard to find. Steamships were replacing the big sailing vessels but Captain Slocum didn't want any part of them. For him, the sea was sailing!

One day, while he was strolling with his friend, Captain Pierce, a former whaling captain, his friend said to him, "Come to my home in Fairhaven and I'll give you a boat!"

The next day they went to this village which was also an important fishing port. There, in a field, behind the captain's house, there was a decrepit vessel that looked like a fishing boat that had been abandoned for many years.

Joshua Slocum took up this new challenge, primarily because the boat had beautiful, balanced lines. For 13 months, by himself, he worked to rebuild it, plank by plank, felling an elm to rebuild the keel and the backbone and making what became one of the most famous boats in the world, SPRAY.

You see, Briac, it's the same as ours. SPRAY OF SAINT-BRIAC *is a replica of that boat, and Joshua Slocum was the first sailor to make a circumnavigation of the world singlehanded. Now, it's the 100th anniversary of this event, and we're making the same voyage; you're making the same voyage. That's good, isn't it?*

"Yes," said Briac, his eyes glowing with excitement and dreams.

"Well, Briac, I'll tell the rest another time. We're going to have dinner, now, because I think it's ready."

"Papa!"

"Yes?"

"Thank you. That was a great story!"

"But it's not a story, Briac, it's true!"

Later, while we were jibing, always a delicate maneuver because of the size of the spars, even when we thought we were controlling it well, the mainsail tore. Even though the sailmaker in Fairhaven had assured us that it would get us around the world without any trouble, I had always been rather skeptical, so thanks to help from Carlos, a new sail would be waiting for us in Culebra. We immediately got out the needles and thread and set about sewing it up. It was taking on more and more the appearance of a patchwork quilt.

Just before nightfall, we were able to set full sail again. The jibes were quite frequent, because the wind would change from southeast, through east, to northeast and jibing was the best way to keep a steady course, and give the crew some exercise besides.

In the afternoon of the 13th day, a red freighter, coming from Europe, altered course, not to avoid us but to pass very close by our stern. Curious, I turned on the radio and listened in case it was calling us. It was the NIEUBURG, and its radio officer asked us if everything was okay. They had been asked to be on the lookout for a red sailboat reported missing. Reassured, it quickly resumed its course and was soon just a speck on the horizon.

The tradewind was not very stable and varied in strength and direction. Quite often, we had to break out the slickers to keep off showers or squalls, and that upset the smooth rhythm of our passage.

Then, one day, there was not a breath of wind! Perhaps at 20°N and 48°W we were too far north? The whole crossing would be like that, alternating between fine and less fine weather.

Friday, December 20 was a little different and the excitement on board grew. It's always like that on the approach to land. It was our 26th day at sea. We expected to see it and perhaps even smell it. We planned to pass between St. Barts and St. Martin, and we sighted them at nightfall. As we passed between them in total darkness, a small military vessel approached. A black shadow with only the navigation lights, it was both disconcerting and intriguing. After following in our wake for a while, like a shark stalking its prey, it passed us to starboard and went its own way, very slowly. It seemed to be on patrol, or perhaps on exercises. Anyway, it was utterly silent.

We continued on our way and soon after daybreak, after a few clouds and black, wet, squalls had gone by, the sun, which was never far away, returned to cheer everyone up.

Quite soon, we saw the Virgin Islands. We came closer to them and eventually passed by St. Thomas in the evening. The island was brightly lit, under a perfect, starry sky, and it added a magical touch to the sailing that night. We had a few more hours of peace, and then, at about two in the morning, the anchor settled on the sandy bottom in the ferry port at Culebra, on the west side, from which you can watch the sunsets. There were only four sailboats there. The rest, dozens of them, were inside the superbly protected lagoon.

At first light, we were curious to take a look at our surroundings. Nothing seemed to have changed very much since our last visit 15 years before, except that the ferry docks had been rebuilt and were larger than before, even though the ferries were still as small as ever. On the other hand, there was a much greater number of boats in the lagoon. The time before there had only been three or four.

We preferred to anchor in this small bay, in front of the tiny beach and the village. We were in the lee of the land so the water was quite calm. Occasionally, a swell would come into the bay for some reason, but it was never really uncomfortable.

A certain nautical lifestyle has developed here, with several bars and restaurants being only accessible by dinghy. Culebra had a reputation as a hurricane hole, at least before Hurricane Hugo went through. That storm caused tremendous damage, probably because too many boats were assembled in one small place, and some were simply anchored and left to fend for themselves.

The island is part of Puerto Rico, so the customs authorities are American. To perform the formalities, all you have to do is telephone or, as we did, go to the new, small airport. After some research and several telephone calls—the advent of Christmas didn't help much—we tracked down our sail to the office of the UPS agent. We arranged to meet on the dock, but I was taken aback when he demanded to be paid the local tax, which he collected on behalf of the government of Puerto Rico. I considered this quite high handed on the part of UPS. Despite making several phone calls, it became obvious that, if I wanted to take possession of my sail, I would have to pay up. Two hundred and fifty dollars gone on Christmas Eve!

I later obtained the name and address of a government official and wrote him a letter. To our surprise and pleasure, a year later I received a check reimbursing me for the tax which was never due in the first place because we were in transit and the sail wasn't made in Puerto Rico.

Because of the holidays, the mail took a while to reach us, especially from Europe and Australia. While we waited for it we made the most of the peace and beauty of this lovely island. Cows grazed at their slow and reassuring pace on its grassy hills and the birds charmed us morning and evening. We took comfort in hearing the crowing of the cocks and the cackling of the hens, and in watching the regular comings and goings of the small passenger boats under their clouds of black exhaust. We watched the antics of the fishes swimming around SPRAY's hull and we could always clearly see the seabed that was but ten feet under the keel. And there was a beach a hundred yards from where SPRAY was anchored. But it was the walks we took in and around this island which brought us to love it. We met and chatted with the locals who spoke a very pure form of Spanish.

The only problem was replenishing the boat's stores. There were several reasonably well stocked small shops and by going from one to the next, we could satisfy our daily needs. For the rest, there was a supermarket in Fajardo on the mainland of Puerto Rico. We could have made the trip there and back in a day by ferry, but we took SPRAY because the cruising is wonderful around the islands and along the barrier reef as far as Cape San Juan. We stopped behind Palomino Island where there are free moorings for cruising boats, probably to protect the coral seabed from damage.

Part of this island belonged to "El Conquistador Country Club and Marina," one of the grand hotels located just north of Fajardo. I don't think I've ever seen a group of buildings as well suited to their surroundings. The architecture, the pastel colors, the physical arrangement of the structures, including the private marina, blended perfectly with the countryside, the forest, and the sea. At the marina, wedged at the foot of the cliff, there were several docks, bars, restaurants, and luxury apartments. A superb cable car system connected the sea level to the top of the cliff which was smothered in lush vegetation. Finally, two miles away, on the south-southwest side of the island was a magnificent beach with an adjacent tiny sand islet that had nothing but a few coconut palms on it.

All around us, the underwater scenery was so varied and beautiful that we had to dive among the lovely corals.

Behind the beach was a bar and restaurant, sports facilities, and even a ranch with horses. Quite often in the mornings, before the tourists arrived, the horses would be let out from their enclosure beyond the border of palm trees to roam free on the public part of the beach.

Overlooking all of this, perched on the cliff above the Caribbean, was a little pastel-pink wedding chapel.

The whole place was perfectly managed and quite idyllic.

While I'm no great fan of organized holidays, I must say that it would be a nice place to stay a while. We took advantage of the lovely public beach, spending a good part of our time in the water and living a little like the vacationers. It was a world very different from ours and our stay there reinforced why we like our life as sailors.

Briac was completely enchanted by the place, what with all the activities and things to see, not to mention that he made friends with a red parrot with a green, blue, and white head. Every evening, he would pay the cockatoo a visit and they would exchange the news of the day.

After several days of perfect contentment, and after promising ourselves we would return, we sailed on to Fajardo.

We anchored right behind Isleta Marina, two islets which have been transformed into a marina with two large, plain apartment buildings. With the inflatable, we crossed the bay to the port of Fajardo. Port is rather a generous description of this place that consisted of nothing more than a ferry terminal.

We were dismayed to learn that the supermarkets and commercial center were eight miles away, which meant taking a "colectivo," a sort of small bus, in order to get there.

Coming back, we took a "shopping car" which is a special taxi with tightly regulated rates. Fajardo itself wasn't of much interest except as a starting point for visiting the interior of Puerto Rico and its capital, San Juan. We decided we'd rather go back to Palomino and use its beach before going to Culebra to pick up our mail. To get there, we had to beat into the tradewinds. Luckily, they weren't very strong early in the morning. With patience, perseverance, and some help from the engine, we made it there.

We were ready now to continue our voyage. We were at a fork: From here, we could head back to the United States or we could head down to Panama and our circumnavigation. Once on our way, it would be difficult to turn back. Unanimously, we decided to press on with the great voyage!

11

The Panama Canal

On January 19 we left Palomino, where we had returned, drawn by the marvelous spectacle of horses running free at the water's edge in the early morning. Once Puerto Rico was astern of us, we were back in the tradewinds which blew a good 20 to 25 knots steadily for the entire passage. SPRAY OF SAINT-BRIAC averaged 140 to 150 miles a day.

During the first three days, we caught one dorado, then nothing else. Then, off Cartagena, in the middle of the night, and in a solid wind of 30 knots, the miracle happened. SPRAY OF SAINT-BRIAC surfed!

I was speechless, because I didn't believe it could happen. Just as I was coming out of the aft cabin, I felt her take off, as though picked up by an invisible force. Horizontal sheets of spray jetted out from both sides of the boat and water gushed onto the deck through the scuppers as if from a fire hose, made a circuit around the aft deck sweeping up everything it could find, then escaped through the same openings it came in by.

It lasted a very short time, but what an exhilarating moment it was. A gust of wind and a big and powerful wave must have coincided and, presto, our 20 tons took off. From time to time I had tried to make her do it and there she did it, all by herself. It reminded me of the great times aboard BISCUITS LU, BNP/BANK OF THE WEST, and OKAY when we took off on unforgettable surfs with the speedometer needle stuck on 26 to 27 knots. It was quite intoxicating, beautiful and so easy, the boat needing no particular help and that night, SPRAY OF SAINT-BRIAC wanted to do it too! However, that would be the one and only time.

Freighters now began to be more and more numerous. They weren't really a problem and were even a comfort, as long as everybody maintained their proper course. The color of the water became emerald green, even though there was still about 1,500 feet under the keel.

We entered the port of Colón at night and in the rain. On the way, we passed one of the PONANT, the sailing cruise ships, all lit up and no doubt heading for the San Blas islands, a little higher up the coast.

There were quite a few boats in the anchorage area but we found a spot from which we wouldn't have to row too far to land at the yacht club. After a fine Chinese soup, tired and happy, we took to our bunks, comforted to have the Atlantic behind us and already dreaming of the great expanses of the Pacific and above all, of its islands.

In the morning, after making sure everything on board was in good order, I went ashore to take care of the paperwork. Immigration was no problem because there was an immigration officer at the club. After that I had to go to town to get the visas. A taxi dropped me off and, after paying the 10-dollar fee per visa, I made my way through the narrow streets to Customs.

"Ah! You don't have an exit permit from your last port. That's a problem!"

They like it when there's a problem. The officer enthusiastically explained the situation to his young, female colleague, to show what a great job they were doing. The way to handle it is to remain calm, attentive, and patient and, soon enough, the problem goes away and you can leave with your papers embellished by a fine rubber stamp. I next had to pay a call on the charming, stout lady in charge of cruising permits. There, more discussions were needed on whether we planned to go through the canal from Colón directly to the Pacific or if we would stop in Balboa, and in the end it cost me 70 dollars. I got the money from the bank across the street, but the good lady had no faith in my 50-dollar bill, so I had to once again join the queue in the bank to change the said greenback. It was almost lunch time, which is followed by the siesta, and I was barely able to complete the business, otherwise I would have had to return the following day. We parted friends with a smile.

Next, it was the turn of the canal administration. Because they don't have an office in Colón, you have to contact them by telephone so that an official can come to measure the boat. That takes only about a half hour and at the end of it there's another bill, of course. Then you talk about what day, what time, and how you would like to make the transit, which in the end they will decide anyway, and always at the last moment.

Before finding out what day you will make the passage you have to pay, and to do that you have to go to Gatun, which is half an hour one way by taxi.

Finally, you have to gather up extra crew; four are needed for the mooring lines in addition to the skipper and the pilot. You can hire Panamanians at 100 dollars a head, or you can try to recruit from the other cruising boats. Some years ago that would have been the natural thing to do, everyone helping each other out and having a great canal party, but times have changed. Eventually, Jacques, Dominique, and Janet, Daniel's Colombian girlfriend, made the transit with us. We only paid Jacques and Dominique. Janet wouldn't accept money on the grounds of friendship, and we left her, tearfully, in Balboa.

Our passage through the canal in 1997 cost us almost 700 dollars. I believe the cost has doubled since the Americans handed it over to the Panamanians. It will soon be less expensive to go via the Strait of Magellan, and it would certainly be more pleasant and more interesting, as long as you take along enough sweaters!

We stayed several days in Colón, first in the anchorage and then at the yacht club dock, not far from Daniel's boat.

His boat intrigued us with its Portuguese flag and the emblem of the Vendée on the transom. *We of Laif,* which translates to "Way of Life" was a fine-looking 39-foot Jeanneau. Daniel is Belgian, and we ended up great friends. We shared several meals with true Belgian frites and galettes from Brittany.

To walk around Colón requires a certain amount of ignorance, or even recklessness, and a taste for adventure. Suffice it to say it didn't have a lot going for it and the bad luck stories of sundry sailors would fill a book. That didn't deter Annick and Briac from going about their daily errands and venturing into the Chinese market, with its bounty of vegetables, meat, and fish. It was our third passage through the canal and, like the other times, we had no problems there. Of course, we never wore so much as a necklace, a watch, a ring, a camera, or even shoes.

For Briac, the club made an excellent playground, not just because he made some friends his own age, but he spent a lot of time there watching the superb, large iguanas that lived among the rocks on the shore. He also got to stroke the cold body of a boa which a young American boy had as a pet.

After a final inspection of the boat and putting lots of provisions on board, because the Pacific is big, we left Daniel, took aboard our three extra crew, and headed back to the anchorage area where we were to meet with our pilot.

He was a young man of Spanish descent, and immediately took charge. We were one of three sailboats making the passage together. Just before entering the first lock, we brought the boats three abreast. The biggest, an American, was in the middle. On its starboard side was an Italian boat of 43 feet, and we were on the other. The middle boat provided propulsion. We were quite happy about this since our motor wasn't very powerful and could only give us 5 knots in a flat sea. However, the skipper of our tug didn't seem quite so pleased with the arrangement.

The passage through the first three locks, which is always an awe-inspiring event, went without a hitch and after the last, each boat was free to go under its own power. We were very quickly by ourselves taking in the scenery as we passed spindly trees and lush tropical vegetation, all of it home to many exotic birds.

Because we couldn't make the whole transit in one day, we had to anchor for the night in Gamboa. When it was time to sleep, Janet found a spot under the upturned inflatable on top of the cabin roof, and Jacques and Dominique took turns in the aft cabin.

The next day, the new pilot, a very likeable guy, brought ice. Since he liked his drinks cold, that was very smart of him because ice is a rare thing on SPRAY OF SAINT-BRIAC.

When we were on our way to the last set of locks, the officers of a freighter, recognizing SPRAY's lines, waved at us from their bridge and blew the ship's horn.

Just before entering the Pedro Miguel lock, to everyone's delight, we saw two magnificent alligators sunning themselves off our port side. They didn't bother even to open an eye as we went by.

This time, we were by ourselves and responsible for the entire operation. Despite a certain amount of tension, and not all of it on the warps, it all went without incident, which pleased everyone. From the moment the last lock opened, we were bound for Balboa and the Pacific.

We really felt that we had made a great leap and had now firmly closed the door on the Atlantic. We were also relieved of the worry about the passage through the canal. A great feeling of freedom swept over us now, as the Pacific opened its arms to greet us.

We disembarked our extra crew, who went back to Colón on the train, and then we were on our way again.

Instead of picking up a mooring at the Balboa Yacht Club, we preferred to anchor a bit farther on, just before the island of Naos. We didn't regret that decision because the view of Balboa and especially Panama City is fabulous. At night it's a fairyland. It's also a hundred times more pleasant than the Colón side. We felt ourselves much more in the Panama of South America, with its wonderful markets and its characteristic atmosphere. We also discovered tides again, which allowed some boats to careen quite easily.

Each evening, a magnificent sunset would spread out and embrace the whole great, mysterious Pacific Ocean, which was now enticing us to continue our voyage to the islands that had been in our dreams for so long.

12

◆

Pacific Ocean, Here We Come

Sunday, February 9, in fine weather, with little wind and the barometer steady at 1014 millibars, the anchor came on deck and was then stowed below. With the bow firmly pointed toward the west-southwest, we set the sails.

"Oh oh!" the peak halyard must have chafed through, because it parted. I got out the needle and thread and fashioned a temporary repair which, to my great surprise, went around the world without giving us any further trouble.

"The best repairs at sea are the quickest ones," said Joshua Slocum, and he seemed to have been right about that.

In the afternoon, we heard a great blast of a horn. It was the DARIO ANDES saluting us, or, more likely, rendering homage to SPRAY.

The weather deteriorated the next day and the sun disappeared behind the clouds. The north-northwest wind veered slowly toward the east, bringing rain and lightning, and the barometer fluctuated all over the place.

"Yiee!"

The fishing line screamed off the reel.

"It must be a big one!"

"Tell me about it!"

It was a marlin, and it took every bit of line without so much as a pause. That was going to be the story for our entire Pacific crossing. We often caught fish that were too big. We lost a lot of lures and in the end, we didn't fish very much: In 43 days, two tuna and a dolphin, a small haul and hardly worth the lures and fishing line we lost.

On the afternoon of February 11, shortly after we passed the island of Malpelo, we noticed we were in a strong and turbulent current. A large amount of debris was caught up in it, and what gave us particular pause were the tree trunks and a swamped fiberglass fishing boat about 18 feet long. We only saw the boat, and thus managed to avoid it, because of the birds standing on it. What would have happened at night?

After these three days of variable winds and squalls, fine weather settled in but there was a catch: the wind was in the south-southwest, right on the nose! I decided to dive south of our planned course in order to reach the tradewinds as soon as possible.

Two days later, on a beautiful day, we found ourselves among a small fleet of handsome, wooden Ecuadorean fishing boats under sail. It was like being in a dream. As we passed, we waved madly and gazed at each other in mutual admiration.

The days went by and blended one into the other. Except, that is, for one special day, when we crossed the Equator. This was a moment we had long anticipated, and not without a certain amount of trepidation, on Briac's part anyway. He was anxious, and he became more and more apprehensive each day.

"You know, when you cross the line for the first time, King Neptune comes aboard to baptize you. But first, you have to pass a few tests to see if you're a good sailor. For example, you'll have to drink a little seawater, tie a few knots, and know north from south."

Briac took the training seriously. He didn't want to disappoint the king, and he asked us a lot of questions.

The weather was perfect for the ceremony. Annick and Briac got dressed in the main cabin in preparation. When he climbed up the ladder to the deck, Briac was surprised to see, waiting on his throne, played for the occasion by a garden chair, King Neptune, with his white beard, draped in tartan, a crown on his head and a trident in his hand. To his young eyes it was a truly impressive sight.

Smiling conspiratorially, Briac and his mother came forward to take the various tests. Then each of them drank a spoonful of seawater, grimacing with distaste and grinning at the same time. They were thus baptized and Briac solemnly accepted his certificate for crossing the Equator.

The principal actors in this memorable celebration then took part in a grand feast around the table: sardine paté, squid in armoricaine sauce, delicious on a bed of rice, crème au chocolat, and not forgetting the Colombian coffee with chocolate chip cookies.

After a week of absolutely magnificent weather, the wind deigned to go southeast. The day before, the water had been much greener in color and colder. That morning, it was more blue, but still cool, perhaps from the effects of the Humbolt Current.

We were definitely on the edge of the tradewinds, because huge squalls came down on us throughout most of the day. These "Irish hurricanes" either contained no wind at all, or the wind would be light and all over the place, which was a lot of fun for the navigator. We broke out the slickers, adjusted the sails, and caught rainwater. In ten minutes, with the help of the fold made by the first reef, we were able to fill the tanks. Never turn down gifts from the heavens.

Then the clouds disappeared, the sun returned with all its strength and the wind came back from the east-southeast. Was this the trades at last? "They're holding! Yes, great!" The trades were there, at 5°South and 86°35' West. Course south-southwest for the Gambiers.

Why the Gambier Islands? During our stay in Tenerife we had met our friend Christian. He had warmly recommended this archipelago over the Marquesas when making a passage to Polynesia. He had stopped there the previous year and from his description, it sounded as though it would suit us best. So, no Marquesas, they would be for another time.

Two days later, with the breeze firmly established, we were once more in our at-sea routine, when a strange noise brought me up on deck. I couldn't quite make out whether it was a boat or an aircraft. It was coming from the sky. I saw a speck astern of us, growing rapidly larger as it came in our direction. It was a little, two-seater helicopter, occupied by two men wearing caps and sunglasses. I couldn't read the writing on the caps, but I soon would have if they'd maintained their course! One of the men looked like an American.

They circled us at a low altitude, the rotor was kicking up spray and making the sails flog, then they fell astern and came down almost to sea level, probably to read the boat's name on the transom.

"Maybe they're in difficulty," I thought. "Will we have to fish them out of the ocean?" I wasn't enthusiastic about that idea, remembering a story told me by a couple of guys from Brittany who'd rescued two American flyers who'd had to ditch their small plane in the middle of the Caribbean.

Eventually, the helicopter climbed, circled us once more and then went on its way, with only a token wave from the pilot. This left us pondering, and not without some anxiety.

"What was that all about?" On the cockpit there was a number and a small Ecuadorean flag, but we were 500 miles from the coast and 300 miles south of the Galápagos. This little chopper couldn't have come from so far away. It must therefore have come from a ship. But it wasn't military, it was a civilian aircraft.

We came up with all kinds of theories, some of which didn't reassure us very much, especially those formed around tales we'd heard of piracy.

In the end, I settled on the idea that it must have come from a tuna boat. I recalled that some of these are very big and use aircraft to spot schools of fish. We confirmed this later when we got to Pago Pago where there is a large tuna fleet and some of the vessels were carrying helicopters like the one we'd seen.

Meanwhile, it took a while before we settled back into the serenity of our ocean routine. The event had the same effect as seeing an extraterrestrial in the back yard.

During the entire crossing, the tradewinds never really settled in. We had light and variable winds and areas of showers and squalls then, in the last days, fronts coming from the west. Conditions weren't exactly ideal! West-northwesterly winds, squalls, lightning, thunder, followed by another "Irish hurricane" and, to top it off, we were becalmed for nearly 24 hours.

The expression "Irish hurricane" used by American seamen, and probably the English too, is pejorative. The adjective "Irish" is used in several other expressions. An "Irish hurricane" has all the characteristics of a hurricane except wind. For our part, though, we saw our fair share of waterspouts. An "Irish pennant" is a small piece of unraveling line. An "Irish reef" is to take a knife to a sail when it won't come down any other way. An Irish coffee, on the other hand, helps you to forget all the others.

During the calm, when SPRAY was reflected in the sea as in a mirror, and when the only movement was the heaving of a significant swell, our "Jonathan Seagull" made a series of timid approaches to come close, as though looking for food. This handsome bird had been following us for 22 days. Twice a day he would come by to make sure we were there. We would call him, and he would turn his head toward us. From time to time, he would shiver from head to tail and send us his calling card which would spatter, white and yellow, over the table or the deck. Now we watched him closely, and if we saw him quiver, we would be ready to dive under the table to avoid his good intentions.

It was quite incredible that he had followed us for nearly 2,500 miles, visiting us occasionally in daytime and at night. Eventually, Jonathan left us one morning a few days before we reached the Gambiers having met some friends who seemed to have come as a reception committee.

We can't say that this crossing left us with much great sailing to remember. El Niño was perhaps upsetting the weather patterns. It seemed to us that ever since we had left the United States, everything to do with the weather had been topsy turvy.

A little friend comes aboard

Something very strange happened one night: the moonlight appeared to be getting fainter. It turned out there was an eclipse in progress. I can now understand why people in ancient times wrapped these events in superstition. It was a weird feeling, and we felt chills run up our spines when the moon disappeared completely. We half expected the fishes and other marine animals, ourselves included, to break out in panic, and we tried not to think about giant octopi and their enormous, long tentacles. But no, all remained calm. There was a short spell of total darkness and then the moon very slowly reappeared until she finally assumed her regal position as though nothing at all had happened.

On the morning of March 24, after 43 days at sea, with a great relief and joy, we sighted the peaks of the Gambier Archipelago. A few hours later we entered the wide and easy passage on the northwest side that leads to the port of Rikitea. To call it a port is a bit of an exaggeration because there was only one quay and it was barely large enough for one small freighter.

This is the site of the village and the principal anchorage; the other islands are mainly uninhabited.

There were only six other cruising boats, so we had no trouble dropping the anchor in the area to the right of the quay. Being on the windward side of the island, this bay was quite breezy, and when the trades blew hard the water could get quite choppy in spite of being protected by the surrounding coral reef. We needed plenty of chain, because the water was about 30 feet deep, and the bottom of coral sand didn't offer very good holding—as we were to find out later.

At last the dream we'd held for so long was fulfilled: the Polynesian islands were laid before us with all their beauty and their charm, their gentle way of life, their clear, calm waters, and their luxuriant vegetation. The island begged to be explored in long walks along the shore and across the land, and this was made easy thanks to the old stone paths that the Foreign Legion had restored. A special adventure was the climb, very steep in places, up Mount Duff, a large rock jutting 1,500 feet above the bay, just above Rikitea. Beautiful flowers bloomed everywhere, and there was abundant, magnificent fruit: grapefruit, acidulous oranges, green lemons, papaya, avocados, pomegranates, bananas. Many of the trees had been abandoned to the wild for years. We prepared to indulge in a healthy regimen of fruit juice, starting with the grapefruit and the slightly tart oranges.

It was beautiful, magnificent, better than the postcards and every day we set off for long walks on well shaded paths. On rare occasions, we met Polynesians riding in cars who, beaming, would invite us to get in. We had to thank them while explaining diplomatically that, having spent such a long time at sea, we needed to walk.

There were few tourists, because there was no hotel and no restaurants, just a few shops selling groceries, one of them Chinese. We had to go from one to the other to find what we wanted. Fresh vegetables were rare because they were flown every ten days to the islands of Ahe and Muroroa for the military. Eggs were five dollars a dozen, even though there were chickens everywhere, running about in the bushes. Only one person, a Frenchman, had thought to pen a few hens. When he wasn't collecting the eggs from his proud, clucking layers, or delivering them on his moped, he took care of the geological center. Otherwise, all the food was frozen and arrived by the island freighter that visited twice a month. Most of the meat, which was excellent, came from New Zealand.

We were surprised to find there was practically no fishing industry. The culture of pearls brings in more money, requires less effort, and leaves more time for beer drinking. After five p.m. the effects begin to show in some people and it's a good idea to be back on your boat!

Herds of wild cattle and goats have taken up residence in the hills. From time to time a hunt takes place, organized by their former, and therefore presumably current, owners. They have to use all their skills to track and capture them, and the slaughter of an animal is always a big excuse for a celebration.

Mail was delivered regularly every ten days by air from Papeete. Everything else we needed would come on the cargo ship, and that included diesel fuel. This came in 55-gallon drums. To refuel, the cruising boats would share a drum and decant the contents into their tanks.

The officer in charge at the gendarmerie welcomed us upon our arrival. He was very friendly and guided us smoothly through the paperwork, and we soon saw how his eagerness to help the cruisers had put him on good terms with everyone. His approach and manner were in pleasant contrast to what we'd experienced in mainland France. He was working patiently toward his retirement, upon which he planned to go cruising. We wish you fair winds, Stanley, in your future voyages.

There's a weather station outside the village, on the high ground that overlooks the lagoon from east to south. We went there often, to visit the meteorologists and to learn about the region's weather patterns. It was also a good excuse for a bracing walk, because it was quite a climb, and that was surely excellent exercise for the heart.

One of the meteorologists, Dominique, had been there for many years. He had first come during his National Service when he was stationed at the air base, which no longer exists. He returned to live in the archipelago which he had grown to love.

I thought I knew quite a lot about meteorology, but I learned that the Pacific isn't as simple as I was given to understand. I thought that the tradewinds blew ceaselessly over this ocean. I was partly wrong, because they are divided into two parts, associated with two high-pressure systems, one named for Easter Island and the other for Kermadec. There's a corridor between the two running from Samoa down to French Polynesia and ending up in the high south latitudes. It's in this corridor that tropical storms and cyclones roam. At the same time, low pressures and their associated fronts can come up from the south. All these phenomenas can interrupt the regular tradewinds. Normally, cyclones don't form after the end of April, and the depressions then begin to come up from the south. The name Papeete means "bucket with a hole" after all the rain that falls there. It's quite possible to go there for a vacation in the so-called "dry" season and have bad weather, with high winds and rain, because of a depression front coming up from the south.

From studying the weather patterns in the area, we began to understand that, if we were to find steady following winds and less chance of bad weather, we would do best to go north of the Tuamotus before trying to head west. That didn't prevent us from encountering westerly winds, with showers, before reaching Samoa, or from finding ourselves 300 miles from a cyclone when we were off Fiji. It seems that that was a product of El Niño!

We waited two weeks for a suitable weather window. During this period, we experienced a series of fronts of varying degrees of violence, with squalls and gusty winds pouring down the surrounding hills. In one of these, SPRAY, despite having two anchors down, dragged rapidly, stopping only a few yards away from the shore and another cruising boat. We happened to be coming down from the meteo station at the time.

Fortunately Daniel, who had arrived singlehanded two weeks before, took everything in hand. With help from several other cruisers, he secured SPRAY by putting out our 150-pound fisherman anchor as well as a 30-pound Fortress borrowed from a big Brazilian catamaran.

What a strange sensation it is to discover, through an opening in dense vegetation, that your boat is no longer in its usual place. We ran madly down the hill until we were panting. Fortunately, a Polynesian driving in the opposite direction made a U-turn and took us to the dock where our dinghy awaited us, no doubt relieved that the distance to its mothership was so much shorter.

We got there just in time to thank everyone, and we re-moored SPRAY OF SAINT-BRIAC a little farther off, on the fisherman anchor. During this maneuver, a water leak in the engine cooling system not only raised the engine temperature dangerously high, but the sight of smoke also briefly elevated the atmosphere on board to panic. The anchor went down a little more quickly than planned. Within the next half hour, the leak was sealed, to everyone's relief. "You know what it would mean if that had happened in the channel!"

"When you think about it, it's a good thing that SPRAY dragged when she did," said Daniel as he stepped into the dinghy where Briac was waiting to row him back to his own boat.

"Thank you, Daniel, very much. We'll see you later for the oranges!"

Daniel is an interesting guy, always optimistic and congenial. He went through two hurricanes in the West Indies, after which his wife and young daughter chose to stay on dry land, and then he was robbed in Venezuela.

He was anchored in a bay there and, at about four p.m. one day, while he was having tea in the cockpit with a girlfriend, four men in a small fishing boat approached, saying they had a fuel problem. Daniel, white knight that he is, went to the rear of his cockpit to fetch a small jerrycan. When he turned back, one of the "fishermen" held him at bay with a shotgun while blocking the companionway. Two others rifled the cabin, even taking away—unforgivable crime—his electric fryer. For a Belgian, that was the unkindest cut!

While at Rikitea, we weren't able to swim very much. The beaches were surrounded by coral and rocks and were hard to get to from the sea. Also, the harbor was infested with jellyfish. These can't have been dangerous, though, because the children would catch them and throw them at each other's heads. When you don't have custard pies, you use what's available . . .

Briac was in seventh heaven. He rowed his Optimist around the boats in the anchorage and he even learned how to scull it. At other times he would fish from the boat and catch remoras, little black fishes with rough patches on the tops of their heads, like Velcro, with which they attach themselves to sharks so that they can live off their waste. Briac would throw them back, because they don't taste particularly good.

Briac also tried to go to the local school. That didn't work out too well and after a week of it he came back on board.

13

◆

From the Tuamotus to Cairns

On May 10, with the promise of very good weather, we raised without too much difficulty our big fisherman anchor. To get it on board, we had to use a block and tackle attached to the mast. Once it was on deck, we had to fold it and, again using the tackle, lower it into the boat and secure it.

The long-awaited break in the weather had arrived which meant it was time to head north of the Tuamotus in search of favorable conditions. Daniel had left for the Marquesas the day before.

We set the sails as we went through the channel in the passage to the northwest. The easterly breeze quickly carried us to sea and as we left the island astern we began to feel the effect of the swell. It was pleasant sailing and we soon rediscovered the pleasure of watching the setting sun's slow but inevitable descent behind the horizon.

The next day was a different matter, treating us to sudden downpours, lightning, and a wind that wanted to go into the north before turning at the end of the day to blow gently from the east-northeast.

On this course, which took us to the north and east of the main islands of the archipelago, we would see only one island, Tikei, from closer than a mile. We would have to jibe to avoid it before resuming our course. It was eagle-eyed Briac who saw it first.

"Hey, Dad, there's something ahead that looks like an island!"

"Yes, I know."

"Yes, but right ahead. You ought to come and look!"

In the time it took to mark my page in my book and climb the ladder, I was up. I looked in the direction he pointed, toward the low, green form of the island.

"I think you're right. It's a little bit too ahead. Crew! Stand by to jibe!" I could almost hear Al Bundy, of *Married With Children.*

Ten minutes later, the maneuver completed, I took up reading again while at the same time watching the speck of land.

It was a calm crossing, with winds of less than 15 knots. It usually blew from the east, but just before we got to Pago Pago in American Samoa, it went west behind a passing front, causing us to make a two-day long tack to the north.

Taking advantage of what was for us unusually good weather, Briac, in addition to reading with his mother, would come to see me every afternoon so that I could read to him, tell him a story, or give him an English lesson.

"Say, will you tell me the story of Joshua Slocum's SPRAY?"

We settled on the edge of the bunk, and I began.

You remember that his friend Captain Pierce had given him the SPRAY, which was lying derelict in a field just behind his house.

Joshua Slocum began to rebuild it, plank by plank, replacing the keel and constructing the cabins. Because he intended to make ocean passages, he raised the freeboard. That gave the deck this sweet curve but more important for him it made the boat more seaworthy. He built her to be very strong.

Then he built a mast, made sails, and soon he launched her and she sat "like a swan on the water." To begin with, he tried fishing to make money, but without much success. Perhaps he spent too much time simply enjoying sailing around the bay. Then, he decided to make a circumnavigation of the world.

In April of 1895, he left his friends in Boston and put to sea. For three years he cruised around the world, through storms and calms, and returned to Newport in June of 1898.

You see, we're making the same voyage, except we're not doing the South American part because we lost too much time in Portugal. In this way, we're commemorating the centennial of his voyage and rendering homage to this great man because, just as he was a great sailor and navigator, he was also a boatbuilder, a shipowner, and a husband and father. His entire life was a struggle, Driven by enormous energy, he strove for perfection throughout, and remained faithful to sailing ships in that difficult era when steam was changing the very nature of seafaring.

He eventually disappeared with his boat. He might have been run down by one of the steamships he refused to command. Perhaps he simply wanted to remain true to himself to the end.

Soon, Briac, you'll be able to read his book Sailing Alone Around the World. *Simple, human, and full of humor, it's one of the best books ever written about the sea.*

"Look out, a fish! Quick, get up and bring in the line!"

We cleared the decks for action and quickly hoisted a fine dorado aboard, to the delight of everybody, especially the cook.

On the 23rd day at sea, we were running along the south coast of Pago Pago. A large swell was pounding on the shore. We needed to be on our guard, because the powerful rollers were breaking well offshore.

The port appears to be the best protected from hurricanes in all of Polynesia. It's actually a deep volcanic crater that's open on one side to the ocean. After negotiating the entrance channel, we steered to the far end where it opened to our port side. We then passed under the cables of the cable car which made the island famous in a movie in which it rained a lot. We finally found a spot at the end of the anchorage area.

What can I say about Pago Pago? We stayed there only five days. We dragged, surprisingly, in 25 knots of wind with two anchors set. The bottom, of a stinking and glutinous mud, was covered with all kinds of plastic and the anchor needed little prompting to imitate a luge when pulled by SPRAY OF SAINT-BRIAC's 20 tons. Once again, the 150-pound fisherman put an end to that kind of behavior. The anchorage was just downwind of the fish processing plants, and the smell at times was unbearable.

The port and the town were dirty. Many Samoans, victims of the consumer society, were obese and depended on welfare. Several cruisers there had created their own little clique, but they were boatbum types who just hung out there and didn't appear too concerned about maintaining their boats. The atmosphere was unpleasant; it remained one of the worst memories of the whole voyage. After what we later heard about Apia, in Western Samoa, we should have chosen to go there. Oh well, next time!

The only advantage, and this was one reason for our going there, was that reprovisioning and refueling were easy and cheap, communications and mail were good. We were disappointed, though, that there was no Australian consulate to issue us visas.

With a feeling of great relief we put to sea again. After passing Blunt's Point, we were once more in the huge Pacific swells. It must be quite something when it blows there!

Although it was June 7, supposedly in the heart of the "good weather" season, that didn't prevent the next day from being overcast with a fine rain, sudden downpours, and strengthening winds. On the third day these reached 30 to 35 knots, and we had to keep an eye on the sails while we steered all night in a sea that was building steadily. The one consolation was that during this dank and dismal weather we made days of 150 miles. Moreover, from the day we left, the barometer remained steady at 1014 millibars.

The Fiji Islands, to our south, were now less than five miles off our port side and, from time to time, we could see the coast. I was half listening to the local FM radio and I couldn't believe my ears: "Cyclone warning." Surely it must be a joke! It was quite startling, and I was alert in an instant with my gaze focused on the receiver. It turned out that Cyclone Kelly was 300 miles due north of us, stationary at the moment but according to the experts, likely to move west-southwest. That explained our awful weather of recent days.

"Damn, that's all we need. The season has supposedly been over since the end of April or the beginning of May. What do we do now?"

Go to Fiji? It would have taken 24 hours to get to the pass far to our south. No, our best bet was to stay at sea.

After what we had learned at the weather station on Rikitea, I had a feeling, in spite of the latest commentary on the radio, that this storm wouldn't go to the west-southwest and catch up with us. I thought it would more likely head to the east-southeast or south. Accordingly, I decided to continue on our westerly course. The atmosphere on board became tense, to say the least. We listened to the radio bulletins without learning anything new. It didn't help the mood on board to hear the advice being given out: "Stay home. Buy food and candles. Above all, stay tuned to your favorite radio station." I switched off the radio and watched only the barometer and the sky which was, no doubt, the smarter thing to do.

The following day the wind eased to settle around 20 knots, then went a little more to the south. The sky cleared for a few moments and a few rays of sunshine came through to warm us. Then, there was some more rain and the wind backed to the east. The barometer remained stable. I figured that the cyclone was moving to the southeast and the radio confirmed it. In fact, Kelly crossed our track at right angles in the place where we'd been four days before.

At the same time that this information was bringing smiles of relief to our faces, a lovely tuna had the very good idea to take our bait and provide us with our ration of needed vitamins.

The wind continued to drop and eventually stabilized at about 10 to 15 knots, which took us as far as Vanuatu. We made the passage north of Efate in headwinds that went from north through west to south, accompanied by a heavy drizzle that cut visibility to 200 yards. That made navigation even more unpleasant after dark.

Once we'd passed between the Vanuatus, the trades came back, strong enough that with two reefs and the helm lashed, SPRAY made daily averages of 155 to 160 miles, much to her skipper's delight.

In this stiff breeze, jibing became tricky and in the course of one jibe, the mainsail ripped just above the second reef. There was probably a little too much tension on the sheet when the boom went across. The tear was too big to repair, so we just tied in the third reef and got on with it. We set off again at almost the same speed. You have to deal positively with these setbacks and not let them get you down. The next day we bent on the new sail. It was a short two-hour job and once it was done, we were under way again in the kind of fine breeze square rigger captains dreamed about.

As we approached the barrier reef which rings the northeast part of Australia, we ran into a pattern of showers and unstable winds alternating with sunshine and good tradewinds. In SPRAY's book, the term "good" means force 5 to 6. Even though we had little success fishing, perhaps on account of our high speed, we never had time to be bored.

After passing between rocks and offshore islands, we reached the entrance to Grafton Passage which leads through the reef. A few hours earlier, a Coast Guard aircraft had appeared just as I was finishing my shower on deck. A few moments later, a female voice came over the radio, asking that we identify ourselves and our destination.

"We will advise the port authorities that you will arrive at the end of the day." That was a nice welcome!

The sea wasn't quite so gracious. Once we got in the pass, with the rocks close by to leeward, we had to come hard on the wind in a nasty and sometimes vicious sea. Some of it hit me full in the face so I put on my oilskins. To minimize leeway and to try to avoid the coral heads to leeward we used the engine at low speed. We made it, just!

Eventually, two hours later, after leaving Fitzroy Island to port and Green Island to starboard, we were at last able to bear off a little toward the channel into Cairns. A large number of sail- and powerboats coming out of another channel were converging on the same point. The charter boat fleet was returning from a grueling day at sea.

We made radio contact with the port and were directed to the anchorage on the left of the river, next to the mangroves and opposite The Pier, a commercial complex near Marlin Marina. All along the riverbank there were numerous sailing boats, moored between wooden pilings or anchored close to the mangroves. We found a spot. The anchor went down and buried itself in the muddy bottom. The current there could have been troublesome, but it was neap tides so it wasn't too bad. Because it was a bit late when we got in, we had to wait until the next day before clearing in, and we weren't permitted to get off the boat. That didn't bother us as all we really wanted was a good meal and a night's rest.

While dinner was cooking, I sat near the wheel. As I watched what promised to be a truly magnificent sunset unfolding behind the hills that surround the town, a great feeling of happiness swelled within me. We were in Australia.

We were on the other side of the planet. I couldn't get over it. After all the delays at the start, here we were!

We were contented that June 28, imbued with a feeling of well-being, of a job well done, and happy to have arrived as planned and without any problems so far. We thought about Debbie and Jacques who were expecting us in Sydney and we dreamed about the Barrier Reef. Above all, there would be no more capricious oceans for several months as we would be sailing coastwise and protected from the ocean swell by this natural necklace of coral.

That morning we had to be on the dock at the marina early for the formalities. We were pleasantly surprised by the courtesy, the smiles, and the friendliness of the two young women who processed us. We can't say the same about the zealous, though courteous, quarantine officer who left with some of our food and even a dried pine cone, a souvenir of our walks in Alvor. That was one way, I suppose, to clean out the lockers.

Because we didn't have entry visas, which had been one of the reasons for going to Pago Pago, unfortunately without success, we had to go to the airport to meet with an immigration officer. The two customs officers gave us a lift there and back. Entering without a visa isn't appreciated. After we explained our situation, they gave us a month, which isn't at all long enough to sail around Australia. That would take at least three months, so we would therefore have to renew the visas, at a cost of 300 dollars.

That was a bad start financially and it took a bite out of our purse. More expenses were to come in the following days with medical and dental exams and repairs and modifications to the sails. The old main was finally repaired and we were able to keep using it, prudently, until we reached North America. Soon, a large part of the budget we'd assigned to visiting Sydney was gone. To make matters worse, we foolishly hadn't paid attention to how far it was from Cairns to Sydney. By bus it would be an expedition and would take too long and the cost of airfare was very high, especially when multiplied by three. We had expected the cost of living to be similar to that in the U.S. but we found out it was closer to that in Europe.

So, unhappy and quite upset, we had to advise Jacques that we couldn't visit them. I'm sure he was deeply disappointed. It wasn't only the cost of the trip, but we would have to pay to leave SPRAY in the security of the marina.

After the long months cruising the Pacific, Cairns was a dream port of call, a welcome return to civilization. Everything we needed we could find nearby and we were able to restock our food supplies, buy antifouling paint, repair the sails, refill the gas bottles . . .

It's a friendly town and its focus is on tourism, especially for the Japanese. They have apparently invested heavily here. The day-charter industry was the most extensive I had seen anywhere. Every day around nine a.m. there was frenetic activity all over the water. Dozens of boats, among them several catamarans over 100 feet long, two of which had sails, loaded with passengers and headed for the Barrier Reef, to return at about 4 p.m. The shoreside facilities which occupied the lower level of the shopping mall offered the tourists every service imaginable.

On board the boats, they sold all manner of merchandise, and they did an especially good business in windbreakers because the return trip was against the wind! Restaurants and bars occupied all the choice locations. The most important advice to heed was "Don't forget your credit card." Once at the reef there were barges with shops, restaurants, and bars and, by flashing your credit card again, you could go on an accompanied dive.

For us, though, the pleasures were simpler and less hectic. How wonderful it was to take a long shower in hot water with lots of pressure! Our last real showers had been in Tenerife, because those in Panama had been cold. We stayed there a long, long time, letting the hot water run over our bodies. It felt so good.

There were sailboats moored all along the river, for two solid miles, but it didn't feel as though they were on top of each other, and some weren't lived on all the time. The dinghies were clustered in groups at the several pontoons installed for their use at intervals along the bank.

Briac was thrilled with all the new activities, all the charter boats, the futuristically styled catamarans like his favorite, the QUICKSILVER, and the commercial and fishing boats. In the air were seaplanes, a blimp, parasailers towed behind motorboats, as well as the traffic at the airport on the left bank of the estuary.

Though we searched hard for them, taking the dinghy all along the mangroves, we saw no caimans, only big lizards. There were many animals to beware of: jellyfish, though it wasn't the season, stonefish, coral, water snakes, sharks, sea caimans. The sun was particularly strong.

In the end, as always, the time passed too quickly, especially for a town like Cairns. SPRAY demanded a certain amount of maintenance and preparation in readiness for her coming passages.

Shopping for gas was easy, as the Australians use the same fittings as the Americans, so we were able to fill the large bottles. We weren't sure what kind of gas it was, exactly, that they sold us. Small matter, after all, just as long as the burners got hot!

14

Behind the Coral Reef

On the morning of July 24, we set off toward Cooktown and arrived there at dawn on the third day of sailing. We doubled the watch during the nights because there was a lot of maritime traffic—trawlers, brightly lit cruise liners, and many freighters. Curiously, sailboats were practically nonexistent. Some way off the entrance to Cooktown we passed, close enough that we could smell the foul odor from their spouts, three superb whales gliding slowly and majestically along. Briac, though a little apprehensive, was utterly delighted to see these monsters of the sea.

The inside of the harbor is small; the river which forms it is divided in two by a sandbar. There was little room for transients and I wanted to moor as close as I could to the spot where Joshua Slocum brought SPRAY. When he was here I imagine there was plenty of room.

The anchor went down and hit bottom.

"Uh oh! Not a lot of depth . . ."

That didn't matter, we'd stay there for the time being. At low tide, SPRAY OF SAINT-BRIAC took the ground and assumed a heavy list. But, as it was on sand, it wasn't serious. We were happy and excited because SPRAY was back in the same spot, just in front of the green square where the statue and plaque stand that commemorate the passage of Captain Cook.

We liked Cooktown very much and regretted that we had not come sooner so we could have stayed longer. Far from anywhere, it was a bit like a town in the Far West with its wide main street flanked by

Cooktown, Australia. Admiral Cook's statue.
A hundred years ago, SPRAY was visiting.

old wooden buildings from the previous century, probably the same ones that were there in Captain Slocum's time.

The local newspaper devoted a page to us and its owner took us to visit the old Grassy Hill Lighthouse and the new regional airport. As he was driving us he pointed out, and described vividly, the amazing work of the termites and their unbelievable structures. On the way back we stopped by his home, to quench our thirst and also to see a few of the animals that he and his wife took in to nurse before setting them back in the wild. Among the convalescents was a wallaby that had been injured by a car. Briac was thrilled to be able to pet it and have it eat out of his hand.

We moved and moored on the other side of the sandbank where there was only one cruising boat. It was a little farther to row, but it was much quieter.

At the local supermarket—its recent opening had been a major event—we were surprised by the number of people going barefoot and shirtless. As for the Aborigines, they normally lived in villages within their reservations. They have a very hard time sustaining their way of life and often those we saw in the towns looked like derelicts.

After spending three days in this great place, we set off again, this time for Lizard Island, one of the most beautiful and interesting stops on our Australian cruise. Most of the islands around there are low, mangrove covered and of little interest. Lizard Island was enchanting. It has two main anchorages. One is in the lagoon and breezy, its only drawback being its entrance on the windward side of the island. The other, Watson Bay, the preferred one, is to leeward, calmer, has easier access, and is fringed by a nice beach. All we had to do was avoid a few easily spotted coral heads and drop the anchor on the sandy bottom.

It was a wonderful place to kick back and relax. We would dive in the waters along the rocks, take long walks, and climb to the top of the hill for its panoramic view of the island and its surroundings. It was from there that Captain Cook spotted the pass that would take him back to the ocean and the Coral Sea. There was no shortage of fresh water, so we were able to collect it for the boat as well as do lots of laundry.

A discreet hotel complex occupied a small corner of the island quite close to an airstrip that served tourist flights. Every once in a while a Cessna brought hotel guests or campers. There was plenty of room for everyone, without being too neighborly!

We certainly weren't going to leave without attempting the ascent to the 1,200-foot summit. What a view! We stayed on the top to rest and recover our breath and eat a snack while we took in the quite spectacular surroundings.

When the cool of the late afternoon caught up with us we started our descent. Half way down, with Briac in front as tour director, we heard something run off through the bushes.

"Hush! Not a sound!"

Eyes peeled, ears pricked for the least noise, we searched for whatever it was had made this sound of flight.

And there, under a thorn bush, its head turned toward us, two small golden eyes looking at us without fear, was a lizard. But, it was about the size of a poodle, as tall but longer from head to tail. It was quite astounding, like a creature from prehistoric times, a small descendant of the dinosaurs. After watching us for a long time it resumed the stroll which we had accidentally interrupted, and, with its elegant reptilian gait, disappeared into the vegetation.

Near the campground at the bottom of the hill it wasn't unusual to see these animals come begging for handouts or foraging for scraps around the trashcans. They are, of course, protected. So, too, are the alligators, which is too bad for the hapless people who, from time to time, become dinner for these guys.

After this idyllic stay, we continued northward in a nice following wind. An hour of peaceful sailing had gone by when we heard the characteristic sound of our fishing line. This time it was a new kind of fish, a superb Spanish mackerel weighing about 20 pounds.

"Excellent," said the cook, smiling, and with the skillet already in her hand. "That will take care of dinner!"

We ate this meal behind Cape Melville. This point is very recognizable because it's made up of large, rounded rocks, like giant pebbles, stacked one on top of the other. We imagine that a long time ago, it must have been the outlet of a prehistoric glacier. We were perfectly sheltered behind this point and we anchored close to shore, where it was shallower and we would be better protected from gusts of wind. This entire coast is practically uninhabited, except for a few fishermen, but we arrived too late in the day to mount an expedition ashore.

One hour before daybreak, SPRAY was already under sail, on her way northward. Captain Slocum had sailed night and day, allowing himself only one stop during this whole stretch. That was a remarkable feat, because, while there is room to sail, some passes are tricky, the currents can be strong, and it's essential to maintain a vigilant watch at all times, even when hove to for a spell.

Our route took us past the Flinders Islands, which would be a fine place to hang out for a while; another time, maybe. We pushed on under power because the wind had died completely. It didn't come back until the late afternoon, and then from the north-northeast, once more on the nose. Since we were off Hanna Island, a coral outcrop covered with mangroves, we decided to anchor and wait for the wind to go back into a favorable direction.

There was already a fishing boat resting there. It left at dusk, and a small wooden cruising boat flying a Swiss flag came and anchored a polite distance away.

Even before first light we were under way again. The wind had gone back to normal and was blowing from the southeast, which was much more pleasant. An hour later, as the sun's first rays were breaking out, a full breakfast made its appearance on the cockpit table.

After a lovely day of sailing, we decided not to stop for the night. We had to maintain a constant watch. Several freighters came down along the coast and, from time to time, we had to steer by hand as we passed between islands and later, to go around Cape Grenville. At last, Clarke Island was abeam of us to port and I was able to set our new course, due northwest, which would make the navigation a little easier. But that was before taking into account the change in the weather. We were soon enveloped in a fine and penetrating rain that proved difficult to see through, especially in the darkness. It's in conditions like this that a radar would be a comfort. We reassured ourselves that the freighters had it and, in such closed-in weather, they would intensify their watches.

At daybreak it was still raining. Like in a bad dream or a good movie, three freighters appeared one after the other, like ghosts, and passed us or crossed our course before disappearing just as enigmatically. Eventually, the gloomy weather broke and the sun reappeared, at first wanly, and then boldly, and filled us with its wonderful warmth, to everyone's great joy. It's silly how such a small thing can make us happy.

At day's end, after slaloming between the last rocks, we approached the Mount Adolphus islands. They lie seven miles to seaward east of Cape York, which is the last main headland before heading west. After that, the navigation is much easier. Just before we got there, a coast guard plane flew over us. We identified ourselves and exchanged a few words and then it went off. The sea had become rougher and quite uncomfortable, shaking the rig every which way. Under the snatch loads this created, the mainsheet horse broke free on one side. We quickly secured it and the boom, and continued on under motor for the last mile to a most pleasant anchorage that we found in Blackwood Bay, behind the western point of the island.

In front of us, on the far side, was a huge, splendid rock shaped like a cat lying down. A few little shrubs clung to the rock where the cat's whiskers would be, and that's the only place they grew. Briac was enraptured by this spot. His joy grew all the more when we told him we wouldn't be leaving for a couple of days, time enough to recuperate, to repair or modify the horse, and to take a walk or two around the bay. Anchored nearby was a black Swedish sailboat, ONYX, which we would have the occasion to see again on our voyage.

Joshua Slocum's SPRAY in Australia
(Sheridan House Archives)

We were quite relieved to have behind us the passage from Cairns. The constant pressure of navigating in restricted waters, in the presence of fishing boats, freighters, and the occasional sailboat, was hard on the nerves. It can't have been easy for Joshua Slocum. He had perhaps less traffic but everything else was the same except that it was probably less well buoyed. Despite all that, he hit only one coral patch in all this very difficult passage, and that caused no damage.

I inspected the sheet horse and saw it needed welding. I left it, lashing it as best I could, and rigged the sheet with a system of blocks. I was sure I would find a welder in Darwin, and the repair held until we got there.

It was time to make the most of our anchorage and put the Avon in the water. As usual, the shores of the isles were ringed with coral which made them difficult to approach and, especially, to land on. We found a small pass, just at the mouth of a little stream. After an attempt at penetrating inland, we swam for a while before returning aboard.

Our next leg, which entailed a week of sailing, would bring us all the way to Darwin. Half of the passage would be coastal and half, the crossing of the Gulf of Carpentaria, offshore.

A few hours after raising the anchor, and in a fair breeze, we rounded Cape York, the northernmost point of Australia, leaving to port Eborac and York islands. We could now point the bowsprit due west. The sandy bottom wasn't very deep and gave the water a beautiful emerald green color. Lovely Possession Island was soon astern of us to quickly become no more than a happy memory. We reached the gulf in the evening and were able to get back into our tranquil, offshore-sailing rhythm, disturbed only by the occasional passage of the customs airplane surveying its domain.

In the morning, for the first time in a while, a magnificent sunrise slowly filled the sky right behind us. The temperature quickly began to rise. The farther west we sailed, the hotter it became—and the thirstier we became—because the tradewinds, in passing over the land, heat up and become drier. Under the influence of this good breeze, SPRAY tirelessly thrust her way forward through the ever green sea. As always, I watched with amazement and a deep admiration as she sailed by herself, without any assistance. At times like this, I go forward and sit at the bow, and I watch as her bow cleaves the waves with a steady rushing sound. All is calm, all is tranquil, I'm alone. The deck is unmanned and empty. Astern, the wake is quite straight and smooth.

That was one of those days. Briac was with Annick. It was reading hour, in the heat of the early afternoon. Right then, he was particularly interested in and captivated by Richard Henry Dana's remarkable book, *Two Years Before the Mast*. These were times of wonderful freedom and we felt a great attachment to the elements around us. To live such moments is probably one of the reasons we like to sail and continue to be at sea. They have to be experienced to be understood. They are difficult moments to duplicate and they make it hard to live ashore. That's how the call of the sea seduces you and pulls you inexorably back.

When we reached Cape Wessel, which marks the departure from the Gulf of Carpentaria, the sea became rougher. We might have been a little too close, and we had to start paying more attention, especially to the currents agitating the sea and their unpredictable eddies. After a while, things returned to normal. We would have liked to have heard the singing of our fishing line, but these shallow, sandy-bottomed waters didn't seem to attract fish. Too bad!

The wind became lighter and lighter as we forged our way farther west and we were treated to beautiful weather. At Darwin, the tides have almost as big a range as in Brittany and the Bay of Fundy, and the closer we got, the more noticeable the currents became.

Soon, the high tower of the Cape Don lighthouse appeared. From that point on, we had to employ the careful coastal piloting practices we use along the Brittany coast. Navigating across the Van Diemen Gulf with its shallows, islands, rocks, and above all its tidal currents, was tricky but interesting. At the beginning, the current was against us, setting slightly across our course and even while we steered to keep Melville Island, on the far side of the gulf, to our port side, we drifted down toward it. Other than being rather tense from concentrating hard, we crossed without difficulty. When the tide turned, it was in our favor, and let us rethink our position and take the channel that runs under Melville Island. That allowed us, during the following night, to cross Clarence Strait, north of Knight Reef, while passing close by Vernon Island to the northwest. All we had to do then was to bear down on the entrance to Darwin Bay.

The low coastline appeared just after daybreak, but the shallows extend far out to sea, so we had to give them a wide berth and find the beginning of the channel, which we then had to follow. The weather, typical of this region at this time of the year, was absolutely magnificent. There was a nice breeze, so we decided to choose a place to anchor after weighing the various possibilities that this great port had to offer. Starting from the far end of the port, at the end of Francis Bay, and following the natural channel which leads to Sadgroves Creek, there's a yacht club next to the shingle Dinah Beach. There, we had several options: we could anchor, though there wasn't much room; pick up a mooring, assuming there was one free; or even put the boat ashore in the boatyard. There were pilings on the beach for careening. After consulting with the crew, we retraced our path and went to anchor in Fanny Bay, just opposite the Darwin Sailing Club and quite far out because of the tide. A new marina had just opened at Emery Point with access through a lock.

"Well then, here we are," the three crewmembers seemed to be thinking, excited to have the anchor down and looking around to check out the neighborhood.

It's a big bay, open to the west, but partly closed off by a sandbar running down the middle which was completely uncovered for about a mile. At some states of the tide, the current circulating inside the bay and running out at its ends could make the anchorage quite rough.

The second drawback was the distance between boat and shore, and despite SPRAY's shallow draft, we still had to go a mile back and forth in the dinghy. At spring tides, the bay was very shallow, and uncovered over great distances. We therefore had to calculate carefully where to leave the Avon so as to avoid long, hard portages. Fortunately, we had wheels to attach to its transom. It was the only time we used them, and they made the task a lot easier.

All in all, everything went well and we enjoyed this marvelous spot, made especially pleasant, once again, by the kindness and generous hospitality of the yacht club.

It had a family atmosphere, with a children's playground, game rooms, and television. It also had bars and restaurants, a reading room, and a terrace under the palms beside the beach where there was always a refreshing breeze.

Out front, the view of the great bay stretching as far as the eye could see allowed us to dream already of the next leg, because, no matter how pleasant Darwin was, there had to be a next leg.

We had at last chosen our next stop. We would go to Rodrigues Island, just before Mauritius, in the Indian Ocean.

Why not stop at Christmas and Coco Islands? We thought about it, but we figured there would be too many cruising boats and anyway, we preferred to spend more time in one place rather than chase after many. While we had been told many good things about the Cocos, we wouldn't be sorry about missing them. We had to make choices, and leave some places for the next time. It's a good thing to hold onto places you can still dream about.

A difficulty we faced in Darwin, as elsewhere in Australia and all the Anglo-Saxon countries we visited, was the distances we had to cover between one place and another, especially in the industrial areas which stretched for miles. It wasn't easy on foot, or even by bus, when there was one. Looking back, it wasn't such a bad thing, and quite healthy after a long passage during which there's minimal physical activity. We found everything we needed, and by going from one shop to another, I was able to find spares for the engine. Among them, I found a fuel filter which I had been looking for three years and another for the Racor. I had been draining this one from time to time without being aware there was an element inside that needed changing! You learn something every day. I also found a welder to repair the mainsheet horse.

Near the nature reserve, which was home to lots of kangaroos, we found a lovely beach that was well sheltered from the usual afternoon surf. We careened SPRAY OF SAINT-BRIAC there, happy to let her rest the bottom of her keel in the soft sand. One coat of Jotun antifouling paint sufficed as it had been a just year since we'd careened and the hull was still relatively clean. We did it more for reasons of safety, so we could inspect the anodes and check for any sign of teredo worms. Everything was in good condition and the hull was perfectly healthy. We could have used sheer legs, but it was easier doing one side and then the other rather than having to crawl underneath. The only drawback was having to do it on two tides. We did one side at night, so we could get back to the anchorage at daybreak.

We took advantage of the time between tides when we couldn't work to enjoy the wildlife park. There were cold showers for the use of visitors. They enabled us to wash off the sand and paint and, in the heat, they were especially refreshing. Sitting in the shade, we could study the magnificent curves of SPRAY's lines. At the time she was conceived, boats were built largely by eye from experience passed from generation to generation, which must go a long way to explaining why this boat is so successful and so beautiful.

The town of Darwin was five minutes by bus from the club, so we had no difficulty running our errands and storing the boat.

Usually, we spent a few hours every afternoon at the club. Under the shade of the trees that gently swayed and rustled in the light late afternoon breeze, we met other cruisers following the same route.

The most pleasant times were, without any doubt, those spent there on the terrace, contemplating the magnificent bay and watching the sun slowly disappear behind the horizon in a pink glow. It reminded me of being on the beach of la Salinette, at Saint-Briac, so many years ago. I could imagine myself there, especially at low tide. It reminded me also of being with my grandfather on board BARYNIA, a little Carantec cutter that I took care of. Jean David was always ready to offer me advice or a suggestion, and always had time to share some of his knowledge. Afterwards, we would go to the water's edge to collect sand eels with which we'd fish for bass on the rising tide.

At la Salinette, too, one of the prettiest times of any day was the fantastic sunset, over there, toward Cap Frehel, especially when the wind was in the north.

In all my voyages, Darwin is one of the few places in the world that came anywhere near Saint-Briac. Full of regrets, we had to get ready to head once more into the unknown of the great ocean that awaited us.

15

◆

The Indian Ocean

On the first day at sea, August 26, a nice 15-knot breeze pushed us westward. It soon left us, leaving in its place calms punctuated by little puffs that riffled the surface of the water. Happily, the motor was healthy after being serviced, and nudged us quietly along at four to five knots, just enough to catch a fine tuna. With the help of Japanese ingredients we'd found in Darwin, it made delicious sushi.

"Come see, Briac, there, a snake."

The color of sand, and striped with black, it wriggled furiously to escape this unexpected mass that we had brought into its world. It was as long as my arm. This kind of snake is poisonous, but it has to bite a fleshy part of your body for the fangs, which are set well back in the mouth, to penetrate.

A little later, a whale breached just astern of us, blowing noisily. Its great tail described a broad arc as it sounded again to disappear in the depths, leaving no trace but an area of disturbed water.

The weather remained fine, and the sea was flat, without even a wrinkle. SPRAY was reflected in the water, taking on a magical air, and we saw our faces when we leaned over the side.

Once more, the sunset was fantastic. We never tired of watching the glowing sky. Each one was unique, and their features varied according to the geographic region. In our experience, the East Coast of the United States produced the greatest number of really beautiful ones.

When we rounded Browse Island, first one, then a second native sailing fishing boat tried to approach us and cut in front of us. In the end, they were only able to cross our wake, and we continued on our way undisturbed but not without a little uneasiness. We found out later that they were fishermen from Timor who come there to set their lines. After an enthusiastic wave, they slowly disappeared behind us and went back to a bigger boat anchored in the lee of the island.

On Saturday, August 31, the weather was still beautiful. A few jellyfish, which propelled themselves with prodigious, supple movements of their translucent bodies, going only they knew where, were the only sign of life in the water.

Twice, Australian Customs flew over, perhaps to reassure themselves that we were indeed going west, even though we were by then 500 miles from their coast.

Little by little, the wind backed to the north, then to the west, creating a rough and quite uncomfortable sea. During dinner, we learned of the death of Princess Diana. This sad news, which would not have affected us in quite the same way on land, took on a special poignancy in our solitude at sea.

This crossing was by and large blessed with good weather, and the maximum wind was only 25 knots. Frequently, though, a southerly swell on our beam made life on board quite uncomfortable. The 37-day passage brought no surprises but was hard on the boat because of chafe and fatigue on the rig caused by the rolling motion in the calm weather. The Indian Ocean was, as an Australian had told us it would be when we were taking on tax-free fuel the day we left Darwin, "a piece of cake."

It was close to paradise, or it was another world, anyway, where I could read for six to eight hours each day and where life rolled along quietly, without hiccups; we were far from anywhere and especially from people.

In time, I became accustomed to living to the rhythm imposed by SPRAY, and it was the best way to be. It was a different way of life, more like that led by our ancestors in the days of sailing ships. There was no end to time, it stretched out to infinity, and nothing tied us to the present. It was a hundred years since Captain Slocum was in these same waters and life was the same for us as it had been for him. It was SPRAY who let us feel so utterly free. That was one of the greatest lessons I discovered. That and the beauty and serenity of the seagoing life.

For the first time, I began to feel the true and deep contentedness that comes from being on the water and from being in perfect harmony with my surroundings. I had the wonderful feeling that I'd achieved what one could call happiness.

In addition to our tuna, we ended up catching two dolphin and two wahoos, one of which couldn't have been far short of 50 pounds. Each time, the latest tasted better than the previous. Every day, we watched with interest and curiosity the activities of many sea birds. Some of them were new to us, like the little cape pigeons.

Freighters were rare, and we saw no cruising boats because they were farther north, heading for the Cocos and Keeling Islands.

Briac, now six years old, was ever more curious about everything going on around him and he was always asking questions. At sea, he liked his classes and followed them assiduously. When we stopped, however, he spent his time getting to know the places and the people.

On October 2, just after daybreak, the high, rounded island of Rodrigues rose in front of us. A few hours later, we were piloting SPRAY toward the pass and the entrance channel across the extensive coral plateau that in some places stretches five miles from the shore. The chart, dating from 1830, or more exactly the copy I'd made in Darwin, didn't overwhelm me with confidence but, for all that, turned out to be correct.

Viewed from the sea, the island didn't appear very exciting and Port Mathurin not very appealing, at least what we could see from the channel. The main dock, used by the freighters that mainly shuttled to Port Louis, was free. We elected to moor there while we performed the entry formalities. About ten sailboats lay at anchor in the man-made basin. We stayed on the dock three days before joining our cruising colleagues and setting our anchor in a bottom that provided good holding.

The day after we arrived, we had a very pleasant visit from the reporter for the local radio and television which were, in fact, those of Mauritius. Word gets around quickly, and a journalist from the Rodrigues weekly paper was the next to appear. He was very friendly. After a long interview, he invited us to visit him at his in-laws' home near the harbor. It was a wonderfully warm, simple, and convivial welcome.

During the evening, Nicolas, our new friend of the written press, invited us to go on a country walk the following Sunday with a group of his friends. For a few moments we were undecided. After 37 days at sea, and with Briac, we weren't sure it was such a good idea to engage in an adventure of that nature.

"How far, Nicolas?"

"Two or three miles."

We had to accept. That didn't scare us!

A magnificent ramble among mountains and valleys made it a day to remember. The island is beautiful and alluring when seen in such a way. We left the cars in the interior and walked to the beach, where we drank from coconuts cut fresh from the trees. Thankfully, we took a bus to get back to the cars. The two or three miles were as the crow flies; on the ground we covered close to seven or eight. We were exhausted, but happy that we were able to explore the island this way and share the walk and the picnic with very friendly young people; one of them had gone to university in France, at Nancy.

For us, Rodrigues was a revelation and was certainly one of the best island stops.

First of all, there were few tourists, as the only three hotels on the island, two on the coast and one which had just opened in Port Mathurin, could only take 50 people between them. The shoreline, in places rocky and in others sandy, is fringed with sea pines and "filao" and the water in the many white sand coves is incomparably pure and clear. The huge lagoon, with its multiple hues of blue, surrounds the island and is bounded by a coral reef, against which the big ocean swells break incessantly. In some places, the reef extends five miles from the shore and it forms a magnificent protected sound dotted with several small islets and crisscrossed by the little white sails of fishing boats and the occasional windsurfer. This island was for us a peaceful haven bathed in awesome natural colors and with a deep human warmth like that found in Africa. It's the land for forgetting time, the anti-stress, the complete rest for body and soul in a place with unforgettable natural beauty.

Port Sud Est is not to be missed. At each turn, the long, winding road that leads to this settlement offers spectacular views. Stretching to the horizon is the sea in its countless shades, from turquoise to emerald, to deeper blue shades where there are channels and passes, and to the royal blue immensity of the ocean beyond the fringe of white foam where the breakers crash on the coral reef. There are also the romantic little sandy cays and the brown rocks topped with luxuriant vegetation. It's a paradise for painters and photographers.

A multitude of birds and a variety of plants, some indigenous to this location, add to this timeless land where animal husbandry, horticulture, and fishing are the way of life.

On Saturday, at about five in the morning, the thing to do is to go to the weekly market which is a clue to the soul of Rodrigues. It is held close to the harbor, and from the anchorage, beginning at about four a.m., you can hear the squeals of a pig being slaughtered. That would be the first one and there would be more to follow, according to demand. We counted five or six each week. It's done the same way with cattle and goats. You won't find meat any fresher!

We always found it interesting to walk between the stalls of fresh fruits and vegetables that are grown in the neighboring gardens without chemical fertilizers. We were taking in the native atmosphere and meeting the villagers, stimulated all the while by the tangy aromas of the citrus fruits, and the scents of flowers and spices.

To be sure of getting the best cuts of meat and the best selection of vegetables, it's best to be at the market by five a.m.; by nine there's nothing much left apart from the local crafts. But the pleasure can be renewed every Saturday.

The kindness and generosity of the locals isn't artificial. Everywhere you go, you're greeted with a smile and a good word. You can converse with your neighbors on the rickety bus in perfect French. We found that surprising given that Rodrigues and Mauritius have been under British administration for two centuries, having previously been French. English is the official language, but everyone still speaks a very pure French, as well as a creole with a charming lilt. Their music is like no other; the newspapers, radio, and television are in the language of Molière—except for the American sitcoms, that is, but there aren't many of those.

The anchorage is surrounded by the coral plateau that extends several miles to seaward. It had been blasted and dredged to make the harbor. At low tide, when it uncovered completely, it became the scene of tremendous activity. Looking like a medieval army launching an assault on a mythical castle, women in long skirts or smocks, scarves on their heads, and armed with long pikes, spread out to forage for whelks and octopus while the men, pants rolled up, spears in hand, hunted fish.

Port Mathurin consists of a few commercial streets with that slightly faded charm typical of small colonial towns. The wooden buildings are roofed with corrugated iron and among them are shops and restaurants of every kind: Chinese, Indian, Arab, African, and European. The mixture of peoples, in the town alone, is remarkable. They all have kept their customs, costumes, and religion. An atmosphere of friendliness prevails. Racism doesn't seem to be a word in their lexicon and, anyway, many of them are of mixed blood. Activity in town comes to a halt at about three in the afternoon; after that, it's quiet, tranquil, and soon deserted.

This was the only port of call where, every day, we took to the road by bus, getting off one in one place and getting on another after a long walk. Often our breath was taken away, not from exertion, but by the beauty of the scenery that would unfold before us at the top of a ridge or coming round a bend. Every feature was dubbed with a charming and poetic name: Pointe Cotton (Cotton Point), Roche Bon Dieu (Good Lord Rock), Rivière Banane (Banana River), Jardin Mamzelle (Spinster's Garden), Petit Gravier (Little Pebble). And so, a little more each day amid all this beauty and friendship, our minds and bodies were purified and rejuvenated.

Our friend Nicolas as well as being a journalist was also the deputy representing Rodrigues at the parliament at Mauritius. Together with members of his party, he organized a sports day at Petit Gravier. There was a soccer match for veterans, a sailing race in pirogues for fishermen, and a demonstration of pétanque. By introducing pétanque (a game similar to bocce) and creating a league, he was trying to develop the game on the island as a way to get people out of the bars. We had a wonderful time as Nicolas's guests, and felt welcome in the friendly atmosphere.

I declined to join the team of local veterans but I was sorry afterwards because the game was very spirited and very sporting.

We ate sitting on the grass, and afterwards, Nicolas made a very simple, short speech. He proposed erecting a plaque to commemorate the centennial of Joshua Slocum's voyage. We were thrilled when it was enthusiastically and unanimously approved. In the ports visited by

Captain Slocum during his voyage, we always brought up this possibility so that he would be recognized.

Unfortunately, we were being squeezed by the cyclone season and we had to think about moving on toward Mauritius, and then South Africa. We had expected to stay only a week at Rodrigues and we had now been sixteen days in this little paradise. Reluctantly we bid an emotional farewell to this wonderful island.

Three days later, after an uneventful passage in a nice southeasterly breeze, we came in sight of Port Louis. We could pick it out from a long way off by the yellowish cloud blowing downwind from the town and the refinery. As we got closer, we found that it stung our eyes and made them water, and the acrid sulphur smell made breathing difficult. Unhappily, this was only the beginning.

Normally, to carry out the formalities, you can go alongside the docks at the new shopping and hotel complex at Caudan, above the port. But that's without the Expo Rally 1998. The space was all reserved for that, even though it wouldn't arrive for a week, and we weren't allowed even to take on water. We had to crowd in to the end of the harbor along an abandoned, filthy, trash-covered quay in an area where there was a lot of traffic and room for only two boats.

Needless to say, the cruising community takes a dim view of this rally-race-combination and everyone tries to plan their route so as to avoid it. This one gathered together 45 boats, and their crews added up to close to 200 people, not counting the guests who fly in at the end of each leg. They all travel in a group, supposedly for reassurance and safety. Everyone gets together for parties and excursions ashore in chartered busses, and they speed around all the harbors in brand new, outboard-powered inflatables without any consideration for other boats. This is the anti-cruise, and it's become a lucrative business for the organizers. It's a bit of a racket.

Worse, it's the opposite of the true spirit of a circumnavigation. Think of 45 boats arriving all at once in a tiny Pacific island. What would the inhabitants and their administration think about such a flouting of wealth? Prices would rise! Afterwards, they wouldn't know the difference, except perhaps by the quality of his T-shirt, between the real circumnavigator and this kind of "cruiserist."

Apart from a few irresponsible ones, who are sadly growing in number, around-the-world sailors have a profound respect for their surroundings and for the local people and their customs. At the root of his personality the cruiser is a pure ecologist, respecting the environment and husbanding nature's bounty. This is how Briac learned to save water and energy on board, not to throw anything away that would harm the environment, and to have respect for it and the local community wherever he was. In this way, he learned how to be a voyager.

On the rat-infested quay we met the Swedish sailboat, ONYX, which we'd seen in Australia. Tied alongside each other, we had time to exchange impressions of this last passage while we waited for the officials to come. We quickly discovered the unpleasant side of this country. To begin with, they only issued 15-day visas, after which they have to be renewed and they demanded photocopies of passports and photo IDs. Then there were the standing instructions if you wanted to move your boat. It's close to being a police state!

Once the officials had left the boat, we departed for Grand Baie, where we found a very pleasant anchorage off the hospitable and friendly yacht club.

SPRAY at Grand Baie
(Mauritius)

Here again, we were visited by a journalist and a photographer from *L' Express*. The magazine published a very fine article which told the story of the time my grandfather, Emile David, stopped in St. Louis in his three-master, DE LA FORCADE LA ROQUETTE, in November 1879, several years before Joshua Slocum's visit. It was an indescribable sensation, and I was proud and touched to find myself here so many years later.

You cannot fail to be moved by a visit to Port St. Louis. The creator of the port, and subsequently the small town, was Francois-Bertrand Mahé de la Bourdonnais, of Saint-Malo, Brittany. The English held him in such esteem for his genius and the works he created here that they erected a statue to him in a square that bears his name. It was during his governance that the remarkable structures of magnificent architecture were built.

The town teemed with all manner of activity and in addition to the vibrant market, merchants all along the sidewalks and even in the streets offer a broad variety of goods, including food, clothing, electronics, and books.

We went into Port Louis from Grand Baie only twice. Both times, we had sore throats and our eyes smarted and watered from the pollution caused by the exhausts of vast numbers of busses and trucks which, while painted in a great variety of colors, all belched the same dense, black smoke.

We were also smart enough to take advantage of the yacht club's beach, which was a good place to meet other sailors. This is where we got to know a marvelous couple, Anne and Jean-Claude, on their pretty steel sailboat, COMME UN CHEVAL FOU (Like a Crazy Horse), and whom we were lucky enough to run into during subsequent stops.

One of the club members we got to know was Mr. Maurel. Just before we sailed, he called to give me a portrait he had drawn of Captain Slocum and to show me a newspaper reproduction of an article and sketch published when the captain visited Mauritius.

Unfortunately, the island is all in all disappointing and its vendors too aggressive. As soon as they see you coming, they have the calculator out and are all too intent on making a deal. It's quite unpleasant.

We were quite happy to leave this place, before our allotted 15 days were up. We have no great urge to go back any day.

It was already November 6. How quickly the time passes! The cyclone season was bearing down on us and we had to head farther west. We elected to go directly to Richards Bay, South Africa. We had thought about stopping in Madagascar, but we were short of information and, to our great surprise, we didn't hear any cruisers talking about it or expressing a desire to go there.

The first day's fair breeze quickly faded, just when we were sailing along the coast of Reunion, and gave way to light and variable winds. This signified the end of the trades.

That evening, while we watched a magnificent sunset, we dined on two small dorado, still quivering, with a side of sauteed potatoes.

We were on the freighter route, which was a bit worrisome. When they approached from ahead, they came on us rapidly. At night, since we no longer had our electric navigation lights at the masthead, we used kerosene lanterns or, frankly, the strobe light, a flashing white light. This last isn't strictly within the rules, but it doesn't drain the batteries too much, it attracts attention, and can be seen from far off. I confirmed its effect in several conversations with passing freighters. They often passed so close that when they were to windward of us we could smell the strong odor of diesel oil.

From the time we left Mauritius, we had mostly fine weather with a few stormy fronts that brought lightning, thunderclaps, and showers; usually much noise about very little.

Several boats of the aforementioned rally overtook us on their way to South Africa. One night, we noticed one to port. It looked as though it was going to gradually pass us and carry on its way. Satisfied, I went to stretch out for a while on my bunk and get some sleep after a long watch. All of a sudden, the hideous racket of a handheld airhorn woke me and the beam of a very powerful searchlight flooded the cabin and blinded me. I immediately thought of fishing boats, like the one that almost rammed me amidships in the middle of the night off the British Isles when I was finishing a singlehanded Atlantic crossing (aboard BNP-BANK OF THE WEST). I went up on deck, covering my eyes, and could see the stern of a sailboat a few yards off our beam. While I was still trying to grasp the situation, a voice called out.

"Are you the SPRAY?"

"Yes," I replied slowly and pleasantly.

"Is everything alright?"

"Yes!" I replied, a little less friendly and in English.

Apparently, the question answered to their satisfaction, the interlopers went on their way, stepping on the gas and putting away their wretched searchlight. It's really irresponsible to do a thing like that in the middle of the ocean, at night, and without being asked.

We found out when we got to Richards Bay that it had been one of these "new wave" cruisers. That's the kind of hyperactive crew that gets you so irritated you want to break out the water cannon.

In the Mozambique Channel, winds preceding a depression turned to northeast at force 5 and it got up to close to 95 degrees in the cabin and very humid. Then the wind built to 35 knots and was accompanied by big squalls. SPRAY OF SAINT-BRIAC under two reefs charged along with a bone in her teeth, bound for the African coast.

After a calm, which left us on tenterhooks, followed by a front laden with thick clouds, lightning, thunder, and rain, the wind went south-southwest and reached force 7, gusting to 8, in sunshine. We had an intoxicating ride. The wind on the beam made it difficult to keep her steady with the helm lashed, and for many hours I steered by hand so as to keep SPRAY on course while getting the best speed with the great press of sail we had on her.

There are limits, and for the sake of prudence, we should have taken in another reef, but occasionally the racing bug gets hold of me, so off we went! It was wild; great piles of seawater crashed all along the hull, flooding the deck under tons of water. Spray flew aboard, hitting me full force in the face. At the bow, it formed beautiful rainbows. SPRAY had never so joyously lived up to her name.

We were going at between seven and eight knots. Suddenly, the cringle of the second reef let go. I had been watching it for some time, telling myself that I should reinforce it the first chance I got. After thinking about it for a moment, I decided to drop the sail and repair it right away. With traditional sails, repairs are easy and last well. So we dropped the mainsail. The wind seemed to be building, I didn't feel like steering all the time, there was a limit to how much discomfort we needed to endure, at this speed we would all too soon be on the African coast and moreover at the edge of the continental shelf with its gloomy reputation, and we weren't racing. In short, all of these factors convinced me to haul in the headsails flat, sheet the staysail on centerline, trail warps astern, and lash the helm. The pace dropped, but we gained tranquility. We had our books, we got our rest, and SPRAY couldn't have been more comfortable.

During the course of a beautifully clear and starry night, we put the mainsail back up and resumed our course, which became easier because the wind went back into the east and settled down by morning.

As dawn broke, an incredible spectacle revealed itself to us: the coast of Africa, magnificent, enigmatic, and shrouded in mystery.

Because of how we had drifted the night before, we were north of Richards Bay and near the estuary of the Saint Lucia River. Pushed quickly by currents which were quite turbulent in places and which we could spot by the swaths of all sorts of flotsam on the surface, we reached the harbor's breakwaters by mid-afternoon. We had to wait a full half hour there for authorization to enter the channel behind two freighters. A good twenty more were waiting their turn in the quarantine anchorage in the roadstead. The wind filled in, bit by bit, from the west, then north, then veered northeast. These were signs of another front coming up the coast. It was time to be in port! The following day, a strong southwesterly front swept through the area. We had timed our arrival well.

Once inside, we found there was no room at the yacht club because of the rally. We ended up in a second marina located toward the head of the port, along a big pier where quite a few cruising boats and local sailboats were tied up in rafts. Between two rafts of boats there was an empty space on the quay just a little longer than SPRAY. Getting in there looked impossible given our poor handling under power.

However, as we started to back out of the basin, I noticed that with the wind on the starboard side and the rudder hard over to counter SPRAY's tendency to turn to port, she was gently crabbing directly toward the space we had spotted. She put the port corner of her transom on the tip of the bow pulpit of the outside and lee boat. I was holding onto the pulpit with one hand, afraid that at any moment I would tear it out, when a guy ran up and took my mooring line to the dock, jumping across three boats in the process, and tied it to a bollard. All I had to do then was ease in on the line, keeping tension on it with a touch of astern to counter the effects of the gusty wind, and continue to crab in. Once alongside the quay, we just had to make fast the remaining docklines and thank our good fortune and those who had given us a hand.

A few moments earlier, I would never have thought I could get in there, and I humbly insisted that I didn't mean to do it. The trouble is, no one believed me!

Once over the excitement, we were delighted to find Anne, Jean-Claude, and Arnaud, who had joined COMME UN CHEVAL FOU in Noumea to accompany them to Richards Bay. Our friends left Port Louis three days before we did and had just got in two hours ahead of us. They had spent three days hove to so as not to find themselves on the continental shelf in bad weather. That was a wise precaution, given what strong winds can do in this region.

Soon after, they came and tied alongside SPRAY. So we were not only on the right side of the cyclones, we were also in good company. However, what lay in store for us between there and Cape Town didn't fill us with boundless optimism. Suffice it to say that in Richards Bay there were a hundred boats trying to get back to the South Atlantic, and there were more in Durban. . . . We would stay there a month waiting for the right opportunity.

What impressed us the most was the bustling activity in this port, and in particular the superb, brand-new tugs. Eyeing the pilot boats gave us an idea of what a gale must mean in these parts. Richards Bay was in a full economic boom, judging by the factories, the commercial zones, and the new town in the country far from the old town which seemed now to be the residential quarter. In the good old Anglo-Saxon way, each was separated by long distances. The new town with its shopping center, for example, was six miles from the port where we were. We couldn't even think about going there on foot. We had to hitchhike, which went relatively well, or take a taxi.

Beyond the marina and the port area, bands of silver gray monkeys roamed fearlessly all over the road. From time to time a crocodile ventured into the small river that ran by the yacht club. Farther away, in the big lake in the old colonial town, hippopotamus went heavily but gracefully about their ponderous business. And there were birds everywhere.

We were in the middle of Zulu territory. The next Sunday, there was a local festival with dance competitions attended by the king. Apart from a few cruisers, there weren't many white people there.

We spent a fantastic afternoon among a very gentle people. The men, ebony black, carried themselves with a proud, erect bearing and the women were cheerful and full of good humor. All were colorfully dressed in their finest clothes so as to look their best in the competition they had looked forward to eagerly and for which they had minutely prepared. Most of the dances were by origin war dances, once used to arouse the people by King Shaka, who founded the nation and organized its administration and the formidable army that gave the English so much trouble. Prince Louis, son of Napoleon III, lost his life in 1879 in one of those battles.

Sitting on the ground at the edge of the dancing area I was transfixed by the energy emanating from each dancer: the fierce, hypnotic gaze of their fiery eyes that transported you far into a world where real and unreal merged, the rapid and jerky movements of their arms and legs which convulsed their entire bodies in rhythm, and above all the stamping of their feet on the dusty ground. Only ten yards from them, I could feel the formidable shockwave that accompanied the deep and terrifying sound. There were but twelve dancers. I tried to imagine how

◆

Zulu dance in Richards Bay

the poor English soldiers must have felt before an attack, hearing the sound created by thousands of feet pounding the ground and punctuated by awesome war cries. How petrifying that must have been.

That afternoon remains for us an indelible memory of this marvelous people. Our relations with them were friendly and it was easy to engage them in conversation. The way I saw it, any problem that arose with them did so mainly because of the attitude of certain white nationals. To have respect for these men and women is, for certain, the first step toward better mutual understanding.

During the course of the festival, we got to meet Richard and his wife, simple people who were having a hard time surviving in this new country. They are examples of those special people who have a high regard for all human beings, of whatever race, and it was they who had helped organize the competition. We made their acquaintance because Richard asked Annick if she would like to present the prizes. She happily accepted and, accompanied by Briac, stepped up on the podium to distribute several trophies and congratulatory kisses in a very relaxed atmosphere.

One of the reasons we chose Richards Bay is because it's situated in the heart of the nature reserves, and a few days later, in the company of Richard and his wife, we visited Umfolozi Park. We saw all kinds of creatures in their natural state: pink flamingos, eagles, egrets, different species of gazelles big and small, giraffes, zebras, gnus, warthogs, numerous monkeys singly and in bands, rhinoceros (very impressive at a few tens of yards from the vehicle—we would have liked to hide under the windscreen or even in a mousehole), buffalo, hippopotamus with their odd little ears. Briac, his eyes boggling with curiosity, couldn't get over his outing in this earthly paradise.

We picnicked above a meander in the river. A short distance away, a solitary old buffalo pawed nervously at the soft, muddy ground.

To enter the park is to enter another world. On the return trip, shrouded in melancholy, we rode back to reality along a track that was so full of ruts it demanded great effort from the driver.

That evening, back on board, we went over and over this beautiful, rich day. It was the kind of day that had been a dream since childhood. It had come true at last!

In the middle of the wasteland, as though it had miraculously sprung from the ground, the new town offered its glittering and well stocked halls of merchandise. We found everything at attractive prices because the local currency, the rand, was at a very low value. We took advantage of it by restocking with provisions and the bits and pieces needed for the boat's maintenance. On top of it all, on our departure from the country, at Cape Town, we were reimbursed, and in the currency of our choice, for all the taxes we'd paid.

With the heavy pollution, the sun was strong enough to cause severe and potentially dangerous burning. On coming within a hundred miles of the coast, I had already noticed a difference in its effect. Even though I was tanned from several months at sea, my exposed skin burned very quickly. It became necessary to protect our bodies, including our eyes and lips. We felt this phenomenon all round South Africa. Richards Bay turned out to be a great playground for Briac. Many of the waiting boats had children aboard and since the part of the harbor where we were wasn't very busy, they could play in perfect safety. Very quickly, Briac met Pierre, a young boy from Brest, some Swedish and Norwegian girls, and a sweet little Belgian girl. Their shouts and laughter soon mingled with the calls of the birds. It was the first time that Briac had had so many boys and girls to play with and it did him a lot of good. Over the month, he acquired a certain maturity. In addition, the common language was English and his command of it grew quickly.

He and his playmate, Mike, a young South African, were invited to visit one of the very modern tugboats.

"Yes, yes, by all means go," I encouraged him. What started out as a brief visit ended up lasting three hours, with a trip to sea to assist a freighter. What a wonderful experience that was for such a young child!

The next day, they visited a fast patrol boat of the South African Navy. Every day presented another novel and fascinating experience.

We also met Gilbert and his Senegalese girlfriend, who were drawn to our Breton flag. At over 70, he was realizing his life's dream of sailing around the world. The atmosphere among the boats took on that of the cruising world: everyone taking the time to visit their neighbors, exchange a few words, help each other out and form friendships. This is one of the benefits of being on the dock, rather than anchored out. As the days pass by, an international community forms. Then according to their own timetable and the weather windows, each puts to sea again, bound for their next destination, like so many migratory birds.

This coast of South Africa, because of the weather patterns, the geographical configuration, and the currents, is probably one of the most dangerous in the world. On average, there's a gale every three or four day, even in summer. They start in the northeast, veer suddenly to the southwest and build rapidly. The Agulhas current, coming down from Mozambique, can flow at up to four or five knots and the edge of the continental shelf is only 10 miles from the shore. The 250-mile passage from Durban to East London is barren of harbors and safe shelters. All of these facts were food for thought, especially after we'd seen the monstrous swell created by the last gale. We really wouldn't have liked to find ourselves caught in those huge and violent seas. Compared to this region, Blanchard Race in the English Channel is a joyride. We needed to collect and understand as much weather information as we could and not hesitate to set off the moment an opening presented itself.

There were only two ways to go: try to make Cape Town directly, which would mean enduring three or four depressions, or leapfrog from port to port between lows. Captain Slocum decided to take the direct route, and took 14 days to cover about 800 miles through some very bad weather.

16

South Africa

We had to go to Durban anyway, since Joshua Slocum had made a stop there. It was a 90-mile passage.

Anne and Jean-Claude, who were still alongside us, decided to go with this plan which had been taking root over several days. We went to action at four in the morning, the idea being that, with some help from the current, we would arrive there before night.

The day before, a strong southwesterly front had passed through leaving just a light wind under a gray overcast. An awesomely large and powerful swell greeted us as soon as we left the shelter of the breakwaters. From time to time, COMME UN CHEVAL FOU disappeared completely from our sight in the troughs.

Impressed by the long swell, we cast questioning glances at each other, and saw the worry on each other's faces. Christmas being on its way, Santa Claus had come by a little early in Richards Bay, bringing in his big bag a little four-legged companion, a cute black and white kitten answering to the name Chaka. On his first trip, our new crewmember was confused about what was going on, but it didn't take him long, though, to find his sea legs.

Somehow or another, we managed to hoist the mainsail and, after Annick had caught a few duckings on the bowsprit in the big swell, the yankee took its station, followed by the staysail. That at least gave the boat a little more stability. Since there wasn't much wind, we decided to go farther out to sea, to the edge of the continental shelf, where we would get more assistance near the axis of the following current.

Chaka, the new crewmember

———◆———

Little by little the fine weather returned and the day turned out quite pleasant. Anne and Jean-Claude stayed closer to land and reached Durban a short time ahead of us.

The day before, I had called to tell the harbormaster of our coming and he had advised me to await daylight tied up to a barge just off the marina. The entrance to Durban is quite narrow and not easy to follow at night. It's therefore preferable not to encounter a freighter coming in the opposite direction. For that reason, contact by VHF radio is compulsory.

Eventually, after groping our way through the dark, we found the barge and tied up to it just as the 12 strokes of midnight carried to us from somewhere in town. One leg completed! The sea conditions we'd come through made such an impression on us we dared not think about what it might be like in a serious wind. That's the stuff nightmares are made of.

We were therefore quite pleased to be alongside this pontoon in the calm water of the harbor.

In the end, since we didn't intend to be there very long, we decided to stay where we were and not deal with maneuvering between the pontoons in the marina. It was a quiet spot and we were able to use the water taxi for our comings and goings.

In the afternoon, once we were done with the entry formalities, representatives of the magazine *Mercury* came by to take photographs and to get material for a story. After that, we had a pleasant time exploring the interesting and beautiful town. Briac and I spent several hours at the Museum of Natural History looking at a superb collection of stuffed animals, each mounted in realistic surroundings. All Africa's fauna, of both land and sea, was there, as well as a good part of the flora.

The next day we were surprised to see Richard and his wife waiting for us on the dock. They had come down from Richards Bay to see us, and they took us to see an exhibit of snakes, crocodiles, and turtles. Every snake on earth was there, and we could study them at extremely close quarters and in complete safety. All the same, they gave us chills up our spines.

From the start, I went every morning to the Sailing Academy where, by consulting the weather maps and listening to the synopses offered by the instructors, I could get a picture of the local conditions.

Christmas arrived, and with help from the weather forecast we decided not to leave until the day after. Briac had sent his letter to Santa Claus well ahead of time. After helping to decorate the inside of the cabin, he waited excitedly for the evening.

"Santa Claus will come tonight for sure, so you have to put your shoes at the foot of the mast!"

By lucky chance, this is on the sole of the forward cabin, and it was quickly surrounded by shoes, boots, and sandals; the more, the better.

Briac was the first awake next morning. Driven by curiosity and excitement, he made his way forward and was thrilled to discover on top of the anchors and lines a pile of brightly wrapped packages. His friend Chaka wasted no time helping him to open them.

For us it was a day on which we could relax quietly before we had to think about the next stage of our voyage.

Ahead of us lay the worst leg of the entire trip: Durban to East London, a 250-mile stretch to be done in one hitch. We needed a weather window of a minimum of three days. The problem was complicated by the necessity to get exit papers. That began with a visit to the harbormaster, a mile and a half away, followed by a visit to Immigration, three miles in the opposite direction, then back to Customs, in the same direction as the harbormaster, then back to the first one only to find it closed because of Christmas.

Well, too bad, we left anyway. We couldn't wait or we would have lost another four or five days and we'd then have to do both the entry and exit papers all over again, because the exit papers are only valid for 36 hours!

At first light, we cast off from the barge. A few minutes later we were once more heading into the big swell left behind from the previous day's wind. A short while later, a large pilot boat came abreast of us. It didn't seem to care about the effect of its wake which, catching us abeam, rocked us violently, making it difficult to control the boom.

"The harbormaster isn't very pleased. You didn't call to say you were leaving."

"The radio isn't working."

It left, digested that information, and came back, coming too close and treating us to another rollercoaster. It was beginning to make me nervous.

"You have to go back into port. You didn't get your exit papers."

"I did get them. It's not my fault you were closed yesterday." Then, "Even if you were on holiday, me, I'm working." Annick and Briac looked surprised at the last comment.

"I'm not going to turn around."

It left again to absorb this and get fresh orders, then came back, still paying the same scant heed to the mayhem it created with its wake.

"You have to turn back!"

They were beginning to annoy me with their insistence.

"No! We have a tight weather window, we're making a dash for it."

SPRAY probably couldn't believe her ears at these last words.

What could they do? Sink us? Call out the Navy? I thought to myself that they probably could, which wasn't very comforting.

A few moments later they came up again, and appeared a little more friendly.

"Okay! Your papers are in order. Bon voyage!"

That was the least they could wish us. Relieved, we at last found ourselves alone and the boat commenced burying her bowsprit in the long swell. The weather was still heavily overcast, the cloud ceiling low, and now and then a fine rain considerably reduced the visibility. The wind was five to 10 knots and still in the southwest. Slowly, it turned to the west, then northwest and then on the next day, went back to the southwest, bringing with it drizzle and thick fog. As long as the wind stayed like that it gave us some respite, though at the same time we weren't going very fast.

Each mile was hard earned. We were hoping that the fronts would take their time to reach us. The usual pattern is for the wind to blow first from the northeast for one to three days while getting gradually stronger. Then, after a brief lull, it goes to the southwest and blows hard against the current. That's when the fun begins! As long as the wind stayed between west and southwest, and not too strong, we could make time and distance toward the next shelter while making the best use of the current. We went to between five and 10 miles from the coast to find it and it gave us a good boost.

In this region, it's essential to make progress whatever it takes, which means using the engine whenever possible.

For the first day, we made an average of six knots. On the second, seven, with hourly posts of eight and even nine knots, in ten knots of wind. That was tremendously satisfying and encouraging, especially in that miserable weather.

A freighter appeared suddenly out of the fog, then just as mysteriously disappeared. It was a ghostly sight, but a true warning of the very real dangers at sea.

During the night, a sailboat very slowly overtook us. We found out, later, in East London, that it was a Canadian boat. Its crew saw us leave early in the morning from Durban and followed about an hour later.

The wind backed to the northeast, through east, remaining weak for the time being but strong enough to assist us toward East London. We reached it at night and heaved a great sigh of relief.

It had taken us 36 hours, which was an average of about seven knots. The hardest part was over, but we still had a long way to go in unpredictable conditions, so we had to remain focused and vigilant.

To reach a place to moor, we had to go up the Buffalo River in the dark. Just before the bridge that crosses it, was a wooden dock built on tall pilings. We would be quite content to spend the night there, but we had to tie up to it carefully because the current could be strong and the water choppy. There was plenty of room but the dock was very high, and luckily the young Canadian couple was there to help with the lines.

Anne and Jean-Claude had decided to spend more time in Durban and we wouldn't see them again until much later, in Cape Town.

Here, nobody seemed to be bothered with official paperwork. All we had to do was inform the harbormaster of our arrival, and I did that via the radio, which I had managed to repair.

The next day, December 28, another front blew through and we were very happy to listen to it whistling in the masts while we were well protected along the quay. It was a rest for the crew. I took the opportunity to service the engine while Annick and Briac went into town to procure fresh food. They had quite an adventure. Walking along the road, they passed through a black area. A chase scene played out in front of them in the dirt paths. Two vehicles were trying to catch a fleeing man, just like in the movies. In the end, the fugitive escaped by jumping a wall and crossing the expressway.

Not exactly confident, they found a small supermarket and returned very quickly. It must have been a long time since a couple of white people had ventured into those parts.

On the 29th, we put to sea again, this time bound for Port Elizabeth 100 miles farther on. Our new Canadian friends had left four or five hours ahead of us. The barometer was relatively high, at 1034 millibars, and after a few hours of south-southwest wind under cloudy skies, the wind went east. The sky cleared and it became sunny and hot, and all the while there was the tremendous swell from the south-southwest. By heading to sea, we found the axis of the current and made rapid progress at an average of seven knots. The east-northeaster stabilized and became a steady breeze in which we sailed with no difficulty. In the morning, as we were approaching the breakwaters, we saw a sailboat astern of us.

We entered Port Elizabeth toward midday, in sunshine and a fair breeze, and took a spot at the Algoa Bay Yacht Club marina, where we found a very friendly and generous welcome. We prepared to take the lines of the boat that was following us. Imagine our surprise on seeing it was the Canadian couple, who had left several hours ahead of us on their 43-foot boat. They seemed a little peeved that SPRAY wasn't as slow as they'd thought!

Port Elizabeth is a pleasant town. We felt we were in the heart of an English country town, with its main shopping street, its church, and its architecturally interesting municipal buildings built of dark red brick.

Briac pointed out a 65-foot aluminum boat with a South African flag. We were surprised to see it there as it had left Richards Bay bound directly for Cape Town with a crew of ten members, brawny enough to have been rugby players. Apparently, they had run into bad weather and broken some gear, which just shows how it makes no sense to set out when there's a front on its way. This region, and I know I'm repeating myself, is truly one of the worst I have encountered in all of my voyages.

To rub it in, the day after we got in, the port was hammered with 35 to 40-knot southwesterlies. Annick had a look about her that seemed to be saying, "It's a good thing we're in harbor."

Early the next morning, we put to sea again and met a southwesterly wind of 10 knots. It went to the east again and the sun came out. Twenty four hours later, under two reefs we were rushing down big, short, and sometimes violent seas. The barometer fell, and instead of continuing straight to Cape Town, Capes Agulhas and Good Hope, we decided to go to Mossel Bay, the only effective shelter on this coast. AR-IJUANA, the Canadian sailboat, which had just passed us, continued on her way. Could they have had better weather information? We were having a hard time getting forecasts. The best way would have been to use a cell phone to call the airport meteorological services, which seemed to me to be the most reliable.

In a 25-knot following wind, we entered the small harbor and ended up rafted with a trawler in for repairs. The place was quite poorly protected and a persistent big surge made it hard on the warps and cleats. But two things made us happy. We had made good progress and it was now time for dinner. All night long, though, the boat groaned against the lines, interrupting our sleep and making us nervous.

The bad weather held us there, eventually, from January 2 to 13, before we were able to set off again. It's possible we could have carried on and saved a week or 10 days, but that seemed a big risk to take without good information to go by.

We left the trawler to go and anchor in front of the yacht club, where it was still rolly but safe and more pleasant. In the end, we didn't regret making this involuntary stop in Mossel Bay because it became one of our most enjoyable layovers in South Africa. For the first time, we were in neither a big town nor a commercial port. This place was more frequented by fishermen in their black trawlers. The medium-sized town lay quietly among the surrounding hills and there was a lovely beach to the right of the yacht club. For once, we could do our shopping without having to walk a long way just to get to the super-market.

We took walks along the rocky shoreline toward the lighthouse and the cliffs that stretched beyond it, following paths above where the sea broke and roared against the rocks. It was then I discovered that I was beginning to suffer seriously from dizziness.

We visited quaint museums that depicted the region's history and the evolution of its way of life. One of them, largely financed by Portugal, was dedicated to Bartolomeu Dias, the first navigator to open up the new sea route via the Cape of Storms, which was later renamed more encouragingly, Cape of Good Hope. It was instructive and interesting, and we went there twice to admire in detail the exact replica of the caravelle in which Dias had made his explorations. This replica was constructed on the 500th anniversary of this voyage at Vila Do Condo, 250 miles north of Lisbon. Commanded by Captain De Sousa, she made the same voyage to Mossel Bay, except for passing west of the St. Helena anticyclone instead of sailing along the African coast. Seventy five and a half feet long and 21.75 feet in beam, she has a displacement of 130 tons of which 37 are ballast, and spreads a sail area of 2,370 square feet. She was sailed by a crew of 17 men. I took the opportunity offered by this stop to change the sheaves in the steering system because the axles of two of them had become worn. We also had to inspect all the rigging and check the mast.

At Richards Bay, James Baldwin, sailing solo aboard ATOM, had come to interview us. He was writing for some magazines, among them *Cruising World* and *South African Yachting*, as well as for the International Slocum Society. He had ferreted out for us some pieces of stainless-steel sheet. During our stay in Mossel Bay, I cut two pieces and fastened them around the mast to protect it from the chafing of the gaff throat saddle. They served us very well.

We were getting impatient with the succession of fronts when, at last, a suitable weather window appeared. We decided to take advantage of it and, contrary to our custom, put to sea immediately after dinner.

We tacked along the shore for a while in a 10- to 15-knot south-westerly before the wind freed up and our course turned to the west, after which we had a pleasant sail for the rest of the night.

A 60-year-old singlehander from New Zealand, sailing on a 26-

foot red-hulled boat, FLAMINGO, had been champing at the bit, and he soon followed us. His wife was flying in to meet him in Cape Town, so he was pretty much in a hurry to get there.

The French artist and journalist, Antoine, was there on his yellow catamaran, BANANA SPLIT, and he, too left the marina in the next few hours. We met up with him again in Cape Town which he reached three hours after us, which shows that SPRAY isn't such a slowpoke.

As a safety measure, we maintained regular radio contact with FLAMINGO, which arrived four days after us in the lovely marina at the Royal Cape Town Yacht Club. Her skipper looked so happy to be there that it brought back memories of my own arrivals during the around the world races via Cape Horn. When his wife arrived a few days later she found him a new man, ten years younger!

Altogether, we had great weather and had no problems, apart from an occasional shortage of wind and meeting several fishing boats. The freighter traffic was farther out to sea. From time to time we would see their lights in the distance, and we didn't ask for more than that.

But it was tremendously exciting for us to round this proud cape, which has such a reputation for stormy weather. We spent a long time gazing in awe at its jagged rocky shores which resembled a little those of the western tip of Brittany.

This was the fourth time I had rounded it, but the first time I had been able to see it. It's a sight not to be missed, like Cape Horn, which I have been fortunate enough to see six times.

As we headed back northward, we sailed at a safe distance from these magnificent cliffs which remain wild because a nature reserve surrounds and protects them. Of all of the South African coast, this is the most beautiful, most majestic, and most impressive part.

Briac was thrilled by everything around him and was especially excited that we had returned to the Atlantic. The water there was much colder and it was full of life and activity. Large numbers of screaming birds soared above the sea, dove into it, or sat on it in rafts. We saw a lot of seals frolicking, hunting, or just resting with their flippers crossed on their tummies and looking from a distance like floating branches.

It was tremendous luck to have such good weather. Perhaps grandfather interceded from above, Thank you grandpa!

We sailed into Cape Town in a magnificent, rosy sunset. After a couple of false attempts due to the encroaching darkness, we found the visitors' pontoon just inside the entrance to the Royal Cape Town Yacht Club marina. We were excited to find right next to us a superb racing machine, an American Whitbread 60. While Annick prepared dinner, Briac and I jumped onto the dock to take a look at her. We learned afterward that financial problems prevented her from leaving. It was really sad to see her like that, when her proper element was the great, long, rolling swells of the Southern Ocean.

Very early the next morning, an official of the marina asked if we would like to move the boat to the guest of honor pontoon in front of the yacht club building. It was a great compliment, and SPRAY OF SAINT-BRIAC and her crew were deeply touched.

To be there, securely moored to that dock at the foot of Table Mountain, the summit of which seemed always to wear a wig of white clouds, was for us a great relief, a great joy, and almost a new birth. The worry and fear instilled by the passage around South Africa were now behind us. Ahead of us, beyond the Cape Town's breakwaters, the great

A family picture in Cape Town
(Barry Lamprecht)

South Atlantic Ocean held its arms open in invitation. We were free again to enjoy peaceful sailing in the warmth of the gentle tradewinds.

We heard about the disappearance of a solo South African sailor whose boat capsized, of a German cruising boat from which four people were rescued, and later, when we were in the middle of the Atlantic, we learned over RFI that Gilbert, whom we'd met at Richards Bay, had fallen overboard just as he reached Cape Town. His body was found on the beach. This is a part of the world to take seriously.

Cape Town, which we already knew from the BOC around the world races of 1982/83 and 1986/87, is a pleasant town, but it's quite far from the club. We called John Martin, a former BOC sailor, who was doing charters out of the Waterfront, a new tastefully designed commercial development on the docks. He was looking for funding for a new racing boat. We also met with Bertie Reed, a veteran of the BOC and the Vendée Globe, who was working at his restaurant at Gordon's Bay, and invited us to spend a day there. An old friend, Tish Simpson, who managed to keep a bold face despite having recently lost her husband in awful circumstances, came for lunch on board and then invited us to her house in Elliot's Bay. There we met Sandra Prinsloo, a South African stage and film artist, who played in *The Gods Are Crazy*. She's a big, beautiful young woman with such deep blue eyes you felt you would drown in them. It was just as well she was wearing sunglasses! And in that part of the world, a meal without crayfish, the local lobster, isn't a meal, especially when all you had to do was dive to ten feet among the rocks to gather a dozen in the space of an hour.

Here again we were visited by members of the press, Eben Human of *Die Burger* among them. We had met him in 1987 and become friends. He often came by the boat, and he took us to visit Bertie's family in Gordon's Bay. We passed a most enjoyable day in the company of this great navigator and seaman without equal whose leathery complexion had earned him the nickname "Biltong," after the dried meat that's so delicious to chew on during night watches at sea.

Accompanied by Anne and Jean-Claude, who had finally arrived, we took SPRAY out so that Barry Lamprecht could to take photographs of her for *Die Burger*.

After being stuck in East London for a while, COMME UN CHEVAL FOU had had a good passage, but just as they arrived at Cape Town,

Maneuvering in Cape Town
(Barry Lamprecht)

they were hit by a 40-knot southeasterly and had to anchor in the lee of the breakwaters and wait until the next day before entering.

On board, they had a young cat, Zulu, which they had been given a few days before Briac received Chaka. The two kittens had a fine time romping on SPRAY's wide deck.

Ray Smuts, a journalist of the Cape Town *Cape Argus*, came to visit us, bringing with him a bottle of port and a selection of photos he'd taken. No doubt, folks in Cape Town know how to live.

Time passed too quickly. Once again, we had to think about leaving, which meant checking over the boat from mast truck to the bottom of the keel. I had to adjust the rigging, and, of course, suffer the usual injuries and indignities at the jaws of the pliers. We also had a new yankee made, so as to have it as a backup, and we had to find paint for the bottom and the topsides. In all, we put on board about 100 pounds of material in readiness for our next spell in the boatyard. We did well, because the exchange rate was very favorable and the prices were about half what they were in America.

Briac found a wonderful little friend in Remi, the son of Mr. Bel-liard, the French Consul, and spent many memorable hours in his company. We too, enjoyed the hospitality and the courtesy of Mr. Bel-liard and the consulate staff. Thanks to him, we met a young French-man, a baker by trade, who had arrived in a small sailboat and had settled in the town. He very kindly gave us several loaves of real coun-try bread which we devoured with relish.

On Thursday February 5, everything was in order and for the first time we had a false start. Bright and early, we had gone to the basin at the Waterfront so as to fill up with tax-free fuel. We waited.

"There's no more fuel. We're waiting for the barge. It should be here to refill us at any moment."

To pass the time, we tied up at another dock and the hours went by in beautiful, baking sunshine. Eventually, at day's end, we went back to the yacht club for the night, hoping that things would turn out bet-ter the next day. We finally received our fuel at two the following af-ternoon, after which we were able to put to sea.

Things actually worked out well. That morning, Annick found a notice in the mail at the club advising her that there was an important letter at the poste restante. Even with this evidence in hand, she had to do battle with the postal clerk before she could collect it. The fuel shortage proved to be lucky for us—the letter contained a check!

"This is Africa!" the club manager said, shrugging his shoulders.

"No, it's not Africa," I replied, "It's bad management." To my great surprise, and some embarrassment, the African secretaries in the office openly expressed their pleasure at my remark.

We had decided to go to Saldanha, about 75 miles to the north, so that we could see something other than a big commercial port.

Antoine, with whom we'd been getting along well, had set off a week before toward Lüderitz, in Namibia. We, too, had thought about going there but some sailors in Cape Town had talked us out of it. At that time of the year, strong winds of 30 to 40 knots were run of the mill all along this inhospitable coast, not to mention the fog. That would have to wait for another time.

At dawn the next day, we found ourselves in the bay at Saldanha and picked up one of the free moorings provided by the local yacht club. This unpretentious place had a very friendly, family atmosphere and offered unparalleled hospitality. The president, Mr. Da Costa, who was from Angola and of Portuguese descent, couldn't have done more to make our stay better.

Two days later, he took Annick to the doctor. Since Cape Town, she'd had a bad cold, then a gastric virus which I, too, had contracted. She returned with medicine for both of us and Mr. Da Costa even paid for most of it.

We were most grateful to him, especially as we were soon cured and quickly back on our feet.

Anne and Jean-Claude arrived four days later, and she, too, caught the virus. According to the doctor, it was probably something in the air. It was an epidemic that appeared every year at the time of the apricot harvest, and some people believed there might be a connection.

We had a very pleasant time in this large, protected bay and in the small village. Because we'd spent several weeks in dirty harbors, we careened SPRAY in her sheerlegs on a small sand spit so as to clean her bottom.

Forty eight hours before we were to leave, we wanted to buy fresh fruits and vegetables, so we walked along the road to the town center. I hadn't slept well, perhaps because of stress or because I was lacking something. Anyway, when we reached the store, I felt dizzy, and had to sit down. I lost consciousness for a moment. Eventually, I regained my senses. The manager drove me back to the club where I could cool down a little, and after a while, I went back on board. That was a weird sensation, and it was the first time it had ever happened to me.

Anne and Jean-Claude careened alongside the small dock at the yacht club. At four in the morning, Mr. Da Costa and his wife were there to help them to get in position and to tie the boat up. They were incredibly generous people, always ready with a helping hand for voyaging sailors.

Saldanha remains one of our favorite stops and probably one of the most significant in terms of human relationships. The club members couldn't have done more to make our stay enjoyable. So it was sadly and with some regret we left for the wide open South Atlantic.

17

◆

Miraculous Fishing in the South Atlantic

Ian escorted us out to sea and waved us on our way from his sailboat. We were immediately surrounded in the air by birds, and in the water by seals which studied us with their dark eyes before disappearing into the cold depths which they like so much.

The first nights were chilly but at dawn, the sun's rays would quickly warm our bodies. It wasn't long before we had to protect ourselves with bandannas, sunglasses, and hats.

After about a week of sailing, when we were some distance away from the coast, the wind went southeast and became the much anticipated tradewind. Flying fish appeared at the same time, to the delight of Briac and his pal Chaka. The first thing they did every morning was patrol the deck to collect the night's bounty of fish. Chaka would play with them for a while before depositing them by the companionway. Two or three times, we gathered enough of them to make a delicious breakfast of fried fish.

During the night before the trades arrived, while the wind was still between south and southwest at force three to four, with no warning at all, an unusually violent wave struck the boat amidships, ripping the dodger and smashing the plastic garden chair, breaking off the arms and the back and leaving only the seat. It was the first and only time we met such a wave. It gave us something to think about!

With the trades well established, we got back into our quiet rhythm. In the South Atlantic they are very steady between 15 and 20 knots and, most significant, there's no swell. I believe it's the only ocean where it's absent, and that's because it's protected by the St. Helena high pressure. It makes for restful sailing and life aboard became close to idyllic. In a fair breeze, with the helm lashed, SPRAY OF SAINT-BRIAC went on her own sweet way.

The biggest miracle? When the trades arrived, we jibed and settled in on the new course. After that, I never had to adjust the lines and SPRAY, all by herself, steered for eight days directly to St. Helena. Not bad, eh?

During that week, we were joined by a school of tuna. Day after day, 24 hours after 24 hours, they were all around and under the boat, darting and jumping out of the water. It was unbelievable. We only had to toss in a line 15 feet to immediately catch one. Once we'd figured out the system, Briac took charge of the fishing, which was a twice daily event. We just had to help him haul the fish over the lifelines, when it would fall heavily and lie quivering on the deck. The tuna struggled, while Briac would try to hold onto to its tail, its other end being wedged under one of the spars lashed to the deck.

South Atlantic, a miracle...

These were certainly the highlights of the day, twice each day, at about noon and again about six in the evening. Everyone gathered together, including of course Chaka, who waited patiently by his dish to collect his due when the fish was cleaned. We threw the scraps overboard where the gluttonous tuna happily threw themselves on them. They did the same with the end of the fishing line, except that the result was then much more in our favor.

In short, we had fresh food, and what food!

Morning and evening, every day, the cuisine became a simple and inspiring matter for Annick, who was always seeking new recipes. . . . Raw, with lemon, with soy sauce, in a potato salad, with rice, with tomatoes; a superb and healthy regimen. We couldn't believe we were receiving such manna.

I tried to figure out what could have attracted them. I think they felt a sense of security. At the slightest warning of a predator, they grouped together under the keel, or swam as close as they could to the hull. There was a huge number of them, as the shoal stretched out a good distance all around the boat.

Several times we saw a large dolphin, or a swordfish, and even sharks, following in the boat's wake. These predators hunted the tuna at the edges of the school.

One morning, I had a fish on the hook when I saw a swordfish surge forward from astern and seize my prize. A few moments later, the line broke and I said goodbye to my nice little fish. Happily, others were waiting.

I think that SPRAY's wide shape, the absence of a fin keel, and her moderate speed afforded them a nice area of shade in which to shelter. In any case, it was great luck and we were close to wishing we had a freezer as we would have rapidly filled it.

I was surprised that Joshua Slocum, who would have had a limited choice of food in his day, didn't mention fishing.

The fish were still with us when we reached St. Helena, and they only left us when the anchor touched the bottom of the bay. We gave a tuna to our neighbor and another one to two youngsters who showed us where to anchor.

It was Sunday, March 1, and the officials were resting. The island seemed as though it should be interesting, partly because of its history, and partly because of its beauty. Joshua Slocum stopped there and a small museum recognizes his accomplishment.

The anchorage proved very uncomfortable during the night because of the current, a big swell, and gusts of wind coming down between the hills. Our neighbor, though quite far away, had put out too much line for the amount of his chain. Lying to it differently in the current, his bow paid a visit to our stern. It was one of those nights.

I admire Napoleon, and it would have been a pleasure and an honor to visit the house where he lived his last days. Antoine told us later that it had been arranged by Mr. Morineau, the French Consul, who had been advised of our pending arrival and was waiting for us.

But in the morning, we put back to sea with a feeling of relief and felt no regret as we watched the high silhouette of the island fade away behind us. Soon enough, we settled back into our seagoing routine and, 24 hours later, the tuna rejoined us. They didn't leave us again during the 19 days of our crossing to Natal. *Incroyable, n'est-ce pas?*

It's just incredible. I have never seen or heard tell of anything like it. It was a truly miraculous fishery! And what a treat, what a delicacy, and so good for the health. We have never felt so well. Where else can you live on such a diet?

We had never been so utterly happy at sea and the days rolled by in perfect serenity and contentment for the whole crew, including the cat. Chaka was now really one of the family. With his rolling old-salt's gait he often gave us frights when, despite the irregular movements of the boat running free, he would run to the end of the boom, out over the water, or to his favorite hideout, the inside of the first reef.

It was something to watch Briac and Chaka playing together, especially after dinner. They played hide-and-seek, or the cat would try to catch a rope end held by Briac. As he teased Chaka, the cat would chase him and try to bat him with his forepaws. If he wanted to escape the claws, which weren't always retracted, the boy often had no choice but to hoist himself onto the roof of one of the cabins.

All in all, I believe that we weren't far from achieving what I would called contentedness. I don't know if it exists on land, but on the water I know it does. The ingredients are quite simple: a day filled with work, study, reading, fishing, and play, far from anywhere and alone on the ocean.

The South Atlantic will always remain for us the most beautiful and the most pleasant. We would like to sail around it for ever!

It became really hot in the last days of the crossing and we often had 95 degrees in the cabin. In this part of the world, radio waves propagate well and we were pleased to hear André's voice on the SSB. We exchanged a few rapid words above the interference and then silence filled the cabin once more. From time to time, Joel and Yannick took radio watch. It was as though all of Brittany was present aboard bringing with them some of its coolness.

During the night before our arrival in Natal, just before the 25-fathom line, I set my line to catch our last tuna. Once we were in shallow waters, I expected them to disappear at any time. I still wonder how far they would have followed us if we'd stayed in deep water and continued north.

We felt their presence without fail, night and day. They jumped all around the boat and you've never seen such a show. It was marvelous to see them at night, silver flashes streaking through the water in the moonlight. On moonless nights, the ocean sparkled with phosphorescence, sometimes enlivened up by the arrival of a bigger fish, which would turn the tuna into underwater fireflies. You could hear them splashing back into the sea after leaping wildly out to escape their pursuers.

It's always a great thrill to arrive in a new land after a long passage. In the preceding days, you try to get a feeling for it by listening to its radio stations. But the anticipation is especially vivid when you approach the shores of Brazil to the rhythm of the samba.

Natal was a pleasant surprise. The yacht club, with a small anchorage off it, lies half a mile up the river on the left, just before the commercial port. It's a well sheltered spot and the current there isn't too strong, but you need lots of anchor rode because the depth, on average, is 35 feet. We re-anchored three times, thinking that there was only 12 to 15 feet. A chart would have been useful; all I had was a vague memory of the one Jean-Claude showed me in Saldanha.

After the formalities, much less rigorous thanks to the help of the charming club secretary, we took the opportunity to explore this fascinating town.

Natal is the principal city of a province of 600,000 inhabitants and has held onto its cultural roots in large part because of the absence of large hotels and tourist development. Just on the other side of the river, at its estuary, the fishing village and a vacationers' village stretch along a superb beach which can only be reached by ferry or by dinghy.

The very congenial club is empty of members during the week, which lets cruising sailors get together around the pool. There, we met a vivacious and enthusiastic couple, the Biquets.

They had left France for a sabbatical year of cruising around the Atlantic, with a detour to Brazil. Their lovely accent from the Toulouse area acted as a catalyst to quickly bring gaiety and smiles. Thanks to them, we discovered Radio Coconut which offers the cruising community a variety of services, great and small. They also confirmed the loss of Gilbert at the Cape. For them, cruising wasn't about covering miles but about encounters and human contact. We shared some intimate moments with these people with whom we had so many feelings in common.

There were only 10 sailboats in the anchorage, so there was plenty of room. Pleasant as our stay was, we could unfortunately enjoy it just for four days, the time to replenish our fresh food. It was just long enough to make us want to return one day.

On March 25, we left this delightful anchorage early, as is our custom, and sailed along the beach to the entrance, which lies between some very striking rocks. We then set a course to get beyond the shallow water before heading north.

Several *jacarandas* were heading for their fishing spots. I watched their progress with considerable admiration and respect. They are usually handled by one or two men, or sometimes more according to the size of the vessel. I am attracted toward the smaller ones; they are the ancestors of a sort to the windsurfer. One, sometimes two, fishermen, their feet in the water that sweeps their miniature deck, sit on their box of equipment or stand, to get the most out of the sail, as they disappear out to sea, beyond the horizon. This ballet of white and colored specks is performed twice a day, in the morning when they go out, and before sunset when they return.

18

---◆---

The Doldrums

We sailed along the white sandy beaches as far as Cape São Roque and, at the end of the day, we left the coast to get the benefit of the following current, if we could find it, that is. The sea had been emerald green since we left and now gave way to a magnificent blue which seemed as though it would draw us into its depths if we stared into it for too long. When we leaned overboard and looked downward, the sun's rays gave the enchanting impression that we were looking through a giant, magic kaleidoscope.

The wind gradually became softer and softer as we left the tradewinds and entered the edge of the doldrums, infamous for their light and variable winds, their powerful and unpredictable squalls, their confused and uncomfortable seas, and, on top of it all, their heavy, humid heat.

It was altogether an exhausting passage, testing for both boat and crew and demanding a diligent watch, both to deal with the caprices of the weather and also because of heavy freighter traffic.

After toasting King Neptune once more, we were again in the North Atlantic, impatient for it to bless us with its northeast trades.

The wind came back very timidly. It really did seem to want to settle in, though it gave us false hope four times.

Despite all the vicissitudes of the doldrums, SPRAY OF SAINT-BRIAC hauled herself out of this region and we managed to make radio contacts. We also caught a wahoo and two tuna at the same time as we passed into a current of green, warmer water. The fine weather returned a few days before we reached the island of Trinidad. We had chosen to stop there because we had heard there were well-equipped boatyards with attractive prices. We left Tobago to starboard, even though it's probably a much more interesting place to cruise.

After 15 days of sailing, we rediscovered the pleasures of being in an anchorage. This one was definitely of the crowded variety, with a hundred cruising boats of all nationalities.

The formalities were quickly dealt with because they were uncomplicated and well organized. We immediately made the rounds of the boatyards, which were mainly set up to provide storage, especially during the hurricane season. Thinking it over, we figured we could find the same prices in the United States, with better facilities.

We were suddenly facing again the anchorages and the crowds of the Caribbean, and felt overwhelmed. After several months of cruising the high seas, it was a bit of a shock.

And so, once we had replenished our fresh food and fuel, we were ready to head back to sea, bound once more for the island of Culebra, which Briac had been dreaming of for a long while now.

On April 15, the day after his mother's birthday, which the entire crew had celebrated around a splendid meal—on board SPRAY so that Chaka could be present—we weighed anchor and headed north toward the open sea. From that point on, we would be heading north, but not without a little nostalgia, which would become more intense as we climbed in latitude.

On the fourth day of a passage which was altogether easy and pleasant enough in easterly winds of 10 to 20 knots punctuated by showers and squalls, and after St. Croix had disappeared in our wake, Culebra came into view. Briac's excitement grew rapidly in inverse proportion to the distance that separated us from the "island of his heart."

Before long, the anchor was down on the sandy bottom and digging itself slowly in. We were very happy to return to the calm and security of this small green island with its quiet pastures.

The circle was now complete. We had crossed our outgoing path. It had taken us 15 months to make the circumnavigation.

If Briac was happy to be on his island again, so were we. Often, at sea, he had asked us when we would get back there. And there we were, anchored in this small, well-protected bay. We plunged into its clear waters to refresh ourselves before having a bite to eat.

Soon afterward, the Optimist was back in its element. Briac rowed, sculled, and then brought it alongside SPRAY so that Chaka could get aboard with him. Then, the two of them made sorties around the boat and toward the beach until the young feline cadet demanded to go back on SPRAY. This became a ritual for Chaka. At least once a day he made his rounds before coming back on deck, satisfied that all was as it should be in the neighborhood.

Under the Stars and Stripes that flies over it, Culebra maintains its Hispanic warmth. We would rise early, after the crow of the roosters and the noisy cackle of the chickens. The first rays of the sun fell on us and warmed away the cool dew from the cabin tops. After breakfast we would work on the boat's maintenance. Then, Annick and Briac would go on their shopping errands. When they got back, we'd have a big swim followed by lunch while listening to news from around the world on RFI or Voice of America.

In the afternoons, our program consisted of a long walk or an excursion in the inflatable, swimming, then tea and free time for everyone, which usually took the form of reading or games. And so the days passed, and all too quickly.

We received mail from our friends Jinny and Bob. They were now settled in Little River, South Carolina, and would be very happy if we would look them up. To back up their wish, we also received an invitation from the Myrtle Beach Yacht Club. It wasn't really on our route, but that didn't matter. A little time spent with friends isn't time wasted.

After 15 wonderful days, we visited Palomino Island and its horses again, before pushing on toward Fajardo for provisions and propane gas. We had no problem getting fresh food, but it wasn't so easy to get our bottles filled. After waiting 24 hours, we left without gas. So what? We had another burner with small butane cylinders.

19

◆

Newport—
the Centennial Celebration

After a final night at Palomino Island, the sails were once again aloft and the anchor stowed down below. An hour later, we rounded San Juan Point and its lighthouse to join the open sea for what would be the last ocean passage in this great voyage we were making in the footsteps of Joshua Slocum. We hadn't followed them exactly, but then he himself didn't always know in advance where he was going, and often decided according to circumstances. We did the same, no less because a hundred years later, the world was a little different.

By the time he left from Boston to cross the Atlantic, Captain Slocum had been debating with himself for two months about what route he might take. He had even considered going via Panama, even though the canal wouldn't be open for another 20 years! He originally thought he would go from Gibraltar through the Suez Canal, Ceylon, Hong Kong, Japan, and California—areas he knew already—and then cross Central America once more. The British Navy dissuaded him on the grounds that pirates were very active in the Mediterranean. He then decided to go round via the Strait of Magellan. It always surprised me that he didn't attempt, or even mention, sailing east through the Indian Ocean and the South Pacific, as that would probably have been easier and less dangerous than sailing through the Strait.

He attempted to sail south around Australia before realizing how difficult that would be, and he ended up going north. He thought about ending his circumnavigation in New York, but bad weather drove him toward Long Island, so he decided to finish in Newport.

Even though we didn't leave on a Friday—superstition has it that that brings bad luck—this crossing was without a doubt our worst and all kinds of troubles piled one on top of the other.

To start with, we had little air, then a weak, rainy front with variable winds. Next, the breeze came out of southwest to west for three days, culminating in another, much stronger front. This brought winds from northwest to north for several days before they at last turned, very slowly, to the northeast, then east, where they died.

Instead of the following winds we would normally expect, we found ourselves tacking, or sailing close hauled in heavy seas.

Because of the effect of the drift, our net course in the northwest to north winds was southwest. That wasn't exactly what we were looking for, since our destination lay to the northwest!

Just as the front arrived, we discovered a leak in the engine's freshwater cooling system, just above the through hull. On SPRAY, the cooling water is piped to the outside of the hull and back. I was able to repair it thanks to an epoxy mastic, Marine Tex, which hardens like iron. Just before it set, I wrapped it with adhesive tape and held it in place with two cable clamps. This temporary repair was still holding a year later.

The trouble was, between this tack taking us southwestward, and the reluctance of the depression to move away to the north, we were day by day getting closer to the Bahamas when we had planned to pass 200 miles to their northeast. However, because of our friends' invitation, we didn't take the direct route to Newport which passes near Bermuda and we avoided the even worse weather we heard about on the radio. So, even though we may not have had ideal conditions, we really had nothing to complain about.

We had to tack to get past Eleuthera. It was during this unpleasant and uncomfortable stretch of sailing that the cry came from the galley:

"We're out of gas!"

"How can we be out of gas? Didn't we fill up with butane?"

"Yes, but the stove burner just broke!"

It was bad news; the prospect of eating cold food isn't something to get excited about. After inspecting the burner and making several tries to light it, I was forced to admit that, from now on, it wouldn't even warm a cup of tea.

"Could we try to use the other two-burner stove? The spare one, from Cape Town."

"Yes, we could, but it doesn't want to know. There's not enough pressure, even for one flame. What a pain!"

At that precise moment, we were startled by the sound of the fishing reel. All hands went on deck to haul in a wahoo. At least for this evening, all was not lost, even though we couldn't turn it into haute cuisine!

For two days we ate cold food, which is neither very exciting nor nutritious. We couldn't, of course cook the staples, such as pasta and rice, which are so important at sea.

Eventually, after a long search, I found a blowtorch with two refills of gas. That improved the situation somewhat and warm coffee made a timid comeback, with a couple of cookies on the side. What luxury!

To prepare food in these conditions is an art, and our skills grew a little every day. Raw potatoes, sliced thin; they're quite crunchy, and in the end, not bad.

"Don't we have a wood stove?"

"The problem is, we don't have any wood!"

"That's not true!"

As luck would have it, Briac, twice a day, would sing his favorite musical numbers to the accompaniment of his preferred instrument, the saw, on any scraps of wood he could find on board. Well, too bad for the oar, this was for a good cause! We used the wood stove to prepare staples for two days at a time, but the problem was keeping them in the prevailing heat.

Fortunately, while we were off the Bahamas, we took dorado every day, and what fine fish they were! One of them was the biggest of the entire voyage. Two of us struggled together to haul it aboard, and then we had to fling ourselves on it to prevent it from fighting free and going back in the water.

As if it had decided to help us, when we were nearing Abaco Island, the wind shifted at last to the east to become a nice light breeze, allowing us to skirt the edge of the rocks and once more regain the open sea.

The next day, feeling the freedom of the open ocean, I was astride the bowsprit, needle and thread in hand, repairing the yankee where it had opened up along a seam. It was a two-year-old sail and had for a long time suffered where it chafed against the inner forestay.

As we approached the American coast, we crossed the confused current of the Gulf Stream, which stymied all the efforts of the electric autopilot. With a dreadful shudder, it died, victim of the violent jerking of the rudder.

We were in the path of another front that came onto us in a night of lightning, showers, and moderate and variable winds. At daybreak, when we were just off the Little River Inlet, the sky cleared and very quickly gave way to a beautiful springtime sunshine. Myrtle Beach is five miles farther south and to get there, we had to use the Intracoastal Waterway.

Several fishermen looked up and watched SPRAY as she struggled under motor against the strong current in the inlet. They might have been thinking she won't make it, or admiring her beautiful lines, or both. Who knows? It was tight going, but we made it through into more placid waters. The scenery was lovely, with tall pine trees thrusting up into the clear blue sky.

We found the entrance to the yacht club basin without much difficulty. We were guided to the guest pontoon where we were warmly welcomed by the many members who had shown up that early in the morning, all of them eager to come to our assistance, or to offer small gifts.

It was hard to contain our feelings as we met our friends after such a long time away. There was so much news and so many memories, and we had just realized Bob's great dream, which was to make a circumnavigation.

Before we left, he had brought me his collection of guidebooks which he had bought in anticipation of a departure sometime in the future.

He noticed my left arm, which was swollen and very painful.

"I'll take you to see a doctor. It's a holiday because of Memorial Day, but there must be a clinic open. Let me arrange it at the club."

"It's no big deal. About a week ago I was bitten by something one night, by I don't know what, perhaps a spider. I treated myself every day with bleach compresses and by applying clay. For a while it helped, but now it's worse than before."

On seeing my arm, the doctor was very concerned, "Perhaps you need to go to the hospital." Well, that put it in another perspective entirely!

"Take these two different types of antibiotics, then come and see me again the day after tomorrow," he said, while putting on a new dressing.

Two days later, he removed the bandage and began to clean and press around the infection. I couldn't believe my eyes! A whitish substance poured and poured out of my arm and, when it stopped, there was a round hole the size of my thumb and a quarter of an inch deep. A second doctor confirmed the first's diagnosis: it must have been caused by a venomous spider, probably a Brown Recluse, which is found in South America and in the southern United States. Its venom destroys tissue but fortunately, antibiotics are enough to stop the damage. Otherwise, you have to cut all around the bite with a scalpel to check the progress of the poison.

At sea, after I was bitten, I had no doubt it was a spider, but where was it? Besides, I had been bitten several times since we left South Africa. Some of the bites were apparently less serious, and left only a painful and swollen spot. After I applied a dilute solution of bleach, they diminished slowly, leaving dark marks which lasted for a while, in particular on my left leg and my left wrist. I thought that their being on my left side was simply a coincidence.

Suffice it to say that since this latest sting, it had become a nightmare and my nights became very short and disturbed. A soon as I felt something on my body, I instinctively slapped it. Because it was hot, I sweated, and the least little drop of liquid that ran slowly across my skin felt like an insect. I couldn't help myself, and the nights became impossible.

I sprayed insecticide everywhere, and poked, prodded, and searched all over. I found absolutely nothing at all.

Just before we left Myrtle Beach, we decided to change the mainsail and put on the new one, so SPRAY OF SAINT-BRIAC could look her best.

With Briac's assistance, I unbent it. I let out the reef that was still tied into it. And were we surprised to see, when the loosened cloth fell on the dock, two spiders, one bigger than the other, probably a female and her offspring. My reaction, I have to admit, was instantaneous, and my fist struck.

The end of the boom is just over the companionway to the aft cabin, and that's where they were hiding. No one thought to look there. Hanging from their threads, they could descend at will and climb back up just as quickly, unseen and unsuspected.

We waited a few days to see how the treatment would work out and made the most of the time by visiting the region and making new friends.

Since my arm was mending well and Annick had taken it upon herself to apply new dressings daily for a month to help the tissue grow back, we decided to leave right after the windy and rainy passage of another front, this one associated with a depression over Canada.

On May 28, after emotional farewells and promises to get together again soon, we motored out through the Little River Inlet and into the ocean once more. The trip would have taken too long by the Intracoastal Waterway.

Fine weather awaited us and it was even very hot after the miserable weather of the previous day. The passage was quiet and posed no great problems. On the second day, around noon, we passed by the base of the Hatteras Light platform, long wooden piles driven into the sand. All around us was tremendous sport-fishing activity, and the big, powerful motorboats filled Briac with envy. Farther on, we crossed paths with several freighters on their way to and from Chesapeake Bay. For many hours, we trailed our fishing line and even though we were at the boundary of warm and cold currents, which should have been good for fishing, we didn't get so much as a bite.

A new front arrived in the night, off the Delaware coast, but it was a weak one, producing lots of rain and winds that were all over the place.

The first flush of dawn revealed the New Jersey shoreline, then Atlantic City and the remarkable spectacle of sunlight reflecting off the many windows suddenly turning its big, glitzy buildings silver.

And then, during the night, for the first time in two years, we had to face the worst . . . the cold! It was truly surprising, the difference between day and night: from 80 degrees to near freezing. The cold was all the more penetrating when a little breeze would ruffle the surface of the water. Even though we were warmly dressed, the cold took hold of our heads, like a vise, and it was difficult to endure.

A familiar image presented itself before us at dawn. Just as it had three years before, Sandy Hook loomed ahead, and then the entrance to New York Harbor. We wouldn't have missed this for anything in the world. To pass under the Verrazano Bridge and enter this great bay that shelters Manhattan, Brooklyn, and New Jersey, to sail among the shipping past the Statue of Liberty, and to go up the East River and enter Long Island Sound is one of the greatest experiences in life.

Once again, the timing was perfect: wind, tide, fair weather, all were in our favor. The entire crew, Chaka included, was on the deck to witness this beautiful and emotional moment. We relived, with the same intensity as before, those marvelous and unique sensations. Then we reached the tranquil waters of Long Island Sound, and we had every sail set as we passed Mamaroneck, another place that holds good memories for us.

Throughout the afternoon and a greater part of the night, we had a fine sail ahead of a new front that the weather forecasts were calling more serious, with a chance of thunderstorms. Southwesterly winds of a good 25 knots pushed us until we were a few miles from the exit in the narrow passage of The Race, north of Little Gull Island, where the currents can be violent. Suddenly, low black clouds were overhead and launched a veritable deluge on us amid thunder and lightning. The rumblings grew louder and louder, giving the impression of an imminent and violent end of the world.

Fortunately, the gusts of wind weren't too strong but we couldn't steer the boat very well as she was now undercanvassed. I turned the engine key and it started. Suddenly, its compartment filled with smoke. The exhaust mixer had perforated. I quickly repaired it, although being encumbered by my oilskins didn't make things easier. I had to be prepared in case something happened on deck, which was now under Annick's supervision. Thanks to experience gained in similar repairs using the same technique, I quickly completed the job. The longest part was waiting for the epoxy to set. At any rate, I was now more confident about dealing with this tricky and dangerous region.

Meanwhile, the front passed and things quieted down. We were relieved when at last we saw the darkness beginning to lift in the east, presaging the arrival of day.

During the deluge, while we were not capable of maneuvering, two tugs towing barges passed quite close by. What a night it was. Poor SPRAY was thrown about in all directions in the confused seas.

At daybreak, with the help of the engine, we made it through The Race despite the contrary current and the numerous eddies. Little by little, the wind came back from the northwest, pushing away the clouds, clearing the sky, and making room for the sun but bringing with it the cold. After trimming the sails, and checking our course, I went below to try and rest, because I was exhausted.

That didn't last long. The wind picked up and blew a good 25 to 30 knots. SPRAY's heart filled with joy and the spray she kicked up created rainbows at the bow. It was time to take in a second reef, because she was really pressed. We did it, but not without some difficulty due to frozen fingers and streaming eyes. But a fine spectacle was unfolding around us. The coast passed by rapidly and we continued to tumble along neck and neck with several fishing boats. I can envision the sight SPRAY made for them, under sail in this wind and in these short, grey-green seas crested with white. I would have loved to have found myself aboard one of them with a camera, or even just to watch. It was a grand and unique moment, one hundred years later.

As we passed Point Judith, in the whitecapped and confused sea caused by the shoaling water, we decided to go under the shelter of the coast where several trawlers were waiting for the weather to improve, and work our way gently toward Narragansett Bay and Newport. Things got rapidly better. The sea was flatter and we had only to suffer the gusts of wind coming off the nearby land.

Calmly, taking the wind somewhat on the stern, we steered for the channel that leads into Narragansett Bay, between Castle Hill and Beavertail Point on the island of Jamestown.

Finally, cold, tired, we dropped sail and took some time to stow the boat before heading for the anchorage in Jamestown.

"What VHF channel is it?"

"71."

"Ah, yes, 71. Good morning! Could we have a mooring? Please?"

"Hello SPRAY, welcome home! Take the red buoy number G2."

The spray creates rainbows
(Onne van der Wal)

"Okay, thanks."

It was almost over. All that remained was to bring SPRAY OF SAINT-BRIAC in and moor her securely. She was soon tugging at her mooring in the gusts, just like three years before.

It was a big moment. We were quite simply happy to be there again after having fulfilled our goal. We were back after realizing a great dream and a great plan. It's the same dream that thousands have. Yet for us, it wasn't completely finished because we had a rendezvous: The celebration of the centennial of Joshua Slocum's voyage in SPRAY was to be held on June 27. We had just enough time left to go to the boatyard and get the boat ready.

In the afternoon, after we'd rested and changed, we went ashore. First on the agenda was a long, hot shower, then we had to advise our friends of our arrival and contact the boatyard in Wickford.

It was June 3. We would need to put the boat back in the water on June 24, which left us 18 or 19 days to do everything. We had to strip the hull, prepare it, and paint it, this time white. Also, we needed to paint the interior and the engine compartment, stow everything, sort through all the gear, replace the standing rigging, service the engine . . . then launch her again. They'd better not lay off the workers!

What a delight it was to see Mame Reynolds, Mamita, the Dumonts, then George and the guys at the shipyard. We had wonderful dinners where we talked about past experiences and shared ideas for the future. Two days later, thanks to George's efforts, SPRAY was on the apron, ready for her great facelift.

This was a marathon of 10- and 12-hour working days in spite of particularly nasty, damp weather which gave us a lot of trouble, especially with painting the hull. June is normally a sunny month but, that year, nearly every day saw foul weather and rain. In desperation, we waited until the last minute to paint the hull. Afterwards, we had to touch it up in places. We almost regretted Trinidad.

Briac gave a hand here and there, but we preferred to see him playing in the boatyard, making friends with girls and boys of all ages, riding a bike (kindly lent by Adelaide) or playing with his cat. Chaka discovered new horizons and only came on board to eat and to sleep a little. He even made a friend, a dog that belonged to a fisherman who was working on his boat nearby. It was something to watch the two of them together, when they weren't three, with Briac.

We were having dinner one night when we heard the awful news of Eric Tabarly's disappearance. This was a shock, and brought tears to our eyes. Tabarly, too, was celebrating a centennial, that of his magnificent PEN DUICK.

Nearly every day at the boatyard, we were visited by the press. We were on the front pages of newspapers and on television. Press agencies and magazine writers called, and all of this took up a lot of our time. For AP International alone, we spent six hours in the yard and another full hour on the telephone. For Agence France Presse and *France Amérique*, we spent not far short of three hours on the phone.

We were surprised by this media frenzy. In the end, it lasted throughout our stay, and 24 hours before our next Atlantic crossing we were out being photographed for *Cruising World* magazine.

Briac had to show patience and self-control when asked the same questions over again. The hardest were the television interviews. We had to talk to him gently, to explain what was going on and to calm him down.

"I already answered that question!" Yes, Briac, you did, but not necessarily to the same person! It's tough, life as a celebrity!

We were pleased when the officers of the Slocum Society came to visit, to exchange ideas and to invite us to dinner. They left somewhat skeptical about our participation in the upcoming events, measured by how our progress in having the boat ready looked in their eyes. We looked calm and confident, but it didn't reassure them a whole lot.

During this dinner, we developed a high regard for Henry Hotchkiss, the president of the Fairhaven Committee. The following day, I telephoned him to thank him for his invitation and to tell him that we would also take part in the celebrations in Fairhaven, despite the tight scheduling that would require. The parade through Newport Harbor to honor Joshua Slocum was to be at 11 a.m. on the 27th, followed by the gala dinner in the evening, then on the morning of the 28th we had to be in Fairhaven, a good 30 miles away. Quite a bit of organizing!

SPRAY in Newport
(Onne van der Wal)

Henry appeared very touched by our offer to be present. We would have been going there in any event, certainly for July 3, as Captain Slocum had done. So, why not make an effort for such a kind and likeable man?

But first we had to get SPRAY ready, and the torrents of water that kept coming down didn't make our task any easier.

And so, by dint of attacking the jobs with the muscle and the mindset of a bulldozer, George put us back in the water on the evening of the 26th. Once alongside the dock, we continued working until 11 p.m., to set the boat up and make sure everything was working properly.

We were physically and mentally worn out, but happy that we had accomplished all that we had to within the allotted time. It brought back to mind the times when I was preparing for races or record attempts. In order to arrive at the goal, I had to keep a level head and crush all the problems on the way, whether they were physical, material, or human. This was one of those occasions when I applied that kind of determination, and it helped to have a solid Breton head.

Wickford is two hours from Newport, and we arrived just in time for the parade of sail, to the great surprise and joy of Ted and June Jones, Commodore and Secretary of the Slocum Society. We had the great honor of leading the procession.

Following behind the harbormaster's launch, with its siren blowing and strobe flashing in the grand American fashion, we led the tour of Newport Harbor, anticlockwise, as is the custom. Cannons saluted us from the various yacht clubs as the port paid its respects to Captain Joshua Slocum in the traditional way.

There were several planned and attempted anniversary voyages, but SPRAY OF SAINT-BRIAC was in the end the only boat to complete one. I think it's only appropriate that I should take this opportunity to offer a big thank-you to this remarkable sailboat, to her crew, and to all who supported us.

After the parade, instead of staying on the Newport side, we returned in company with MAI LING to the Jamestown moorings. Since the weather forecast had nothing good to say about the afternoon, we decided not to leave for Fairhaven until the following morning. A few hours later, a violent thunderstorm with ferocious winds battered the bay. I believe SPRAY was thankful for the security of her mooring, while we sipped a hot tea in the corner coffee shop.

For the gala dinner that night, which was attended by a large number of sailors, men and women, from Europe and the two Americas, Briac put on his navy blue blazer and a white shirt adorned with the SPRAY OF SAINT-BRIAC logo. During the course of the evening, we received the *Golden Circle Award* from Commodore Ted Jones. We also had the pleasure of seeing Yves Gélinas again. He was in Newport on his boat and was accompanied by a television crew from Quebec. I recalled his being in Brittany before he left on his solo circumnavigation, quite a few years ago.

The next day, June 28, the sun paid a visit and slowly burned off the fog that covered the bay. That was the signal aboard SPRAY to cast off the mooring pennant and set course for Fairhaven, the end of our voyage. Just before leaving, I advised Henry that we were setting off and said we would rendezvous on the radio at four p.m.

Parade in Newport for the Centennial
(Frieda Squires, Providence Journal)

It was a pleasant sail, with a nice breeze between northeast and north. As expected, we made contact a mile before we reached the entrance shared by the harbors of New Bedford and Fairhaven. This passes between two huge breakwaters which, in the event of a hurricane, can be closed to protect the inner harbor from a storm surge and the full force of the waves outside.

We had to wait an hour for the road bridge between Fairhaven and New Bedford to open before we could reach Poverty Point, the exact spot where Joshua Slocum built his boat, launched it, and where he completed his circumnavigation. Our voyage wouldn't be truly over until the anchor rested on the bottom there.

We had only 500 yards to go and the tension mounted. Led by the fireboat, the police boat, and the harbormaster's boat, we made a handsome and moving procession to the head of the creek. We were quite overcome to think that, 100 years before, Captain Slocum had brought his SPRAY right here and that it was now SPRAY OF SAINT-BRIAC's great honor to re-enact that great moment. She, too, would enter the history books as an addendum to the incomparable sea story that keeps that great mariner alive in our minds.

On land, more than 350 people were waiting impatiently after a long day of diverse activities. At the sight of SPRAY emerging from behind the bridge pier, a hush fell over the crowd. There was something particularly solemn and moving in the sight of SPRAY as she crept slowly forward behind the fountains of seawater sent up by the red fireboat that fell in a myriad droplets set sparkling by the last rays of the sun. We suddenly felt as though we'd been transported into the past.

Once the anchor was set, those gathered on the shore filled the air with applause and hurrahs, to which we replied from SPRAY's deck. We launched the dinghy and landed on the shingle beach where Henry Hotchkiss received us solemnly and presented us with a citation from the town of Fairhaven. For him, as for us, it was a very special moment.

He was very touched that we had kept our word and that we were there, just in time, to make this a unique and unforgettable day. I believe that at that instant when we came ashore, without fanfare, but just with a look and a smile, a great friendship was born between us.

During the course of the several days we would spend there, we found Fairhaven to be a friendly town with marvelous people and a human warmth that we never expected. We were invited to share many meals, and a car was rented and put at our disposal for getting around. A visit to the Whaling Museum in New Bedford was for us quite magical, in particular because on the third floor, there was a very interesting exhibition about Joshua Slocum. New Bedford and Fairhaven, on either side of the river, are old fishing ports now in decline. They saw their peak of wealth and glory in the days of whaling; New Bedford was the setting for Hermann Melville's *Moby Dick*.

It was with mixed feelings of sadness and gratitude that we left our anchorage off Cosy Cove Marina to head back toward the sea, to farewells from the bank from Henry, Gael, and many new friends. Bob Gracia fired a cannon from his lawn and all too soon Fairhaven was behind us. Nostalgia swept over us as we left this lovely port. We had come to feel profoundly that this was SPRAY's place, that she belonged to this port which had witnessed the beginning of her story and that, one day or another, she would return.

We didn't leave quite alone. The Henry the Navigator Association of New Bedford had entrusted us with a commemorative plaque to take to the officials of Expo 98 in Lisbon. The organizers had invited us to participate, and our next ocean passage would take us there.

At the end of the day, we picked up a mooring put at our disposal for our planned 15-day stay in Jamestown.

Thanks to our friend Jean-Paul Guinard, the necessary contacts and formalities needed for our presence at Expo 98 fell into place quickly. All we had to do was undertake another crossing of the North Atlantic, the third in SPRAY OF SAINT-BRIAC. This time there was no rush. We just had to be in Lisbon by the beginning of September.

We had many opportunities to admire the graceful old America's Cup 12 Meters and the two magnificent and imposing J Class yachts, SHAMROCK V and ENDEAVOUR strutting their stuff on the superb stretch of water that lies in front of Newport. One afternoon, we even saw the elegant form of MARICHA III, a 135-foot sailing boat which several weeks later made a successful attempt on the transatlantic record.

Walks in Jamestown once again became our daily routine, and then it was time to think about our departure. Fortunately, Catherine and Bertrand lent us a car. That greatly facilitated our comings and goings to Wakefield, Wickford, and Newport, in that perpetual search for one last gizmo, or to change something at the last minute. Bob dismantled the autopilot and had Don make a new metal piece to repair it. I didn't expect it to last very long—when you strengthen one side, the other side breaks. It wasn't a long time coming, and broke just at the end of our crossing. Nevertheless, this repair saved us many hours of hand steering when under power.

For several days, I had been following the weather, especially in the south, on RFI and on the American radio stations and charts. I didn't want to run into tropical storms, or worse, on the way. There was nothing significant in the forecasts and we waited for a front to pass so we could leave just behind it, as that would mean fine weather for at least the first few days.

20

◆

Across the Atlantic
to Expo 98

We spent our last afternoon in the company of Catherine and Bertrand Dumont, in the tranquility of their lovely house near the water, not far from Newport.

On Sunday, July 19, we put back to sea, bound for Horta in the Azores, accompanied again by MAI LING, our faithful support boat, which soon left us to ourselves to face this great and unpredictable ocean.

It was without a doubt the most pleasant North Atlantic crossing that I have ever made. The first 15 days were in beautiful weather, in west-southwesterly winds no stronger than 20 to 25 knots and often less. We couldn't remember anything like it, and we were thankful for having had the chance to cross so easily. On the last few days, as we approached the Azores, the weather was calm. Puffs of air came from all directions before settling in the east which, in fact, gave us better progress.

Our best day was 140 miles. During this passage, we caught only one dorado, two days before reaching the island of Faial. It was a dream crossing, and it took 19 days.

Our reintroduction to Horta came on a better day, and with a better perspective. This time, we would have more time, and the pressure of the circumnavigation was behind us.

A surprise awaited us: the paperwork was simpler, probably a result of the united Europe. On the downside, American boats could only stay six months in the entire continent, beginning for us here in the Azores, with only a three-month extension possible before the boat was subject to the Value Added Tax. And just to make things really simple, every country seemed to have its own rules, or its own interpretation of the rules. Under these conditions it was difficult to visit all of Europe. Things may be different now. (Editor's note: They are; the permitted stay is now 18 months.)

Instead of going into the marina, we were granted permission to tie up to a large white buoy in the middle of the harbor. There, we could touch up the paint where it had peeled on the hull, and particularly the bow. This was a result of the extreme dampness of the weather while we were in the boatyard which had left the wood too wet.

Despite some minor disagreements arising from our being moored to this large, metal buoy, we enjoyed the berth, especially the magnificent view it gave us of Horta and its surroundings.

This island is truly a meeting of the countryside, with its cows grazing on lush green pastures bordering the cliffs, and the incomparably blue sea. Several windmills, relics of a past epoch, their cruciform sails stationary, stand watch on the heights. Colored brick red and white, they are distinguishable from a great distance. The fields, separated by stone walls and hedges, resembled their counterparts in Brittany and Ireland. Some of them were punctuated by huge clumps of hydrangeas, in which blue was the dominant color.

Joyfully and hungrily, we found our way back to the market where the fruit and vegetables are wonderfully fresh and of incomparable quality. The butcher at the corner was another of our favorites. The animals were raised in the most natural way possible.

In the course of our walks, we indulged in the simple happiness of being on these beautiful islands, where the air is so pure and where the nearby islands of St Georges and Pico are all that interrupts the ocean as it stretches out of sight. Pico's majestic volcano, with its colors that change with the passing hours, is absolutely magnificent, especially at sunset and when the wind is in the north. At any time of the day, we couldn't help but stare at it and marvel, when the clouds let us see it. Saint Georges, to the north, protects a magnificent roadstead and is celebrated for its cheeses. Each island has its specialties.

We started to dream about what it would be like to cruise this delightful area. You could easily spend a year visiting these nine islands, with their numerous anchorages. You don't have to go far to find a quiet corner, kind and hospitable people, as only islanders know how to be, healthy food, and unpolluted air, which seems to be more and more of a luxury. A German couple, whom we'd met in Rodrigues, had been in the marina in Horta for two months. They were there when the earthquake hit and caused severe damage to part of the island. They had bought a small house and were fixing it up, happy to be there.

Antoine was there, too, making a documentary on the archipelago before leaving for Madeira. We also met Mr. Fraga again, dynamic as ever, and spent some time with him. The Joshua Slocum regatta still goes on, and will be held every year.

From the minute we arrived, Briac had had only one idea in his head, which was to treat us at the one and only Peter's Cafe Sport. We went there and found a free table where we sat and placed our order. This is a particularly pleasant spot, a sort of museum of cruising people and famous sailors and where you can receive mail and send faxes.

The mooring in the middle of the harbor enabled him to amuse himself rowing and sculling the Optimist, and taking Chaka on his daily excursions.

As always, the time came to think about leaving. This time, they were expecting us at Expo 98.

We decided that we would first go to Cascais, to make sure that everything was in order, before continuing on to the Expo marina which was far up the river Tagus. Antoine warned us that the current can be very strong.

After leaving Horta, we tried to make northing whenever possible so as to reach the 41st parallel before attempting to head east. This involved a lot of tacking because of light winds from the north to east quadrant. They finally settled in the northeast, then went north as we approached the Portuguese coast. The Nortada was particularly strong during that summer and there had been frequent gale warnings, yet we met quite feeble winds. The maximum was 20 knots two days before arriving in Cascais, where we anchored off the beach in front of the Hotel Albatroz.

We met once again the friendly reception at the yacht club and partook of the delicious pleasure of its very hot showers. A breakwater was under construction that would better protect the bay and allow a marina to be built.

In the bistros and the outdoor restaurants, we relaxed in the soft Mediterranean atmosphere and the European wellbeing. It was a way of life, with a feeling of comfort and security that we had almost forgotten.

"Okay. We'll leave this evening so as to be at the Expo marina at 11 p.m., at high tide."

We didn't like sailing at night, if it was possible to do it during the day, especially when we had to go up a river or through a channel, but these were the port captain's orders.

Sailing up the Tagus was an unforgettable experience. Following the bank on the Lisbon side, we went all the way past the city before carrying on northward as far as the airport. It was truly unique, especially at nighttime, as all the principal monuments and public buildings layered up the nearby hills were floodlit.

The majestic Torre de Belém commands the entrance to the port. The splendid Praça do Comércio, with its beautifully lighted plaza, was nearly deserted; Castello de São Jorge looked down on the river from its heights. We then passed under the Ponte 25 de Abril at Alcántara before sailing along the docks which were filled with a variety of ships, among them three cruise liners serving as floating hotels for the Expo. Three full hours after leaving Cascais, we arrived at last at the inside basin at Expo 98.

Reconnoitering the approaches to the marina at night with all the lights and noise wasn't very easy and we had difficulty making out the entrance. Fortunately, the marina staff aboard a small and powerful motorboat guided us competently, with the help of a searchlight, toward the narrow entrance and then to our berth. In spite of the late hour, they were very pleased to see us and asked lots of questions. They couldn't believe that we'd come so far. For our part, we were simply happy to be there, our mission accomplished!

Bright and early, we were on deck for the big clean up, tidy up, and to hoist the flags, including those of Brittany and Saint-Briac.

SPRAY OF SAINT-BRIAC stood proud among the vessels present. Among them were several caravelles and a magnificent replica of a

Portuguese frigate, the FERNANDO DA GLORIA. Large numbers of fishing boats, painted bright colors, represented every region of Portugal.

Throughout the duration of the Expo, from May to October, there was a constant coming and going of traditional sailing vessels, both restored and replicas, and all kinds of ships.

The following days we divided between visits to various pavilions and trips to Lisbon and its surroundings. Briac was in heaven, there was so much going on, so much to see and do and hear, and so many countries to explore. A living and breathing geography book lay wide open before him.

One of his favorite memories is of his visit to the frigate, where life aboard was reconstructed to the minutest detail, with a real sense of authenticity. It was really well done and thought provoking. The big aquarium was another remarkable creation. It contained a tremendous variety of flora and fauna of the undersea world, and you could look into it from above and from several levels under the water. There were penguins, petrels, seals, and all kinds of fish among which were some beautiful shark specimens. It was worth the long wait in the line that formed as soon as the Expo gates opened.

In the French pavilion, the photographs of racing interested Briac the most, and in the United States pavilion it was the exhibit on Joshua Slocum.

Expo 98 was a tour around a world without borders and without political and administrative barriers. We could pass from one pavilion to the next without hindrance, from the Russian one to that of the United States without a visa, from Arab countries to African ones, a world without frontiers. Even though it was just a brief dream, it was wonderful. That was one of the great lessons of this very interesting and successful exposition.

We went to visit a modern cargo ship—from the spotlessly clean engine room to the bridge equipped with the last word in electronic equipment—and two warships. In a very few days, Briac saw and did so many things. And let's not forget the live television broadcast from the deck of the frigate when we presented our celebrated plaque from the Henry the Navigator Association of New Bedford.

SPRAY OF SAINT-BRIAC looked great on her dock, right in front of the Cafe Sport, which was a copy of the one in Horta and run by the owners' son. She was getting a lot of attention and her flags cracked proudly in the northerly breeze. She seemed very dignified, in the presence of so many sailing boats and replicas of old craft. She was the only one among them that had really been anywhere. She had completed her second circumnavigation and had never been in better shape for setting off again. In fact, because of the modifications and improvements we had made, and her new sails and rigging, she was in better condition than when we started. For all that, her only plan now was to go back to southern Portugal where she would rest a little before putting back to sea.

On Monday, September 15, after a quiet and pleasant voyage along the coast, we entered the channel at Alvor. We were happy to be in this beautiful place once more and we had a hard time believing we'd been around the world. Could it possibly all have been a dream?

We were excited at the idea of seeing again those who had stayed behind, Michele and Dominique, the old fishermen, the men in the yard. Then after that would be the joy of driving back to France, to see our families, our friends, the schoolchildren, and, above all, Saint-Briac, the starting point of all of my adventures.

Alvor was the real end of this circumnavigation and, why not, perhaps the beginning of another long voyage.

After a few days, we decided to leave SPRAY OF SAINT-BRIAC in the new marina in Lagos. She would be much more secure there and I could stay on board alone, to write this book.

Appendix

◆

A Critical Analysis of the Yawl SPRAY

C. ANDRADE, JR.

Reprinted from The Rudder Magazine, June 1909

"I did not know the center of effort in her sails, except as it hit me in practice at sea, nor did I care a rope yarn about it. Mathematical calculations, however, are all right in a good boat, and SPRAY could have stood them. She was easily balanced and easily kept in trim."

With these words Captain Joshua Slocum dismisses the technique of SPRAY's design.

Considering the unparalleled performances of this little boat, it is remarkable that no one has ever attempted an analysis of her lines and sail plan.

SPRAY was built about the year 1800, and was used as an oysterman on the coast of Delaware. Her original lines were those of a North Sea fisherman. For almost a century she ranged up and down the Atlantic coast, and at length found her way to Fairhaven, at the head of Buzzards Bay. There she was finally hauled out, as every one supposed, for her last rest.

In the year 1892, however, Captain Eben Pierce, her then owner, presented her to Captain Slocum. Slocum set to work with his own hands and rebuilt her from the keel up, so that not a particle of the original fabric remained, except the windlass, and the "fiddle head" or carving on the end of the cutwater. In rebuilding her, Slocum added to her freeboard 12 inches amidships, 18 inches forward and 14 inches aft. The lines published herewith show her as thus rebuilt.

Under a sloop rig, Slocum sailed SPRAY from New Bedford, Mass., to Gibraltar, thence back again across the Atlantic, down the South American coast and through the Strait of Magellan. Then he changed her rig to a yawl, and completed his circumnavigation of the globe by way of the Southern Pacific and Cape of Good Hope, and back across the Atlantic to New England—a gross of some 46,000 sea miles—all single-handed.

One of the most remarkable things about SPRAY is her ability to hold her course for hours or days at a time with no one at the helm. Had she not possessed this quality, Slocum's performance would have been a physical impossibility. For example, she ran from Thursday Island to the Keeling Cocos Islands, 2,700 miles, in twenty-three days. Slocum stood at the helm for one hour during that time. Her average distance made good for the run was over 117 miles a day or about 5

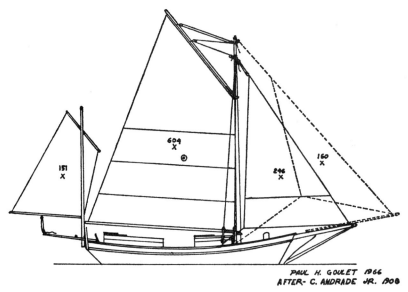

PAUL H. GOULET 1966
AFTER- C. ANDRADE JR. 1908

Sail Plan of "Spray"

miles an hour. This was a fair cruising speed for SPRAY, and she maintained that speed of 5 knots for twenty-three consecutive days, or 552 consecutive hours. The impossibility of steering a boat for that time, or for any considerable portion of that time, is of course obvious. There are well-known men right here in New York City who have seen boats do the same thing for comparatively short distances. Thus, Mr. Day records that after he had converted SEA-BIRD into a keel boat and had lengthened her keel, he laid her on a course and she held that course for an hour and a half, at the end of which time there came a change in the wind. Now if a boat will hold her course alone for an hour and a half, she will hold it for a year and a half, *provided always* that the wind and sea remain unchanged.

Examine an ocean chart of SPRAY's voyage, and you will see that Slocum systematically ran down the trades, not only for hundreds but for thousands of miles, and his wind and sea conditions for whole days and weeks must have been practically constant. This is one of the reasons for SPRAY's phenomenal runs. Perfect balance is the other reason.

After a thorough analysis of SPRAY's lines, I found her to have a theoretically perfect balance. Her balance is marvelous—almost uncanny. Try as I would—one element after the other—they all swung into the same identical line. I attacked her with proportional dividers, planimeter, rota-meter, Simpson's rule, Froude's coefficients, Dixon Kemp's formulae, series, curves, differentials, and all the appliances of modern yacht designing, and she emerged from the ordeal a theoretically perfect boat. For when she is underway, every element of resistance, stability, weight, heeling effort, and propulsive force is in one transverse plane, and that plane is the boat's midship section. I know of no similar case in the whole field of naval architecture, ancient or modern. There may be similar cases in existence, but it has not been my good fortune to know of them.

Before passing to a critical analysis of the figures, I shall take up a few general questions concerning this unusual boat.

GENERAL APPEARANCE

SPRAY's lines appear, in much reduced size, at the end of Slocum's book, *Sailing Alone Around the World*. When I first looked at them, and read Slocum's statement that this hull had been driven at a speed of 8 knots, I thought he must be mistaken.

Slocum, however, is an accurate historian; and I therefore set to work with proportional dividers, and laid SPRAY out to a scale of ½ inch to the foot, in order to acquire an intimate personal knowledge of her lines—merely looking at them in a book will not always suffice. I next swept in two diagonals (A and B in the halfbreadth plan), which are omitted from the lines as published in Slocum's book, and then I realized that he was justified in his claim of 8 knots.

DIAGONALS

If you will look at the drawings, you will see that SPRAY's real working line is the diagonal B, which is a normal practically the whole length of the boat. On the half-breadth plan, you will see that diagonal B is marked by a little cross between stations 3 and 6. At this point she takes the water. From the cross to station 6, there is a very coarse angle of entrance, of which I shall have more to say in a moment. From station 6 to the transom, a run of over 27 feet, diagonal B is as clean a line, as fine drawn, easy running and fair as you will find in any racer of the Larchmont fleet—and that is the line that bears her; it is the line she runs on, and it is the measure of her speed.

Now let us take up that coarse entrance angle of diagonal B from the cross to station 6—a matter of some two feet.

Twenty years ago, Mr. Herreshoff announced that hollow bow lines were not essential to speed.

The Whitehead torpedo, which travels at about 30 knots, has a nose as round as a cannon-ball.

Some of the little scow boats on the Western lakes develop great speed, and they hold this speed through rough water (that is, rough for their size and length), and their bows show hard curves, and in some cases even flat transoms.

Viewing all these things with impartial eyes, I should say that the two feet of diagonal B in SPRAY from the cross to section 6 would be no detriment whatever to her speed.

BOW

Let us now consider that portion of diagonal *B* which lies forward of the cross. This portion of the diagonal runs up to the stem-head at an angle somewhere in the neighborhood of 45°. The waterlines do the same and the buttock lines do the same. The result is a bow of terrific power. With her thirty-five thousand odd pounds of dead-weight and a few more thousand sail pressure on top of that, SPRAY can go coasting down the side of a roller, and then when she turns from the long down-grade uphill again, instead of running under, or carrying a ton or so of water aft along her decks, that bow will lift her. And it is the only bow that would lift her.

STERN

SPRAY's stern is the best that my limited experience could suggest. There is just enough rake in her transom to lift her handsomely over any following sea. Her transom is broad enough and deep enough to hold her waterlines and buttocks easy to the very last moment. And the practice of dropping the bottom of her transom below the waterline finds support in such examples as Mr. Crane's DIXIE II and Mr. Herreshoff's SEA SHELL, and many other master designed craft. It does ease up the buttock lines so; and contrary to popular superstition, it does not create any material drag of deadwater. The Crosbys have been building catboats this way for years. By dropping the transom below the waterline, the water lifts the boat to the very end of the run, and one of the resultants of that lift on the buttock lines is a forward thrust. On the other hand, where the knuckle of the transom is above the waterline, the exact opposite takes place, and the water, instead of lifting the boat and thrusting her forward, is lifted by the boat and holds her back.

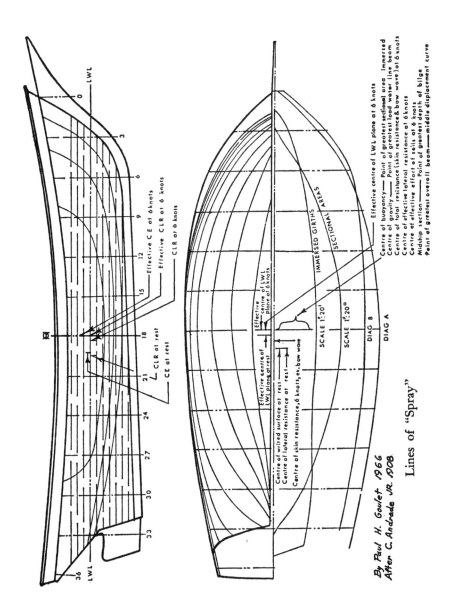

Lines of "Spray"

MIDSHIP SECTION

SPRAY's midsection, at first glance, would seem much wider and shallower than a seagoing model would require.

But like everything else about her, there is a very good reason for SPRAY's form of midsection; in fact, there are several good reasons.

Firstly: I have heard it said, that her immunity from loss is due to the fact that when she is hove to she yields and gives to the sea, constantly easing away to leeward; whereas a deeper, more ardent model, holding in uncompromising fashion to the wind, would be battered and strained into destruction.

Secondly: SPRAY's great breadth gives her no end of deck room. Now when you are living on a boat weeks and months and years, deck room becomes not only important, but essential. Without adequate

TRANSVERSE METACENTERS, LOAD WATER-LINES AND CENTERS OF BUOYANCY YAWL "SPRAY"

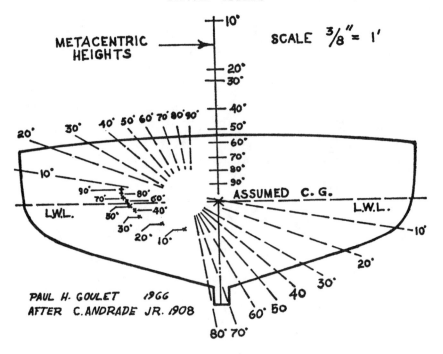

deck room for walking and exercise, a man could not exist for that length of time. He would fall ill of some sickness and die.

Thirdly: The form of SPRAY's midship section insures that she will never heel to an uncomfortable angle. She would rarely go down much below 10° of heel, and in good sailing breezes, she would probably not exceed 5°. Now equally with deck room, this matter of heel is most essential to the comfort and, in the long run, the health of the crew. The strain of living on a boat at 25 or 30° of heel may be borne for the brief period of a race, maybe a race as far as Bermuda. But when it comes to living on a boat thus for weeks at a time, no human being could stand it.

Fourthly: SPRAY is a much better boat to windward than her form of midsection would at first glance indicate. To the casual observer, it would seem almost impossible to drive her to windward at all without a centerboard (and she has no centerboard). But on careful analysis it will appear that there are three reasons why SPRAY should be a fairly good boat to windward.

In the first place, she has an unusually hard bilge and an unusually flat vertical side, and the result is that even at a small angle of heel, her lee side acts as an efficient leeboard of very considerable area.

In the second place, she has a long, fairly deep keel, and as this keel rakes downward from the forefoot to the rudder, it is constantly entering solid water at every portion of its length, and is very much more efficient than if the keel were horizontal.

In the third place, SPRAY has a large lateral plane in proportion to her sail spread.

Therefore, like everything else about her, I should say that her form of midsection was fully justified.

DISPLACEMENT

For a boat of 32 feet waterline, SPRAY's displacement is enormous— 35,658 lb. Of course, this is an essential in her design. Being an ocean-going cruiser, her construction is heavy, 1½-inch yellow pine planking. Her great breadth requires heavy deck beams, 6-inch by 6-inch yellow pine; and her construction in other particulars is equally massive. All this means displacement. Then her crew, even one man, consumes a good deal of water, food and fuel in the course of several months. She must carry a large supply of spare gear and stores. Her large displacement then is necessary, unavoidable; and, besides, it gives her power to carry on through a sea.

By reason of her large waterline plane, her displacement per inch immersion at the load waterline is very large, 1,863 lb. This is a good feature, as it makes little difference in her trim whether she has a ton or so more or less of stores on board. This feature is still another advantage accruing from her wide shallow form of midship section.

CENTERS OF RESISTANCE, WEIGHT, ETC.

We now come to the inner mystery of SPRAY's design.

I suppose that the extraordinary focusing of her centers is the result of chance. SPRAY was laid down about the year 1800. Analytic boat designing, as we understand it, was unknown at that time. SPRAY's perfection of balance, then, must be purely empirical, but it is none the less marvelous for that.

To begin with, SPRAY's center of buoyancy is located exactly at the boat's midship section. This is unusual. In fact, at the moment I do not recall any other design that has even this peculiarity. Axiomatically, the center of gravity and the center of buoyancy must lie in the same vertical line; and thus at the very outset of our investigations we find that the center of gravity, the center of buoyancy, the greatest breadth, the greatest depth of bilge, and the maximum point in the boat's curve of displacement, all fall exactly on the same line, which happens to be station 18.

And what is still more unusual, it will be observed that station 18, containing within itself all these elements, falls at exactly the effective middle point of the boat's curve of displacement. A glance at the curve of displacement will show that for all practical purposes the portion lying forward of station 3, and aft of station 33, can be disregarded. In other words, for all practical purposes, the curve begins at station 3 and ends at station 33, and exactly midway between station 3 and station 33 lies station 18, at which are focused all the points above-mentioned.

Let us now examine station 18 with reference to its position on the load waterline. The old school of designers who pinned their faith to the wave-line theory, held that the maximum point in the curve of displacement (station 18 in SPRAY) should be .60 of the L. W. L. aft from the forward point of immersion. Modern practice has discarded the coefficient .60, and says that it should be .55; and the measurement rule now in force adopts this coefficient of .55. SPRAY's coefficient, however, instead of being .60 or .55, is only .506; which means that her midsection is somewhat forward of the position which has been decreed by modern practice.

Now, all displacement curves under the wave-line rule and under the modern practice show a marked hollow at the bow. Obviously, where the bow portion of the displacement curve is hollow, it is essential that the boat's center of gravity should be thrown as far aft as possible, in order to keep her head from burying when running under a press of sail; and this entails putting the midship section as far aft as possible; all of which doubtless had much to do with the adoption of the coefficients .60 and .55 above-mentioned.

But in the case of SPRAY, it will be noted that the displacement curve of the boat's entrance is not hollow at all, but convex. Therefore, there is no reason for throwing her center of gravity very far aft, because her bow is powerful enough to lift her at all times and under all circumstances. On the other hand, in SPRAY, there is a very good reason for not throwing the center of gravity very far aft of the middle of the L. W. L. And the reason is this: To throw the center of gravity aft, is to throw the midship section aft, and as the boat of necessity has great displacement, the placing of the midship section very far aft would result in hard lines (either buttocks, waterlines, or diagonals), and would produce a form of run that would inevitably create a heavy stern wave and make a slow boat.

The next element to be considered is the center of lateral resistance. This center lies .044 of the L. W. L. aft of station 18 when the boat is at rest. And here it is well to remember that the position of the C. L. R. is not always thoroughly appreciated in all its aspects. The C. L. R. as laid out on the drawings represents the point on which the boat (rudder and all) would balance if pushed sideways through the water. Take the case now under discussion. Suppose you were to make a working model of SPRAY and put her in a tank of still water.

Then suppose you took the point of a knife, and praised it against the side of the model at the exact point marked "C, L, R. at rest" in the drawing. Now, if you pushed the model sideways, at right angles to her keel, she would just balance on the knife point, the boat moving bodily sideways, without turning either the stern or the bow, And that is all that is meant by the C. L. R. as shown on the plans.

The instant, however, that the boat starts to move forward, the C.L.R. starts to move forward toward the bow of the boat. This is in obedience to a well-known law. As the bow works in solid water, and the stern dead-wood in broken water, the bow holds on better than the stern, and a square foot of lateral plane at the bow holds better than a square foot of lateral plane at the stern. The net result is that the effective C. L. R. moves forward. The question of *just how far* the C.L.R. moves forward when the boat begins to move ahead is a question involving some rather tedious calculation. Froude compiled a set of figures, showing the change of resistance per square foot at various portions of a surface located at various distances aft from the leading edge. (They relate specifically to skin resistance, but I assume that the lateral resistance would vary in the same ratio.) A table of these coefficients is given at page 135 of Mackrow's Pocket Book. Froude gives the figures for 2, 8, 20 and 50 feet. By interpolation, using a variable differential to satisfy the points established by Froude, it is possible to get the correct coefficient for any intermediate point. Then by applying the appropriate coefficients to the various stations of the immersed lateral plane, and applying Simpson's formula, it is possible to find how far the C. L. R. will move forward for any predetermined speed. In the specific case of SPRAY, moving at a speed of 6 knots, the C. L. R. from a point 1.45 feet aft of station 18, to a point .4 of a foot aft of station 18, a forward movement of 1.05 feet. This gives us the actual working location of SPRAY's C.L.R, at 6 knots, *disregarding the bow wave.* In order to make our calculation complete, we must further reckon with the bow wave. The question of stern wave may be disregarded, because, from the pictures and photographs of SPRAY underway, it clearly appears that the boat creates no sensible stern wave—she has too clean a run for that. She does raise a moderate bow wave, and the effect of that bow wave is of course to bring her effective C. L. R. a little bit forward.

The question of just exactly how far forward the bow wave will carry the C. L. R. is a matter beyond the ken of precise calculation. Judging from the height of the bow wave as shown on SPRAY's pictures, I should say it would amount to a little over 1% of the L. W. L., and if that assumption is correct, it would bring SPRAY's effective working C. L. R. exactly on station 18. Of course, every heave of the sea, every slant of wind, every touch on the helm throws this center a little bit forward or aft—it is no more fixed and stable than her angle of heel is fixed and stable. Constantly it plays forward and aft, but the central average point of its play must be station 18 or within a fraction of an inch of it.

In order to make my analysis of SPRAY's hull quite complete, I also calculated a center that is seldom considered at all in yacht design, and yet which must have some significance—that is, the center of wetted surface. In other words, I determined the effective center of her curve of immersed girths by Simpson's formula. To my surprise, this center worked out to a hair on identically the same line as the C. L. R. at rest, viz., 1.45 feet aft of station 18—another of the extraordinary coincidences in SPRAY's design.

Now exactly the same considerations which apply to the C. L. R. apply also to this center of wetted surface. In other words, when the boat begins to move forward, the focal point of her skin resistance begins to move forward from the place occupied by the center of wetted surface at rest. Thus, by applying Froude and Simpson, as in the case of the lateral plane, we find that at a speed of 6 knots, SPRAY's center of skin resistance moves forward from a point 1.45 aft of station 18, to a point .6 of a foot aft of station 18, a forward movement of .85 foot—that is, leaving the bow wave out of account. To complete our calculation, we must again reckon with the bow wave.

Now the bow wave will have a more potent effect in carrying forward the center of skin resistance, than in carrying forward the center of lateral resistance. And for this reason—the boat throws off two bow waves, one from the weather bow and one from the lee bow. Both of these waves affect the wetted surface, whereas only the lee wave affects the lateral plane. Of course, the wave on the lee bow is heavier than the wave on the weather bow, and therefore we may safely say that the two bow waves will *not* move the center of skin resistance forward twice as far as the lee-bow wave moves the C. L. R. forward. We thus reach the conclusion that the boat's wave action will throw the center of skin resistance forward further than the C. L. R. is thrown forward, and yet not so much as twice that distance. We have already seen that the wave action throws her C. L. R. forward .4 of a foot. Therefore the wave action will throw her center of skin resistance forward between .4 and .8 of a foot, say .6 of a foot as a mean. And when we do move her center of skin resistance forward .6 of a foot, we land again exactly to a hair on station 18. Another in the series of coincidences.

ELEMENTS OF THE YAWL "SPRAY"

CALCULATED BY C. ANDRADE, JR., DEC. 1908

SCALE $\frac{1}{2}'' = 1'$

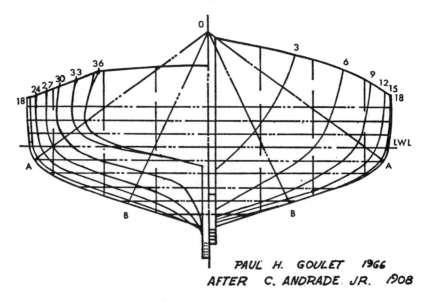

PAUL H. GOULET 1966
AFTER C. ANDRADE JR. 1908

Length O. A.	41'0¾" (36'9" excluding Figurehead)
Length L. W. L.	32'1"
Beam Extreme	14'1" (13'10" at L.W.L.)
Draught	4'1"
Freeboard (excluding Rail)	
Bow	4'1"
Waist	1'9¾"
Stern	2'9¾"

Rail   1'2"

Area Mid. Section Immersed   26.32 sq. ft.

Area Lat. Plane Immersed   111.88 sq. ft.

Area L.W.L. Plane   349.04 sq. ft.

Area Wetted Surface   443.18 sq. ft.

Area Rudder   7.52 sq. ft.

Sail Area Actual   1161. sq. ft.

  Jib   246 sq. ft.

  Mainsail   604 sq. ft.

  Mizzen   151 sq. ft.

  Flying Jib   160 sq. ft.

Displacement   556.72 cu. ft.-35,658 lbs.

Lbs. per inch Immersion at L. W. L. = 1863

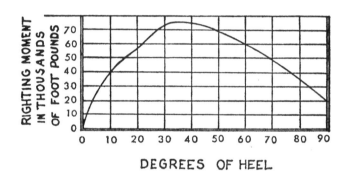

Even the effective center of the L. W. L. plane falls only .4 foot aft of station 18 when the boat is at rest; and the piling up of the bow waves under the bow, when she is underway, must bring this center also just about on station 18. (Unlike the C. L. R. and the center of skin resistance, the effective center of the L. W. L. plane is not affected by the forward motion of the boat—it is affected only by the bow wave.)

From an inspection of the L. W. L. plane, the almost perfect symmetry of the curve of displacement with reference to station 18 as an axis, and the symmetry of the boat's ends, it is quite evident that the longitudinal metacenter for a given angle of pitch forward will be at practically the same height as for an equal angle of pitch aft.

I know of no other conceivable factor of weight, displacement, buoyancy or resistance that can be calculated for a hull, so far as longitudinal balance is concerned, and I shall leave the discussion of SPRAY's hull with the statement that every one of these factors, when she is underway, is concentrated exactly at her midship section (station 18). So much for SPRAY's hull.

Let us now examine her sail plan.

At the outset, it should be remarked that the flying jib will be eliminated from the discussion of sail balance, as it is a light-weather sail, set standing on a light bamboo jibboom, which is merely lashed to the bowsprit when the flying jib is set, and is stowed when the flying jib is stowed, and is never used on the wind.

When SPRAY is on the wind, she carries three sails only, the jib, mainsail and mizzen. The combined center of effort of these three sails at rest falls about .17 of a foot forward of the C. L. R. at rest. This .17 of a foot is only a little over .5 of 1% of the L. W. L. Modern practice calls for from 1 to 3 % of the L. W. L. But it must be remembered that the 1 to 3% coefficient is used for sloops with large mainsails and small jibs. Whereas SPRAY is a yawl with an unusually large jib and a comparatively small mainsail. On this state of facts no less an authority than Dixon Kemp uses the following language (*Yacht Architecture*, Third Edition, page 100): "In the case of yawls it is generally found that the calculated center of effort requires (relatively to the center of lateral resistance) to be a little further aft than in either cutters or schooners, as the mizzen is not a very effective sail on a wind, the eddy wind of the mainsail causing it to lift; also a yawl's mainmast is usually further forward than a cutter's, and it should be noted that the position of the center of effort of the largest driving sail influences the position of the general C. E. more than the calculation shows."

SPRAY's center of effort is therefore amply justified by authority, and the authority, in turn, is justified by SPRAY's actual performance under the sail plan shown. For Slocum says of her: "Briefly, I have to say that when close-hauled in a light wind under all sail she required little or no weather helm. As the wind increased I would go on deck, if below, and turn the wheel up a spoke more or less, relash it, or as sailors say, put it in a becket, and then leave it as before."

Of course, in order to attain this balance, SPRAY's efficient center of effort must be over her effective C. L. R. And as we have already seen that the effective C. L. R. at 6 knots falls exactly on station 18, so her efficient center of effort also at that speed must fall exactly on station 18.

It is obvious that, just as the effective C. L. R. moves forward as the boat moves forward so the efficient center of effort moves forward on the sail plan when the boat sails forward. This has long been known by naval architects; and the recent activity in aeroplane flight has led to much experiment on the subject. The C. E. seems to move forward more slowly than the C. L. R. as the boat's speed increases; and the result is that although the C. E. at rest is forward of the C. L. R., yet when the boat is at her normal speed, these two centers, advancing at unequal rates, come into exact balance; and when the boat's speed is increased still more by a harder wind, the C. L. R. continuing to work forward faster than the C. E. makes the boat carry a harder and harder weather helm as the wind increases. This is a matter of common observation.

CURVE OF STABILITY, TRANSVERSE METACENTRIC, ETC.

The curve of stability shows that SPRAY is theoretically uncapsizable, because of 90° of heel, she still has left a righting moment of over 20,000 foot-pounds or over 9 foot-tons. This is most remarkable for a boat of her shallow draught; doubly remarkable in view of the fact that she carries no outside ballast whatever, and even her inside ballast consists merely of cement blocks. (All boatmen of experience say that stone or cement ballast makes a livelier, "corkier" boat than the same weight of lead or iron.) Her maximum stability is at about 35° of heel, where she has a righting moment of 75,000 foot-pounds or over 33 foot-tons.

As she should never be sailed much lower than 10° of heel, it will be seen that she has an ample margin of safety at all times.

In plotting the curve of stability, I assumed the center of gravity to lie exactly at the L. W. L., which, I think, is conservative.

I have also plotted the transverse L. W. L., transverse center of buoyancy, and metacentric height for each 10° of heel up to 90°.

CONCLUSION

I conclude my analysis of SPRAY's lines with a feeling of profound admiration and respect. She is not only an able boat, but a beautiful boat; using the term "beautiful" as defined by Charles Elliott Norton, "that form most perfectly adapted to perform its allotted work"—beautiful in the same sense that Sandow, or the Farnese Hercules is beautiful. From the man who loves boats and the sea, and in some measure understands them (for it has been given to no one yet to know all their ways), SPRAY will receive the recognition that is her due.

She is the perfection of her type—a perfection demonstrated not only on paper, but by the ordeal of actual achievement. She is an oceangoing cruiser, in the largest sense of that term. After sailing 46,000 miles, and weathering a hundred gales, some of which foundered great ships in his near vicinity, Slocum says of her: "I have given in the plans of SPRAY the dimensions of such a ship as I should call seaworthy in all conditions of weather and on all seas." These words coming from such a source are not lightly to be disregarded.

The question is one of such interest, that *The Rudder* invites the opinions of all amateur and professional designers and practical boatmen, to see if they would suggest any departures whatever from SPRAY's lines in a boat intended to circumnavigate the globe single-handed.

Of course, if the question were to design the best possible boat to race on Long Island Sound, or to Block Island, or even to Bermuda, there is no question but what other characteristics than those of SPRAY would be adopted.

But let the question be clearly apprehended—what would be the best boat with which to circumnavigate the globe single-handed? Would the ideal boat for that purpose depart in any measure from SPRAY's lines; and if so, why?

On this question, a full discussion will be of the utmost interest.

We trust that all who are interested will contribute their views, and not only their views but their reasons for their views.

Glossary

◆

anode A sacrificial piece of metal, usually zinc, fixed to the outside of a boat's hull and connected to other metal components to protect them from galvanic corrosion.

antifouling Special paint used on the bottom of a boat's hull to deter the growth of marine organisms, barnacles for example.

asymmetrical spinnaker A *spinnaker* that's not symmetrical in shape and that can be set with or without a pole. Used when *reaching*.

beam 1. An athwartships cross member supporting a deck. 2. The width of a boat. 3. With "the" or *abeam*, a position relative to a boat as if sighted along the main deck beam, therefore directly abreast.

block A device containing a free-wheeling *sheave* or pulley used for changing the direction of the pull of a rope or line.

boom The spar that supports the *foot* of a sail.

bowsprit A spar that projects forward from the bow of a boat.

careen To set a vessel on its side on a exposing part of the hull that's normally in the water in order to do work on it. Often done on a beach but sometimes alongside a wall or another vessel.

caulking Material used between a boat's planks to prevent water from seeping between them. Also used under hardware where fasteners penetrate the hull or deck.

clew The aft, lower corner of a sail to which the *sheet* is attached.

close hauled Sailing close to the wind, with the *sheets* hauled tight.

companionway An entrance from the deck to the living quarters of a vessel.

cringle A metal ring sewn into a sail for attaching a line.

davit A small crane used for hoisting, lowering, and sometimes stowing a *dinghy* or *tender*.

dinghy A small boat. Often one carried aboard a larger one and used for transport to and from shore and for other tendering purposes.

fender A cushioning device used to protect a boat's *topsides* when tied alongside a dock or another boat.

foot The bottom edge of a sail, running from the *tack* to the *clew*.

forestay The foremost *stay*. Usually supports a *jib*.

freeboard The distance between the top of a vessel's hull and the waterline.

furl To stow a sail on a spar or a stay by rolling or folding or a combination of both.

gaff 1. On a gaff-rigged boat, the upper spar on a fore-and-aft sail. 2. A pole with a large hook on one end used for hauling fish on board.

GPS Global Positioning System by which a vessel's position can be determined by data obtained from a number of artificial satellites. Also the device on board that communicates with the satellites and displays information.

halyard The line used to hoist a sail.

head The top corner of a triangular sail to which the halyard is attached. On a gaff sail, the upper edge, between the *throat* and the *peak*, that's supported by the gaff.

heel The leaning attitude of a sailing vessel caused by the action of the wind on the sails.

helm The device used to steer a boat, usually a *tiller* or a wheel.

helmsman The person steering a boat.

heave to To set the sails and helm in opposition so that a boat lies with its bow pointing at about 45 degrees into the wind without making significant headway. Used with reduced sail to weather a storm, or sometimes just to bide time.

jib A sail set forward of the forward mast on a sailing vessel, usually on a *stay*.

jibe To turn a boat so that the stern passes through the wind.

ketch A sailing vessel with two masts in which the aft mast, the *mizzen*, is shorter than the mainmast and is stepped forward of the *rudder post*.

leech The aft or trailing edge of a sail, between the *clew* and the *head* of a triangular sail or the *clew* and the *peak* of a *gaff* sail.

lifeline Usually wire permanently strung around the outside of the deck on *stanchions* as a safety measure.

list To lean to one side usually because of the way weight is distributed on board.

Loran An electronic navigation system by which a receiver on board a boat interprets the boat's position from a network of radio waves.

luff The leading, or forward, edge of a sail, between the *tack* and the *head* of a triangular sail or the *tack* and the *throat* of a *gaff* sail.

mainsail The sail attached to the aft side of the mainmast.

mainsheet horse A bar attached to the deck to which the mainsheet is attached with a ring, allowing lateral movement in the sheeting point.

mizzen The fore-and-aft sail set on the mizzenmast.

mooring A fixed point, usually a heavy weight or a permanent anchor on the seabed marked by a buoy, to which a vessel can be moored instead of anchoring.

Open 60 A class of sailing yacht used in single-and short-handed ocean races.

Optimist An international class of small sailing dinghies used extensively for teaching children to sail.

painter The line attached to the bow of a *dinghy* or *tender* used for tying it up or for towing it.

peak The upper aft corner of a *gaff* sail.

poop The raised aft part of the deck. When a following wave breaks over the poop, the vessel is said to have been pooped.

port The left hand side of a boat when looking forward.

reach Point of sail between *close hauled* and *running free*.

reef 1. To shorten or reduce the area of a sail while it's set to reduce the force exerted on it by the wind. 2. The area by which the sail has been reduced, first reef, second reef, e.g. 3. An area, usually of rock or coral, that stands higher than the surrounding seabed, making it a hazard to navigation.

rudder The device at the stern of the boat by which it is steered, usually connected to a *tiller* or steering wheel.

running free Point of sail when the wind is well aft of the *beam*.

running backstays Temporary *stays* set up aft of a mast depending on which side the sails are set.

running rigging Components of a boat's rigging, sheets, guys, halyards etc. that are not fixed and are used for controlling sails and spars. Includes *running backstays*.

scull To propel a boat by using a single oar over the stern.

sheave The rotating wheel inside a *block* over which the rope or line turns.

sheer legs Supports to hold a boat upright when it's intended to let it dry out on the seabed on a falling tide. Sometimes used when *careening*.

sheet The line attached to the *clew* of a sail and by which the sail's position is adjusted relative to the wind.

shroud A wire that supports a mast athwartships.

spinnaker A large, usually colorful sail flown free forward of the mast, its tack attached to a pole set off the mast.

SSB radio Single Sideband radio used for long-distance communications ship to ship and ship to shore.

stanchion A vertical support for a *lifeline.*

standing rigging Fixed rigging, a combination of *stays* and *shrouds,* that supports a mast.

starboard The right hand side of a boat when looking forward.

stay A wire that supports a mast in the fore-and-aft plane.

staysail A sail set on a stay.

sternpost The member in the vertical plane at the aft end of the hull to which the *rudder* is often attached.

sweep A large oar used to propel a vessel like SPRAY in calm water when there is no wind.

tack 1. The lower, forward corner of a sail. 2. To turn a boat so that the bow passes through the wind. 3. A point of sailing. When a boat is on *starboard* tack, the wind is blowing from the starboard side and the sails are set to *port.* On port tack the wind is blowing from the port side and the sails are set to starboard. Starboard jibe and port jibe have similar meanings and are used when the wind is aft of the beam.

tackle A combination of *blocks* through which a line is rove to gain additional purchase.

tender A *dinghy* used for the express purpose of tending to a yacht.

throat On a *gaff* sail, the forward upper corner between the *luff* and the *head.*

tiller A lever attached to the head of the *rudder post* and used by the *helmsman* to deflect the *rudder* and thus steer the boat.

topsides The area of the hull between the *waterline* and the deck edge.

tradewinds Winds that blow fairly constantly in certain parts of the world and so named because trade routes for sailing ships were developed to benefit from them.

transom The flat or slightly curved panel at the stern of a boat that terminates the hull.

VHF radio Radio used for short-range communications, ship to ship and ship to shore.

watches A system of dividing time so that crewmembers can stand watch at regular intervals and for specified lengths of time.

waterline The line along the hull of a vessel at which it floats.

windvane A part of a self-steering device used to steer a sailing vessel by the action of the wind and without a *helmsman*.

yankee A type of *jib*, large but with a high *clew* so that it doesn't catch water when the boat is *heeling*.

Bibliography

Le Chasse-Marée Numéro 77

Roberts-Goodson, Bruce, *Spray: the Ultimate Cruising Boat*, Dobbs Ferry, NY: Sheridan House, 1995

Slack, Kenneth E., *In the Wake of the Spray*, Dobbs Ferry, NY: Sheridan House, 1981

Slocum, Joshua, *Sailing Alone Around the World*, Dobbs Ferry, NY: Sheridan House, 1999

Slocum, Victor, *Captain Joshua Slocum: the Life and Voyages of America's Best Known Sailor*. Dobbs Ferry, NY: Sheridan House, 1993

Teller, Walter Magnes, editor, *The Voyages of Joshua Slocum*, Dobbs Ferry, NY: Sheridan House, 1995

Useful Addresses

◆

U.S.A.
Conanicut Marina
Jamestown, RI 02852
Tel 401 423 71 58
Fax 401 423 71 59
VHF 71

Fort Myers Boat Yard
2909 Frierson Street
Fort Myers, FL 33916
Tel 813 332 7800

Joshua Slocum Society
    International
Commodore Ted Jones
15 Codfish Hill Road Ext.
Bethel, CT 06801-2315

Onne Van der Wal Photography
5 Marina Plaza
Goat Island
Newport, RI 02840
Fax 401 848 5187
e-mail Klehman@Vanderwal.
    com.
www.vanderwal.com

Wickford Cove Marina
PO Box 436
North Kingstown, RI 02852
Tel 401 294 1540
Fax 401 294 1541

AUSTRALIA
Cruising Yacht Squadron
Cairns

Darwin Sailing Club
Fanny Bay
Darwin 0800
Northern Territories

GUATEMALA
Mario's, Suzanna or Catamaran
    Hotel Marinas
Fronteras
Rio Dulce

HONDURAS
French Harbor Yacht Club
French Harbor
Roátan
Bay Island
Tel 504 45 14 78
Fax 504 45 14 59

PORTUGAL
Marina de Lagos
Apartado 18
8600 Lagos
Fax 351 82 770 219

Peter Sport Cafe
Horta
Faial
Azores

SOUTH AFRICA
Point Yacht Club
PO Box 2224
Durban 4000
Tel 301 47 87
Fax 305 12 34

Royal Cape Yacht Club
PO Box 772
Cape Town 8000
Tel 211354
Fax 216028

Saldanha Yacht Club
Atn: Jeff da Costa, Commodore
Saldanha

Zululand Yacht Club
PO Box 10387
Meerensee 3901(Richards Bay)
Republic of South Africa
Tel 351 32 704
Fax 351 31784

Barry Lamprecht
Die Burger
Cape Town
Fax 021406 2913

About the Author

◆

Guy O. Bernardin was born in Brittany, France, in 1944. He is a citizen of both France and the United States and when not at sea, he divides his time between the two countries. His great-grandfather, a Cape Horner, and his grandfather were tall ship captains.

In 1975 while living in New York, he decided to keep on with the family tradition and became a sailor. He has a very impressive sailing and racing record: 350.000 miles, 4 around the world voyages, 3 solo racing among them, 6 passages round Cape Horn and two world records: 6 times solo around Cape Horn and the fastest time around the world on a boat under 40 feet.

1974-75	From Los Angeles to Brittany (France) on a PIC 26 (Californian sailing class)
1979	AZAB (Falmouth-Azores-Falmouth) singlehanded
1980	OSTAR (Transatlantic Observer-Europe 1) on RATSO 38'
1981	Two Star (Transatlantic two crews)
1982-83	The BOC Challenge Around Alone on board RATSO-BNP
1984	OSTAR: on board BISCUITS LU 44' second in class 2
1984	Quebec-St Malo: Winner in class 4 on BISCUITS LU
1985	TWO STAR on board BISCUITS LU 2 (60 footer), finishes second
1986-87	BOC Challenge on BISCUITS LU, finishes 4th
1988	January 20-March 2 Cutty Sark record. Attempt to win the sailing record New York-San Francisco via Cape Horn (10 days ahead at Cape Horn, two days after that he loses his mast, has to abandon ship and is luckily rescued on his liferaft by the Chilean Navy.
1988	Gives a lecture at the US Naval Academy in Annapolis
1988-89	Second attempt at the Cutty Sark record, between New York and San Francisco. After many problems, the internal keel structure breaks two days after rounding Cape Horn in a big storm. The Chilean Navy is able to rescue both Guy and his boat BNP-BANK OF THE WEST

1989	He gives a lecture at the French Naval Academy in Brest
1989	One of the greatest adventure starts: The Vendée Globe, single-handed round the world race, non stop on board OKAY, a 60 footer. Bernardin finishes the race after one stop in Hobart for medical treatment
1990	Guy Bernardin receives the Médaille de l'Elysee from François Mitterrand, the French President
1990	Route du Rhum (St Malo-Guadeloupe) second in class 2 monohull
1991	He participates in the 1000-mile race around Valparaiso. Then via Cape Horn to Nantes non stop with a 62-day new record plus the record around Cape Horn, with 6 passages (2 east to west and 4 west to east, 5 in 5 years)
1992	Across the North Atlantic aboard SPRAY OF SAINT-BRIAC
1994	Circumnavigation around the North Atlantic aboard SPRAY, including the West Indies, Central America, Florida and the East Coast
1995-98	Sailing around the world to commemorate Joshua Slocum Centennial voyage. June 1998 festivities in Newport and Fairhaven
1998	North Atlantic crossing via Horta to Lisbon invited at the EXPO 98.

Guy Bernardin produced a 16mm and video picture: *20.000 Leagues Over the Seas* (published in the United States). He is the author of *Adventures Around Cape Horn.* He has been made honorary citizen of the state of Rhode Island, and the following cities: Elizabeth (New Jersey), Saint-Briac and Cape Town. He received a citation from the city of Fairhaven. His most treasured trophy is the Golden Globe Trophy given to him by the Joshua Slocum Society.

For contacting Guy Bernardin:
Ocean Deliveries, Yachting consultant, Project manager on racing and cruising programs. Representing your corporation on Racing Around the World. Guest speaker.
Bernardin 1@msn.com
Website: www.gbmarine.com